# THE I THAT IS WE

# THE I THAT IS WE

Richard M. Moss, M.D.

CELESTIAL ARTS
BERKELEY, CALIFORNIA

Copyright © 1981 by Richard Moss, M.D.

Celestial Arts
P.O. Box 7327
Berkeley, California 94707

Cover design by Dave Porter
Cover illustration by Marshall Peck III
Book design by Abigail Johnston
Typography by HMS Typography, Inc.
Printed by George Banta Company

First printing, September 1981
Manufactured in the United States of America

**Library of Congress Cataloging in Publication Data**

Moss, Richard, 1946 –
  The I that is we.

  1. Consciousness.  2. Love.  3. Holistic
medicine.  4. Mental health.  I. Title.
BF311.M635        158'.1        81-65713
ISBN 0-89087-327-5 (pbk.)        AACR2

8  9  10        88

# ACKNOWLEDGMENTS

Heartfelt acknowledgment:

Judy Johnstone for expert condensation and clarification of nonlinear material.

Cora Brownell for helping define the cover theme.

Dixie Shipp, Phyllis Galanis, Joan Adair, Jill Morgan, Barbara Rifkin and especially Elizabeth Harlow for typing, retyping and retyping.

Dixie Shipp, Ellen Margron and Gay Luce for helpful feedback and support.

Mary Fisher for keeping up the house and my body with her wonderful meals.

Patricia Carney for her ceaseless love and friendship.

William Brugh Joy, for being.

# Table of Contents

Men's curiosity searches past and future
And clings to that dimension. But to apprehend
The point of intersection of the timeless
With time, is an occupation for the saint—
No occupation either, but something given
And taken, in a lifetime's death in love,
Ardour and selflessness and self-surrender.

T. S. ELIOT

# Introduction

*The cleanest expression is that which finds no
sphere worthy of itself and makes one.*

WALT WHITMAN

WITH THE IRREVERSIBLE FINALITY of an
earthquake's shifting plates, a profound shift in my consciousness occurred in early 1977 and the old Richard Moss, M.D.,
disappeared forever.

Gradually I learned to exist with a new sense of self. This kind
of change has no clear model in traditional Western medicine or
psychology. At the time I considered and rejected all the familiar models, including psychosis, neurological seizures and that
perennial catchall, the nervous breakdown. Yet the new me felt
like an atomic reactor powered by energies so great that I could
not have conceived them before. For awhile I even considered
the possibility of possession, but there was also the love and in-
expressibly uplifting joy when I realized that I was nothing and
existed only by God's grace. Gradually I recognized that a fundamental transformation of my nature was taking place.

For about six months it was impossible to think about or to
categorize what was happening. Any attempt to do so resulted
in a sense of disintegration. The communication link was not
yet established between these new energies and the intellectual
self that resided in the old me, and it was all I could do to deal
with this new sense of myself from moment to moment. In
many ways this is still the case.

1

I was learning to live with sensitivities such as telepathic rapport, clairsentience (the ability to feel things not available to ordinary senses), and a powerful current of energy that seemed to move with varying intensity both within and around my body. Through these heightening sensitivities (a process I now refer to as *awakening*), I found that I could avidly read philosophical and spiritual texts that were formerly beyond my comprehension. A new kind of intelligence was developing within me. Simultaneously, the understanding and compassion for human nature became so markedly increased that it was another man who began to emerge.

When the shift in consciousness occurred I had been practicing medicine for five years, during the last of which I released traditional general practice to concentrate on counseling the severely ill. I also began group work that I called "explorations of healing consciousness." In this counseling work I meditated with patients, attempting to help them shift from a disease/recovery focus to a learning, explorative, self-transcendent focus. Through the power of my own exuberance and charisma I could help a person to shift from fear, confusion and despair into a sense of hope and new beginnings.

Although I knew conceptually that it was wrong to lead a person toward a state of consciousness that I myself had not fully realized, I found that I could employ the energy that is born between people when they are in intense communication to play with consciousness in a way that makes all perspectives relative. Together we could selectively place despair, failure or hopelessness at the background of the awareness and draw the spiritual strengths and new understandings into the foreground. This was very important to me. But was I really helping my patients? Once out of my influence, many of these people returned to their former state of consciousness, often with greater depression.

In the enthusiasm of the moment, and because I really wanted to help, I did not appreciate the depths of this phenomenon. I remained within the good/bad, better/worse, accept/reject polarization that is a natural but nonetheless immature characteristic of human awareness. I selectively empowered the "positive" qualities and minimized the tremendously challenging "negative" forces that surround major life crises and, in particular, certain diseases such as cancer. At this point in my life, "helping" was manipulating consciousness so that someone would feel better.

After the shift in consciousness, all dimensions and facets of human awareness became equally real to me; they could become enormously, sometimes overwhelmingly, amplified during the early phases of the change. Any attempt to augment one facet and suppress another resulted in a tremendous intensification of the suppressed component. I oscillated between the wonder of the new dimensions and the fear of annihilation which the transformation at times seemed to be. This latter manifested as inexplicable anguish as well as dreams of death, usually from cancer.

In working with the fear, I soon saw that what I had been offering my patients was not a true resolution. It was merely a process of displacement, and it grew unwittingly out of my own repressed fear of death. Even though it might be just the key for a particular individual at a particular developmental moment, it was for me untenable because it divided my psyche and obstructed wholeness.

I temporarily curtailed work with severely ill patients. There were those with whom I could not accept the degree to which certain fundamental aspects of the psyche were being undone, and sharing with them accelerated me into spaces I could barely integrate. I was forced to go inward and seek deeper answers.

Two dominant forces were operating. First, there was the radical change in my own consciousness — recognized as both an awakening and a death process — which generated enormous "highs" as well as fear, and which my previous motives and philosophies were inadequate to resolve. Second, there was a sense of integrity that demanded that I be the living representative of what I taught others or else neither truth nor true healing was being offered. It became a journey of almost brutal self-honesty, one of opening the heart and discovering a quality of love that is not housed in the dreams and ideas of the personal me. The love emerged as the old me fell away. It was and is a love that demands a new quality of awareness not based on an egocentric selection process that wants to allow only the ego-sustaining forces into the foreground of awareness.

The writing of this book became a meditation into the depths where mind and soul can blend. It became an act of love, first within myself and now for all of us. In the first draft of July/ August 1977 I had only scratched the surface, had only begun to understand that my own transformation opened the door into collective levels of consciousness. (By *collective consciousness* I mean a higher harmonic of experience out of which the discrete experiences of our familiar reality seem to be emerging. It is the part of consciousness that is discovered as the ego boundaries of personality or individual self-consciousness begin to dissolve into realms of a greater Self.) The personal me was being fostered by a force so incredible and seemingly alien that it defies definition. Yet through this I was being shown directly — not philosophically or conceptually, but in the very cells and molecules of my fleshly existence — a whole other reality. Soon I could no longer view myself as an individual process distinct in any absolute sense from this greater collective force.

I left my home, the conference and individual work that I had established, and my key personal relationships and set out on a pilgrimage to resolve the powerful oscillation or polarization of my consciousness that had begun with the spontaneous awakening. The journey took me to Europe, the Middle East, India and Nepal. One day on a roof in India the resolution occurred. It was a simple, undramatic, uncluttered sense of being. I knew in the simplest sense that I was not my experience. From that point forward a new integration started to develop. It was confirmed in a beautiful dream in which I was healed of cancer and the fear of death. I finished out some traveling and returned to America to begin a new level of work.

Discussion of these dimensions seemed nearly impossible in the early phase, because ordinary words cannot bridge the gap between the personal levels of awareness from which our linguistic mind is programmed and the collective levels that transcend the rational mind. How can a linear flow of ideas communicate a quality of awareness that is not in linear time, but simultaneous? This is the realm of poetry and mysticism. If communication of these dimensions is to happen, an energy must ride on the words. Learning to hold both the energy and the word-making mind at the same time is a tremendous challenge. It was for this reason that no attempt could be made to write about my experience in the initial period without putting undue strain on my rational faculties. Nevertheless, once I had matured in the energies and attained balance, I began the commitment of communicating these areas.

Then I discovered another challenge, having again to do with translation. Moving with a part of Self that is infinite, total, and in one sense uncompromising, into the world of relative experience where each of us has our own perspective, is difficult. All too often I found myself sounding absolutist and making things seem proven and definite, when in fact my deepest intention was to clarify my own thoughts and to leave behind a kind of rope so that others might follow.

It has taken a year to write down these thoughts in the midst of my conference and lecture work, although I began to outline some of the areas over four years ago. Part of the writing was for me a deep contemplation into the collective essence of disease and the ways in which we share the most difficult issues of life. At times I protested "Why me?," for it is impossible to go deeply into such spaces without being shaken to the core of one's mortal nature. But as I struggled to articulate what comes from a place where there are no words, the very effort and intensity of my commitment revealed to me the depth of my own transformation.

With the completion of this aspect of my work has come a great sense of lightness. The effort has been made. Now it is for each of you to feel into the thought and ascend the rope on the climb toward a different way of regarding human nature and the processes we call health and disease.

I am no longer a physician in any conventional sense. What I offer now is a growing strength and a growing love. Any concerns about health or disease that are separate from the much larger context of human transformation feel less important to me. It is the radical transformation of consciousness hiding within these superficial descriptions of the human condition that excites and quickens me and that I want to share with others. It is being human in the simplest and fullest sense that is the miracle and the adventure now.

I could not be expressing these feelings today if it weren't for the love and dedication of many people. I have had teachers who healed my soul with the love and wisdom of their presence, but equally important to me were the hundreds of individuals who joined me in the group explorations. These individuals placed before me the vast spectrum of humanness and demanded the fullest commitment of integrity, courage and love. To the patients who came to the groups discussed herein, bravely revealing their deepest secrets in order to teach us directly about the collective forces that reside within the individual disease process, I offer my special appreciation. You, as much as I, have made this work real.

I suspect that the ideas in this book will be taken for granted in a few years. But the direct experience of the energies out of which these ideas are born will never be taken for granted when the experience emerges in an individual's life. There is an energy in these words, more than the words themselves, that bridges beyond ordinary human involvement.

This book is a spiral returning over and over again to similar areas, but from a deeper perspective and energy. Elements that at first appear to lack cohesiveness gradually begin to be woven into a thought that, if expressed directly, without the foundation of earlier concepts presented at a lesser energy, would lack the power to quicken the expansion and the shift that can take place in you. As you flow along with this you will be in an altered and amplified state of consciousness. The poetry of a deeper wisdom and the rational world of your own experiences will begin to merge. We will be together.

*Richard Moss*
*Sky Hi Ranch*
*Lucerne Valley, CA*
*December, 1980*

# 1 ❖ THE "HEALING" –
A CONFIRMATION

A NUMBER OF YEARS AGO someone asked me why I am so involved with transformation after having trained long and hard to become a doctor. The answer came simply. I have experienced something that is more real to me than anything else, and there is no choice but to honor it.

As a traditional physician I plunged my hands into the abdomen of a man opened from breastbone to umbilicus. Blood was pouring his life into his guts as the result of a stab wound. I squeezed his inferior vena cava (the great vein of the body) against his spine in an attempt to tampanade the bleeding. He died with my hands still in his innards. I have seen the brain gleaming under the surgical lamps as the neurosurgeon prepared to dissect out a tumor. I have been a patient too. I lay upon the surgical table and in the most extraordinary state of consciousness watched the smoke drift up before my eyes from the cautery that was stopping the bleeding as two opthalmological surgeons repositioned muscles to correct a wandering eye that had plagued me for most of my life. Each and every one of these moments was in a very real sense miraculous.

Then one day in the emergency room, as I approached a frightened and pain-gripped man with injections of Demerol and Valium, a voice came into my head. The voice rang within me: "You have nothing to give this man but love."

Handing the syringes to the astonished nurse, I approached the man and placed my left hand on his groin and my right hand on the top of his head. Almost instantaneously I and the room became blazingly hot. Perplexed family members moved spontaneously to the windows to let in some cool air. The patient's eyes rolled back and he went limp and fell into a deep sleep. Thirty minutes later, free of pain and with only a mild limp, the patient rose, thanked me with tears in his eyes, and left the hospital. His pain and hysteria had stopped in seconds with no words and no drugs. Where there had been only hate, belligerence and fear, there now was awe, respect and caring in his eyes.

In that moment, a truth I had somehow always known was confirmed forever in my being. Simply stated, it is that we are multidimensional creatures. There are many dimensions of consciousness that flow through us that we can choose to embrace in our lives. The exploration of these dimensions can be so creative that it renews life, and the miracles of practical medicine seem primitive by comparison.

What is the nature of the energy that passed between us, that seemed to heat the room and everyone in it? To what kind of love was the inner command referring? I stood there in wonder, thinking "What are we?"

Now I know that if we are not profoundly and deeply shaken in our assumptions about what we are, we may remain forever traveling the same path and arguing the same arguments, all in the framework of what we think is happening and who we think it is happening to. And this "who" may be a fiction or, at best, only a fragment of what we truly are.

It wasn't the miracle of that moment that was so important to me, but the larger exploration of consciousness itself. The miracle was a confirmation: It told me that the commitment to open myself and grow by learning about what it means to love was bearing good fruit. It was a cosmic confirmation, a baptism of sorts into a new level of service, and one of the key experiences that led me out of traditional medicine and into the exploration of what it means to be a whole human being.

I moved on, but I do not negate medicine or the gifts to life that science has provided. I believe the greatest potential for healing yet realized by mankind emerges in the wedding of expanded consciousness (more specifically, of deeper love) with the impeccable application of the modern physician's skills.

This adventure is not something for the physician or the healer alone. This is something for all of us. This love can happen anywhere. It is not something that we are born with and have forgotten, as so many like to think. It is discovered through the mature appreciation of the whole of oneself in all moments of life, which finally reveals beyond all these seemingly separate facets our essence as divine creatures.

Make no mistake, this is not a trivial exploration. The quality of energy and the kind of love that manifested as healing in the emergency room is not like any love we are familiar with in our ordinary levels of living and sharing. It is not something we can want with a part of our self like we want a bicycle, or power, or even freedom from disease. This love belongs to the whole of self when it comes. Those who approach naively or from an unconscious selfishness will turn back at the first experience of this love's tendency to bring forward the repressed and the lowly equally as it reveals the beautiful and the lofty. Much that we would never want to think within us will come forth in the light of these deeper forces.

We, as humans, are much more than individuals. It is not merely our individual idiosyncracies and areas of fear and limitation that we must eventually come to embrace without judgment and contraction. It is also the collective areas of human psyche that reveal themselves to the explorer of higher consciousness. It can be terrifying as well as miraculous. One can come to know and feel within one's being the forces that drive the collective momentum of humanity in all its cycles, creative and destructive.

With each of us who begins to realize the level of consciousness in which we discover such an energy, a new capacity emerges. We can for the first time transmute these forces as they pass through us. Just as our body transmutes lettuce and carrots into eye cells and sinew, the same energy that brought us to tears and consternation in adolescence can show us a realm of inexpressible well-being as we learn to carry it harmoniously through an open heart. The opening of the heart, the flowering of the lotus of the chest, the perfect love that casts out all fear, the pursuit of the Holy Grail—herein lie the keys.

This is much more than a metaphorical journey to be theorized and symbolized by alchemists and New Age philosophers. The heart opens and all values change. The appropriate world of yesterday ceases to exist. Relationships change. We cry and struggle with what we can no longer make work in our lives. The body energies course in strange currents and evoke incredible somatic phenomena. Heart attack? Hyperthyroid? Psychosis? Delusions? Possession? Narcissism? Death? These issues press forward. Who is to interpret these phenomena? The traditional doctor knows nothing of energies of other "bodies" beyond the physical and won't allow herself or himself to see. The popular consciousness movement is busy selling methods of feeling good or being more powerful.

Today we frequently take the tricks of yoga, the powers consequent to a heightened consciousness, and package them into behavior training techniques. Consciousness becomes a measure of transactional success, a tool for gain and fame and inner peace. But all too often it is the peace of a shallow pool. The Kingdom is not opened casually. The gifts of wisdom, grace and compassion do not flow simply because we have decided to be better people. They grow in those in whom the very idea of being human has been challenged and undone.

You may well ask "Am I one of those people on the threshold of reaching a new potential, of accepting the challenges of undoing myself?" Who, after all, should read this book? In truth, it is not appropriate for everyone. Those who have not yet reached into life and felt and seen and thought about the deeper issues will not find a home here. Those who cannot participate with the world from a greater perspective than *me, me, me* and *them, out there* are not yet mature or strong enough to begin this journey. Their task is the process of strengthening the statement of *me*, just as the baby must learn how to control its body before it can learn the art of movement. For the mature individual who is ready for this step, the art of living is the conscious loss of control, the letting go of the obsession with self, the surrender into being, the opening of the heart.

We have been seduced too many times by the way-to-be life orientations—to be stronger, or more successful, or more clear. These processes of how to win in life and, equally as dangerous, how to change our world, are just like the excitement of a new lover. We become disenchanted with the old lovers: college education, marriage and family, wealth, careers, retirement at 55. We have found some new lovers. We can "get it," we can learn to be full, to be clear, to be psychic, to be a winner, to feel abundant. In fact we are told that the success of our efforts is measured in our winning. Before, we were told that we could get ahead with a college education, and marriage to our one-and-only. That old dream didn't work, and the dream of personal power is the new lover. In many ways it is an advancement over the old, for the sense of heightened personal power arises through a more here-and-now, in-the-moment stance in life. But the motive is still in the *me, me, me* of the childish psyche that needs to believe there is a way to be and that it can find it. The stimulation of the old dream has become familiar and habitual. It has lost its intoxication. Onward to the next intoxication. . .

The trouble is that you have to do something to recognize your success at this new level of intoxication. You have to push and shove, albeit much more subtly, even psychically. But the sensation of mastery and achievement that one can learn to appreciate through heightening personal power is still following the same theme and the same motivation that fostered our love affair with the earlier dreams. Now is not enough. We must somehow fiddle with the intrinsic harmony of the universe that we haven't even felt.

Meanwhile, the mirror of life is showing us something contrary to this image of triumphant self. The more powerful and masterful we seem to be, the more the experience of living seems to create the incomprehensible and the uncontrollable. We penetrate deeper into the phenomenology of our world and see that the universe does not operate as we thought. Need I qualify this statement with data after all the statements by physicists, scientists, social philosophers and consciousness teachers who have become part of the world scene? Medicine becomes more and more sophisticated. Healers and therapies are springing up like flowers, but cancer is epidemic and not particularly responsive to any one approach, while the world of human interaction grows more and more violent.

Still, we are on the scent of a new flower. We have been moved and quickened by the hope of a better way of being. *Holistic* or *humanistic* or *spiritual*, new labels for our medicine, psychology, or philosophy, have hinted at a new potential, a new reality. But if the fundamental consciousness has not changed, then the incidental energies, the *siddhas* (powers) that emanate from a deeper core reality and that present to our awareness a magic beyond the mundanity of our everyday life, may augment the forms they are added to but will nonetheless remain the servants of the basic psychic structure: the illusion of personhood or individuality that is really the key. A deeper self must be sought and the layers of fantasy shed until we can take an honest look at what we really are. Then, with grace and every bit of will we can muster, perhaps that deeper core can be realized in its essential purity and love. And it can be shared.

I believe we deceive ourselves in the idea that this grace can be approached rationally through control. We run willy-nilly to every process and teaching that presents us with a series of hierarchical steps, planned exercises and specially packaged techniques. If the attainment is incremental and logical, if it is attainable through techniques, then in my experience it is the ego and imagination that grow, and not genuine love, not Beingness. Ultimately there must also be taken into consideration that moment of hiatus, of stepping beyond the realm of the "normal" ego structure, of awakening energies beyond our conception, of falling beyond reason into a new order of reality. This is the transformation of the ego, not winning or success. What emerges is a new consciousness, not a well-polished version of the old.

So who is going to read this book? Who already knows that there is more to gain in letting go than attempting to control and extend the *me?* I believe there are many of us.

There are those who have been in therapy for years. Perhaps they are ready to begin to release the need to understand themselves, to fall beyond their judgment of their situation and feelings to the energetic realm that underlies their experience. There are those who have become blocked or frustrated in their attempt to find meaning and purpose in their own work as health professionals and therapists. There are those who have been purged in the dark night of life's deeper trials, the grief of lost kin or the assault of illness, and they know there is within all this a deeper principle of life.

This book is for those who have always had a sense that there was something else, who were never fully seduced by the material plane. It is for those who have protested, marched and fought to make things better, and who now sense that power in the service of a power-oriented psyche leads to more conflict and more repression. It is for those who care about themselves and about our world but are finally ready to see that there are no fixed answers, no absolute truths, no real issues to fight for, until you have learned how to stop fighting entirely. It is for those who are ready to go deeper.

Define life any way you want and it still escapes your definition. Success, power, gratifying relationships—these are all important and all part of the beauty of life, but equally part of the beauty of life are defeat, failure and vulnerability. The blend of these seeming opposites is where this book begins. It is not for making winners. It is for making men and women who can enter any situation and, having less egoistic perspective to defend, less that has to be won, can infuse their experience with a radiance that presents all of life with a new color and freedom. You can embrace the unknowable, operate without an agenda or goal, and for the first time know what radiant presence means, and the transparency of Self in which such radiance is born. This is the heart of Beingness. It involves the gradual, perhaps radical, transformation of the energies of consciousness that animate our lives. This book is about what happens as we commit to such a journey.

# 2 ❖     LOVE AND ENERGY

HUMAN BEINGS POSSESS a reality of inner space that has been all but ignored in Western civilization's obsessive preoccupation with outer phenomena. Though we are all intuitively aware of the energies beyond the superficial levels of our selves, there is a profound existential fear associated with the journey of self-discovery. Faced with seemingly limitless freedom, we fall back in dismay and opt for a very limited range of experience.

Far from willing to explore our human potential, we are afraid to venture beyond a cautious high, and we quickly reject our lows. Any behavior that might carry us beyond our own narrow band of acceptable feelings is unthinkable, and we banish it instantly. When our Beingness cries out for expression, we are willing only to intensify the *acceptable* emotions: We create some minor crisis; we become angry. We have sex; we become happy. Soon, without noticing, we are addicted to this range of sensations. We have to be emotive, for within the range of energies we permit ourselves there is no other recourse for experiencing contrast and intensity.

In our culture we have an addiction to intensity that is almost always confined to the coarser emotions. Subtleties and nuances are beyond the scope of those who use most of their psychic energy just to avoid inner knowledge. Even with the maximum range of intensity we permit ourselves, we limit the amount of energy with which we empower our consciousness. We stop short of a potential to go beyond ourselves because we imagine that we are in control and must remain so.

Only by extending beyond this self-imposed limitation, by plunging into a profound unconditional state of deep soul-felt love, can we begin to understand the real functions of our emotions and behavior. We can then come to know how they function to create our existence—to define the very psychological space of our incarnation.

Let me give you an example. Recently I went into deep retreat with my closest and most committed students and associates. There were hot springs at the site we chose. A series of tubs contained water ranging in temperature from the low 50s to about 117 degrees Fahrenheit. In the middle range were several tubs containing water from about 98 to 108 degrees. For several days, none of the people would enter either the coldest or the hottest tub. I overheard people commenting on those extremes. "You'll never see me in those!" or "Who needs to torture himself?"

The mind is very tricky. It decides that such extremes represent a context of stress or torture and closes off whole realms of experience from which many benefits might accrue. However, my friends were right in a way. At the level of their awareness when they arrived at the hot springs these extremes *were* perhaps too threatening—even inappropriate.

The limit was in their minds. It represented the range of energy they would allow themselves to experience. Fear of the extremes of temperature was acceptable to them and they had not as yet considered transcending it. However, as the days went on, the strong consciousness that grew out of the group process began to expand their awareness, and the range of what was possible, appropriate and beneficial also expanded.

Finally one evening I announced that, as a ritual signifying our commitment to transcend our limits maturely and wisely, we would all immerse ourselves in all of the tubs. As part of the ritual there was to be silence and no change of facial expressions. We would begin at the most comfortable temperature, move to the 108-degree tub, from there to a pool of 74 degrees, thence to the hottest tub and finally the coldest. Complete relaxation and "allowing" would permit us to sense into the changes, so that from one perspective in consciousness (the place of total acceptance) each tub experience was identical to every other.

All of the thirty-five people accomplished the ritual with ease. They experienced a tremendous release of energy and great joy. The next day many wondered how they could have denied themselves the magnificence of this range, with its accompanying depth of relaxation and sense of inner mastery. Few things make human beings feel better than an experience that stretches the sense of aliveness and shows us we have grown.

The tub ritual was in no way torture, nor did it require the evolvement of stoic self-control. A higher energy state—one could call it love—and a basic well-being had happened within these people through their work and meditation together. This fuller quality made it possible to enter the ritual without any kind of repression. Certainly there were chattering minds doubting to the last minute whether it was safe or wise. But the experience was right, and it transcended the boundaries of the intellectual mind's reaction. Throughout the vicissitudes of the journey of awakening the eventual sense of joy, wholeness and radiance is final proof that we have extended our limits through love.

The initial avoidance of the hottest and coldest tubs is a metaphor for unawakened human life. Most of us are narrow and constricted, so that the love in us cannot flow fully. We confine our experience of love to sex, and our sensations to a small band of emotive experience. There may be a lot of power in these emotions, but the energy is still of a low order. At higher, *finer* levels of energy, our awareness participates in such feeling states as reverence, gratitude, trust, wonderment, awe and unconditional love. To fulfill this potential we need to learn to retain the energies with which we are already comfortable and expand ourselves to encompass energies beyond our usual range. We thus become radiant beings, imparting a quality that evokes an energy all around us. The intrapsychic and interpersonal experiences of these states are entirely different from those available at so-called ordinary levels of consciousness. In the awakening process love transcends the boundaries of our self-imposed or conditioned half-hearted living by incorporating and allowing the whole range of our experience, not by closing some part off.

I have found that the use of the words *energy* and *love* produces anxiety and irritation in some people. This is because these words imply an interior dimension underlying the world we know. It is not a dimension continuous with our present knowing. It is a quantum leap beyond that. *It is a transformation.*

In Newtonian physics the word *energy* is no problem. A block slides across a table and we can measure the force needed for that movement to occur. We never question the energy represented by this action even though it cannot be seen. We are comfortable with the idea that (within a carefully defined system that we are usually unaware of) all energy is measured in its effect.

When I use the word *energy* I am referring to the force (or quality of consciousness) operating at a particular moment that allows us to perceive a particular reality. At one level of energy we have access to certain moods; for instance, if we are exhausted (low in energy) it is easy to become irritable and impatient. At another level of energy, when we are rested, we may feel on top of the world; our senses relay the news that coffee tastes wonderful and the sunlight on the leaves imbues us with great joy and peace. To the ordinary human awareness this is referred to as feeling good or not feeling good, but the underlying energy state is not perceived *directly* — it is recognized *through* our behavior, and *through* our sense of vitality.

Just as the eyes see light and translate it into an image and the ears hear sounds and translate them into signals, there is a largely unrecognized dimension of human capability that experiences energy more directly than as feelings, attitudes and impressions. For this dimension of human awareness, energy becomes a living current. Sometimes this is called *kundalini* energy. In acupuncture it flows in the *meridians*. It is also referred to as *chi* energy or as being in *communion with the Tao*. But even here the energy is often inferred, not directly experienced in the same way we experience with eyes and ears. Very few people who discuss it are capable of igniting this dimension in others. Thus it remains intellectual rather than catalytic. The important thing in my work is to bring the awareness of self as energy into direct experience so that the sense of this energy is a direct bodily experience of a force that transcends what we know ourselves to be. It is alive and real, and once it has been awakened in a human being, that person is gradually dissolved into it, or transformed by it.

This energy or force of consciousness is not easily defined, but with it comes a qualitative shift in how life is experienced. The knowledge of this energy is a kind of cultural myth that is alive in the hearts and souls of human beings, and being born as a direct experience at varying levels in thousands of people each day. The sense of this energy is the revelation of another hidden dimension underlying ordinary consciousness. Despite resistance on the part of science and "objective reason" to such ideas, an appreciation of this hidden reality is becoming increasingly common in collective consciousness: Thus *Star Wars* could talk about "The Force," to the delight of millions of people of all ages.

But the use of words like *love, energy, underlying reality* and *multidimensional* still creates a problem for some people. They may feel the words imply there is something they do not know. A frequent response is "I already know that" or "It doesn't matter anyway." People who are very linear and rational and who exercise a lot of control over their emotions and their daily lives resist these words the most. To embrace the words and the feelings from which they arise might create a sense of illogic, nonrationality or loss of control. Yet the rational and linear aspects of consciousness are really quite limited. They are valid only as long as one has carefully defined and controlled the context being explored and this is not possible in the awakening process. Once a sense of the underlying dimensions implied by words like *love* and *energy* begins to enter the picture, an absolute reality disappears. There is an element of insecurity and uncertainty in the embracing of these words.

I am not interested in making someone uncomfortable or in taking control. The words are unavoidable in the exploration of inner spaces. To appreciate them means that the world is experienced more totally than through limited physical sensation, intellectualization or emotions. A more subtle "body" is needed. We have to sense into experience, and feel into these words. The subtle Self that is responding to energetic forces is infinitely greater than the self of ideas or emotions. It responds and resonates to energies and levels of experience that less-developed levels of consciousness can never know directly.

This Greater Body or Self is the reality that communicates between the formless and unseen underlying aspects and the outer experiences that we once thought absolute or objective. Direct experience of words like *love* or *energy* implies a full-body feeling that includes every level of self. Reality seems to become a dance of energies, and through these energies each of us is connected to experience and to each other. This energetic dimension is so much more inclusive and primary than emotion or thought that if the energy of love sweeps through you, any thoughts or emotions you were formerly experiencing, no matter how powerful, evaporate. To embrace the Greater Self is to become vulnerable to flows of feeling that are quite nonrational and can create tremendous peace when you can finally release into their intrinsic harmony—or tremendous discomfort until this release is achieved.

I use the words *love* and *energy* liberally, but not lightly. They are parameters of my own direct experience. Too casual use of these words is equally as damaging to the person using them as being unwilling to face the insecurity and newness implied by them. *Love* and *energy* can be words of resistance to inner spaces—or of escape into them. There is wisdom bestowed by meditating into the essence of these words and allowing them to grow in depth and meaning with each new day.

We have talked about energy. Now let's take a look at the word *love*. It is *the* word of our time, and perhaps the word of all time. The core of Christ's teaching was the love of our fellow humans and the love of God. Christ consciousness is often referred to as love. But what is this quality of love? Christ said that he came to bring a sword. He also said that those who honored the Law as he did were his family, clearly differentiating personal family and the family of man united through a deeper principle. Certainly very few of us would equate love with a sword or with non-intimate relationships beyond family and loved ones. Yet in my experience, the equation is very real.

To embrace a love that is beyond the level of personal and sensual love is to enter into an experience of such magnitude that the whole personal self is dissolved into it. At every point in my own inner nature where I held to a memory or a need—the old ways of fulfilling myself—the greater energy turned this into pain. I was too small for the energy. I had to let go, to surrender, to grow. It wasn't until I reached harmony within the greater energy that I recognized this force was part of a larger reality. The feeling state of this recognition is a profound love but its existence is not compatible with the rigid grip of ordinary awareness.

We are not talking here about a philosophical embrace of love as a primary way of being that is above all other imperatives of life. In fact, one must do this to initiate the process of transformation. But this philosophical stance is only the first step, though it can go on for a very long time. Often it creates all kinds of troubles, such as avoiding relationships and fearing to explore the emotions fully. We would rather believe that love is something we can do, than something that destroys our doing and takes us into another dimension.

Nevertheless, if the idea of love is not embraced, there is no way to gain objectivity about the reality dominated by personal imperatives and emotional reactivity and need. Transformation begins with the embrace of love and leads to the first essential step, which is the transmutation of emotions. When you begin to tell yourself that your emotional stance in life is a distortion of your potential to love, then you have invited a flame into your life that will gradually destroy and transform you.

Still we have not come to a sufficient expansion on the word *love*. Who is the beloved of Kabir, and of Rumi and Gibran? Who is the lover who came to Whitman? Despite what we think we know about their personal lives, these poets speak of a transcendent lover. The romantics would like to believe that these songs of love are a sanction for personal attachment to another individual, but the lover they truly celebrate is an experience of ecstacy in transcendent consciousness.

I use the word *love* as a koan. The koan is a teaching tool of Zen Buddhism. It presents the rational mind with an unsolvable question, such as "What is the sound of one hand clapping?" The answer is a total state of awareness; another dimension of experience. It is not an answer in any ordinary sense at all. Similarly, I use the word *love* not to tell anyone anything, but to evoke a larger relationship to experience. I use it to symbolize and suggest, to invite the experience of a larger harmonious perspective. Love can be discussed only as a tool to expand perspective.

I spent several years mimicking the philosophy and way of living of the teacher whose presence had kindled in me the first taste of this higher kind of love. I made believe I knew about this love. I was even audacious enough to teach about love. I reached for a sense of unconditional love—a sense of energy and being prior to my judgments and "ideas about" experience, a quality that was intrinsically peaceful and in harmony—as the resolution of every state of consciousness, every feeling and every desire that was not harmonious. I urged myself to this sense of harmony, and I urged others to it. While there is a distortion in this—a trying to force reality into a certain form— there is simultaneously a subtle preparation taking place at another level of consciousness. When a "gate" finally opened and an enormous sense of energy engulfed me, it was the years of striving for a perspective of intrinsic balance and harmony (whose heart was love) that allowed me eventually to gradually trust and stabilize this energy and to survive it.

Throughout this book I use the word *love* in many ways, and sometimes it may seem contradictory of another usage. The point of love is not to pin it down or provide a formula for being so that the rational self can feel safe and secure. The point of love is to invite us to reach deeper into our experience.

I use the guiding invocation of unconditional love as a way to put the rational mind aside and begin to sense into another dimension of Self. Acknowledging the quality of this love to be unconditional, one moves toward a state of consciousness characterized by the intrinsic harmony and well-being of love, but not requiring any qualifying context. It does not require a person outside of ourselves to love. It does not require that someone recognize our goodness. It does not require that the world respond to us just as we want.

When that gate opened for me, and I was swept into worlds that I could never have conceived, I had already set this love alive inside me. Through my seeking for it and my intuition of it, something in my consciousness recognized that the central place at which all experience resolves is love, without regard to any outside condition. Thus I could know that we do not have to earn this love, that it is given to us by life itself, unconditionally. It was not easy for me to awaken into the deeper energies, nor is it easy for others who are beginning to reach into other levels of awareness. But with the embrace of unconditional love, the stage is set for resolution and harmonization.

Unconditional love is the embracing of all experience and the bringing of all the varying intensities to the level of the heart. At the heart level, unconditional love, which is an alive, vibrant, valueless state of awareness, replaces the varying intensities of mood and uncontrolled emotion and lifts the energy of these states into a finer, more radiant quality.

For example, an experience of emotional intensity can be sensed around the solar plexus. The solar plexus is the power center where our "body" extends out into existence through our ideas, beliefs and plans. It is the home of our adrenal glands, of fight and flight, and of the emotional response that results when these ideas about reality set up an interference pattern with actual reality. Think about what it is like to feel jealous or to be caught in the pain and reactivity of possessiveness. Now recognize that the energy (the underlying consciousness force) that is giving rise to these feelings of jealousy can itself be worked with, rather than the content and issues we think are crucial. If this energy, that at one moment is operating from the emotional level, is transmuted to the level of the heart (brought up into another potential, like turning the crude force of a waterfall into electricity), an amazing discovery is made. The very situation in which we are threatened, feel hurt and jealous, can in a moment become a sense of peace and oneness. We can come into harmony with a larger reality—one that was obscured by our earlier orientation. It is then possible truly to resolve the interpersonal issues without supposing that the reasons for the initial feelings are absolute and must be dealt with on their terms.

Recently at one of my conferences a woman shared what she had experienced while she watched me interview a patient. The patient was describing the painful and protracted death of her son. I could sense the pathos growing in the room and reminded the participants to maintain their centers of awareness consciously at an unconditional (heart) level and not move into emotional rapport. The woman listener had found herself suddenly in a fantasy of her own son's death and became emotionally panicked. Hearing my guidance, she was able to release the terrifying fantasy. However, as she was recounting her experience to the group, she was unable to remain clear of the power of her fantasy and began to cry, her voice broken and tremulous, her respiration erratic. I said "Allow the energy in your guts to lift into your chest." Instantly, as if by magic, her voice became strong and clear, her breathing regular, and she cried out "I did it!" She said "Just as you told me to lift the energy I remembered what you had said about listening from an unconditional space while you were interviewing. The moment I remembered I felt the energy lift to my heart and I was free." This is an example of transmutation in which the awareness of the teacher (in this case, me) was necessary to catalyze the process.

The first time I personally had this experience I was profoundly moved. One of my closest friends had come for a visit and an obvious attraction had sprung up between him and my girlfriend. I was feeling contracted, angry and hurt. Realizing this, I shifted my awareness and simultaneously asked my consciousness to release this energy into unconditional love. Miraculously, the contraction of my guts and the sense of anger and possessiveness suddenly lifted away. I was suffused with a radiant warmth that seemed to project from the chest. A wave of heat passed through the room and the others also felt kindled in it. The issue of jealousy no longer had meaning for the rest of my friend's visit, and gradually diminished out of my life.

All emotional states (in fact, all levels of experience) are relative: Shift the quality of the underlying energy and the nature of experience changes. Of course the key to such fluidity is to be able volitionally to move to a higher level of energy. It takes a higher principal to refine the reality of a lower principle of being. Unconditional love is of so much greater fineness and magnitude than the dimension which manifests in emotional experience that it literally dissolves or resolves the emotional configuration of energy.

As these processes, such as the instantaneous ability to shift levels of consciousness, began to open in my life, I began to experience the deep existential question of what is real. For this I have no rational answer, but I can expand to contain the questioner and there rest into a sense of higher Beingness. Thus when people have asked me why this process has to be seen as fundamentally spiritual, my answer is that without love, in its deepest and mystical sense, there is no way to work safely with the forces of reality. Without love there is nothing to let go into. One either willingly moves toward a spiritual center within oneself or, if fortunate, is made spiritual by the evoked experiences. The alternatives, as we shall see, are not good.

The episode of the transmutation of my jealous emotion, which happened years ago, was just the beginning for me of a process in which the transmutation of the energies of my consciousness was guided at the level of the heart. I discovered that the crucial element in the deeper awakening of consciousness is the willingness to allow all discordant intensities of feeling to be transmuted into an intrinsic harmony that is both expansive and uplifting. This must not be construed as denial or rejection in any way. I am not talking about trying to create a prettier reality.

The first step in a genuine movement toward awakening is the realization that all experience is relative and the direct consequence of its underlying energy dynamic. An outer analogy is the experiment in which medical students who learned certain material while drunk later tested better on this material when they were again drunk. They tested poorly if they were sober. Even intelligence is not an absolute based upon the accumulation and retrieval of information. Intelligence and behavior are functions of consciousness that are entirely consequent to the basic energetic state. We are all in a sense drunk within the energy level of our present state without ever realizing it. One must develop the ability to sense into the energetic level and the capacity to alter the quality of this energy.

The second step lies in acknowledging that the ability to refine energy (as opposed to merely increasing it) requires a commitment to and direct realization of unconditional love. Love is the great transmuting force that can take any fixed energetic/existential pattern and allow it to resolve into harmony on a much greater scale. *Without unconditional love as the center from which to consecrate our Beingness, the ability to shift and transmute energies can become just another manipulation of our ego power.* It is essential to understand this. Recall the example of my working with critically ill patients, where their shift in perspective proved only temporary because it was not founded in unconditional love so much as it was in my ability to be persuasive.

Just because we call something spiritual does not mean that it liberates in the unconditional sense. Remember the great religious wars, all of which were based on the assumptions of right vs. wrong, the True Christ vs. the Antichrist, and so on. Such polarities always grow out of judgment and the desire for power. We need to sense into the difference between power- and emotion-bound consciousness and the levels revealed though unconditional love.

The heart, anatomically the midchest area, is at first a metaphorical center of meaning in life and gradually opens into a direct experience of a new dimension. It is the center for the direct sensing of the energies that represent unconditional love. It is metaphorical at first because we cannot make unconditional love happen by thinking about it. I tried over and over to tell myself that I could choose love and release a particular pattern, that I didn't need to feel a certain way, and so on. But that didn't change anything. Finally I began to notice where the energy *was* in and around my body, where sensation was concentrated, and all the thoughts that were part of this state. Then I remembered how I felt when I was in the sense of deep well-being and love. Here, as I said before, the energy emanated from the midchest, the heart center. Thus, I finally learned to place my awareness at the heart and began to learn how to transmute energy consciously.

I called this early process the "knock down-drag out fight" because I was willing to sit with my experience until it transmuted, even if it took a week. At first the state I was working to transmute would intensify and my being would seethe like a volcano, and then as I stayed with this I would become blank. Still I kept returning my awareness to the heart and waiting. It was not enough that I drifted off to other thoughts and the whole process seemed unimportant, or that I had a wonderful creative insight. I soon learned that this displacement of awareness into acceptable territory was not transmutation. I waited until I was suffused with a deep feeling state of well-being that emanated from my chest. Then I would re-examine the issue from this higher state to see the assumptions about reality that had allowed it to configurate in the first place. I found that in this expanded state I could marry divisive issues to each other and could appreciate the energy process inherent in their activation.

Gradually this transmuting capacity became more and more natural and automatic. It even went beyond emotional issues to touch upon issues that, for want of a better word, are of the soul itself. One day I realized that even the existential fear that at times would sweep through me early in the awakening process was in fact a miraculous sensation of embodiment to a higher level of my being. Thus even deeper patterns and reality frames began to transmute into a more and more unconditional and eternal sense of Self. While it is difficult to state what this transmuting mechanism actually is, it seems to be a refining sense of acceptance.

The heart is the point of balance in consciousness through which we become aware of the full spectrum of our humanness—the feared and the hated as well as the loved and revered. *Coming from the heart level is the continuous process of learning to let go of everything and anything that closes the heart to the embrace of Now.* Rather than reacting to a particular situation, one recognizes that there is another level at which the elements of the situation could be allowed to have a new relationship. This overview reveals an energetic force that can be changed and molded by a disciplined and sensitive awareness.

To work in this dimension represents a quantum leap from the dimension of analysis, interpretation and rationalization. It moves out of the realm of ideas and behavior and into an area of formless states where life is an ongoing medley of energetic forces. It is almost impossible to describe the incredible richness and newness that imbues life when this realization is discovered and we begin to live it.

It is a journey of many mistakes and of taking risks. After all, if a sense of a new quality of energy is to be achieved, then some of our favorite feelings will have to be set aside. Few of us are aware of how addicted we are to such sensations as excitement, anger, possessiveness, sadness, righteousness, self-importance and success until we are asked to make room for an entirely new experience. But once a deeper sense of harmony and balance has been embraced, the energies available to our consciousness gradually become so enormous that we could never again safely manifest them in our old limited and conditional ways. A process of radiance and well-being begins to replace the dimension of uncontrolled, addictive emotions and power.

There is nothing conditional or judgmental in the love I am describing. The greatest mistake we can make (and it is a common one when we are new to all of this) is to think that love is better than some other quality of experience. No, love is not better. If you think so, then the love you espouse is personal and conditional. The love to which I refer embraces all experience equally and unconditionally. When it arises for the first time in one's life, it makes all other ways in which we have known love seem crude.

Unconditional love as an invocation is only a way of processing experience and a tool for transformation. It is also a state in itself, and when its tremendous presence flames within you, you are not saying "This is love!" You are not saying anything at all. To talk about this presence later is already a distortion. It cannot be talked about accurately. Unconditional love is quite beyond words. When it is there, you are not.

In embracing unconditional love you surrender all emotions and thoughts that separate you from well-being and harmony. This is the essential commitment in transformation and it must be renewed every day. Love is a daily celebration of aliveness *and* permission to go deeper.

# 3 ❖  THE EXPERIENCE OF
TRANSFORMATION

EVERYTHING I HAVE BEEN SAYING derives from the manner in which my own unfoldment has been guided. It is not that I have come so far. In many ways I am only an infant in the ongoing process of full human Beingness, and as each day passes this realization becomes deeper. This state of infancy is a place of new beginnings that has occurred many times in my life. Sometimes it has been frightening. Usually it is inspiring, and at the same time quite humbling. Whenever there has been struggle and fear on this journey, it has come because I lost the sense of infancy and eternal new beginnings.

I have come to think about myself, and about life in general, as an illusory integrity about which blows a cosmic wind. If we try to hold onto a concrete or absolute sense of ourselves as the wind begins to erode the outer fringes of our being, the change brings fear. It is the illusion of *me* that brings the pain. I believe that all disease and all suffering starts as we begin to recoil away from this deeper intuition of the vastness and indefinable eternity of Self. When the fear or doubt arises, which it does over and over again, it becomes a signal that it is time to let go, rebalance and find an unconditional allowing of life.

One immediately hears the inner question "How do I do this?" The effect of this question is dual. It prepares a path for understanding, but simultaneously it obscures another level of experience. How-to-do-it is important if what we are trying to learn is rational and must be reproduced. But if it is this ineffable quality of Beingness or unconditional love, then the question is an obstacle. It is never enough that someone offers us an energy through their presence, their words and their very being that—if we would just give up our urgent rational inquiry—might infuse us with the answer directly. There is always a part of us that thinks we can learn about love the way we learned to add and subtract.

I have no doubt that the level of communication towards which we are moving is telepathic and that it is through telepathic impress that the deeper learning is initiated between people. Still the questions are inevitable, even though all of us are aware that we do not really know how the deeper things are learned. In fact, transformation is radiated, not rationally taught, and rational processes must be wisely set aside to help receive the deeper impress.

The answer to how-to-do-it is always direct experience. Quite distinct from the intention that motivates us or the expectations we have about what we would like to discover, direct experience implies living the answer. Still, it is hard to tell someone that if they will just let go and rest into the Now the learning will happen automatically. It will also happen faster, but of course with accelerated challenge, in an environment of heightened energy.

This book is not intended to answer all questions and provide the security of understanding. There is no such thing as a handbook for Beingness. We do not learn the more important things by having our questions answered by someone else. We learn by having our present equilibrium thrown off balance so that we can discover on our own a way to return to balance. Thus, my intention is to stimulate, stretch and even frustrate you into discovering new ways to look at life.

But we can go no further if it is not appreciated that there is some kind of energy field or organizing process—call it consciousness—that is operating beyond the reality we ordinarily perceive. If we let go and surrender our outer reason there must be something that we fall into, otherwise the release of our limiting egocentric reality would just result in chaos, the very thing we always fear.

Did you know that there have been experiments with the developing frog embryo where, at a point in its development when it has begun to differentiate the left and right arm buds, the embryo can be cut in such a way as to rotate the arm buds? The left arm bud ends up on the right and the right arm bud is on the left. Yet, instead of going on to develop the displaced left and right arms, the embryo matures and that which began as a left arm turns into a right arm and that which would have been a right arm turns into a left arm.

There is nothing in the genetic material as we understand it that should account for the interruption of a normal process by a human experimenter. If life unfolds simply through the material maintained in the genetic pattern then this realignment should not occur. It is my suspicion that matter as we understand it precipitates from or is defined by another dimension. Then it becomes our quite reasonable concern to know whether human consciousness is capable of reaching past its material configuration and tapping into this deeper orchestrating process through some other level of awareness, some other mode of knowing.

In making this jump one enters a dimension of formlessness governed by feeling states and intuitive knowing that do not respond to, or participate with, our traditional ways of learning. The ego structure through which we perform in our life is constantly distinguishing between ourself and so-called external reality. This process is rooted in the relationship with our parents, against whom the initial sense of distinction and separateness is developed—we having begun as·indistinct from them. We carry the separating and categorizing mode of consciousness, which is the essence of ego formation, on into adult life.

Traditional ego-based psychological thinking identifies a breakdown of this differentiation mode as the underlying process in psychosis. Traditional education believes that accumulation of facts, which are really points of distinction (the ego saying "I am not this"), is the basis for intelligence and mastery of the world. But there comes a natural point in human development where this very process must be reversed, where the boundary between self and experience must be allowed to relax in order for a new level of perception to enter. This is not psychosis, but mystical/spiritual awakening.

The spiritual awakening can in many ways be a razor's edge — its other side being a delusional process, or even psychosis. To move beyond the memory, which continues to recreate the Now through a comparison with what was, is not a task to be regarded lightly. It is a fundamental return to the beginner's mind, to the child state, to Beingness prior to conditioned and memorized images about life. Yet one is fully armed with all the facts, discriminatory faculties and right/wrong prejudices. It is easy for a fool to believe in healing and give heart and soul to it. But when the scientist/physician, knowing what he knows, can rest into formlessness and operate with a part of awareness married to the Void, and manifest this as love — this is a divine state. It is not an easy state to reach. We must surrender to a higher principle within our sense of existence.

Within this deeper, orchestrating consciousness the part of awareness that needs to know and the part that already knows are both available. Therefore, we need a certain shift in attitude and understanding in order to make the knowing part of self equally as available as the questioner. I suspect they must be available equally for the learning process to happen. This is quite a challenge, since, when faced with the new and unknown, we usually try to place our accustomed labels or line up our familiar battery of questions. Despite ourselves, memory takes over. The true Now is experience moving with a Greater Self — a Self that can only be realized directly and never through an idea or memory.

The philosopher Alfred North Whitehead has referred to the natural fact that the future must remain intrinsically frightening, and that any structures formulated by a culture to defer this apprehension are the very structures that destroy the culture. This is also true for the individual. What we do to make ourselves safe eventually creates the situation for our demise. It is the good guy who won't make waves who has the personality profile for a higher risk of cancer. It is the rational, logical self that obstructs transformation when it defends less than its fullest possibility for growth.

If we approach transformation with the dominant attitude of already knowing, it usually acts as a defense against the vulnerability of new learning. On the other hand, the part that desires understanding and asks the questions is filtering the totality of experience into a narrower channel. We have to learn to approach experience simultaneously through a third point of awareness. This third point of awareness is not simply a detached or neutral witness point, although the latter is an essential developmental state. This third point of awareness operates in an entirely different dimension of consciousness. To learn in this dimension, we discover that words like *trust, balance, surrender, allowing* and *love* are more than words, they are reality-defining energies. They allow an essentially Now relationship with that which is beyond form and reason.

Meanwhile, the part of us that requires the guiding directions is valid and leads us toward a door. It is a gift of our nature to intuit a higher potential and to search toward our Greater Self. But there is a kinetics of consciousness that suggests that once we identify with an aspect of ourselves we empower it, and it then resists flowing back into the vastness of awareness from which it emerged. Thus, our "searcher" or "questioner" will never step through the door it has found. Our searching self knows its existence through the process of leading us onward and not by being the resolution we seek. As we approach the door, the searcher or questioner, as well as the "knower," must return into an undifferentiated potential—the third point—so that "all" of us is reconfigurated. It sounds paradoxical, and it is, but you cannot transform only a part of you.

This is what I believe is meant by the injunction "Save as ye be as children, ye shall not enter the Kingdom of Heaven." It is the undifferentiated state of consciousness that belongs to the infant who can perceive and appreciate the whole of experience simultaneously. To return to this openness as an adult is the beauty, the pain and the challenge of transformation. We are asked to intuit the whole puzzle all the time rather than being blindly absorbed with any one individual piece. We must function precisely and maturely *even as we intuit our ultimate ignorance.*

At this point it is essential to grasp the concept of a hologram. A good description of the technology of holograms can be found in *Scientific American* and in the late Itzhak (Ben) Bentov's book *Stalking the Wild Pendulum.* My description will deal with the metaphorical significance of the hologram.

Basically, a hologram is a three-dimensional image created by the interference pattern of two laser beams. The image that results (like the intersecting waves of multiple rocks thrown into a calm lake) has certain unique properties. The image is three-dimensional, not flat like a photograph, and is nonmaterial. There is no "thing" there where the image is seen but we see it nonetheless. Another unique property is that the whole image can be retrieved from any segment of the holographic plate. Each part contains the whole. This is not true of a conventional photographic image. Can you imagine trying to recreate the face of a friend from a section of the foot. Yet this can be done with the hologram, although the resulting image will diminish slightly in distinctness according to how little of the original is used, and the recreated whole will be oriented slightly differently in its time-space properties. The actual relationship of the two beams used to create the image is also very interesting. One beam must be pure, while the other beam must have interacted with the image, before their intersection results in the capacity to foster an image on the holographic plate.

Nature understands the holographic principle quite well, as is seen in the process of tissue regeneration. It is fundamental to the idea of cloning that, starting with certain cells, a whole creature can be reproduced. The idea that some kind of energy or consciousness acts as a holographic force directing the formation of the image of a complete structure when only a part is available is also suggested by the Kirlian photographs that show an aura-like radiance which traces the location of a missing half of a leaf. Even when part of the leaf is missing there still remains some property of the remaining piece that allows a powerful burst of energy, employed in the creation of the Kirlian photograph, to configurate the image of the missing part.

In transformation, human consciousness is seen to obey principles similar to those exemplified by the hologram. For instance, I strongly believe that, as we look at consciousness as a whole, any repressed or weakly developed component of the psyche will effect a subtle diminution of Beingness. One consequence of this may be the inability to master certain forces necessary to the maintenance of full health, forces such as the vitality necessary to reject aberrant tissue. Similarly, those who have rejected and repressed the more elemental and primeval forces of life may be unable to master the powerful unbounded quality of awakening energies. The forces of consciousness that ultimately express as the wholeness of Beingness are all woven inseparably one within the other; none can be discarded. Thus, the awakening process will bring forward all that is latent in order to achieve wholeness.

On the other hand, the personality is no more transformed by the addition of a new behavior than is a house by the addition of a new extension. Addition or deletion in a linear sense is not transformation. In transformation, the change occurs simultaneously at all levels of the structure. If the house were to be transformed, it might suddenly be made of a new material that interpenetrates every aspect of the structure. *Transformation is radical. When it occurs, it effectively integrates and alters one's nature at every level all at once.* The sequential and rational idea of changing one thing here and one there is not what transformation is about. Erich Fromm alluded to this when he wrote that we cannot change only one behavior. Every behavior is permeated with every other behavior.

We all approach transformation thinking that what is needed is to work out a particular problem, such as the area of loving and relationships. Our outer mind tells us that once the relationship issues are resolved there will be fulfillment. But the issues of loving and sharing are part of the whole structure of Self. If they change, everything changes. It often happens that, when relationships begin to resolve, the whole desire process around relationship (often predicated in a sense of inadequacy) is seen for what it is, and the very thing for which the search was motivated becomes irrelevant as a far deeper process is engaged. In a balanced awareness, relationships are a natural given of life and not something to be "worked on" independent of deeper balance. We are, as I have already said, incredibly addicted to certain levels of experience, and, as we move toward an energy that would change the whole basis for our experience, the choice to flee or deny can be quite strong. We want to change just the part we want to change, but this is not possible if genuine transformation is to occur. When we sense that *everything* will change if true change is to happen at all, that sense strikes either hope or fear in our hearts and we open or contract accordingly.

Suffice it to say that transformation, if you commit to it, will change everything. It may be a subtle change or it may be radical, but to approach any single problem without being willing to look at and work with the whole process of Beingness is naive. This is why I am less interested in people's problems and more interested in the process of inspiration and discovery.

Within the imagery of holograms is contained another key component of the transformation process. *Transformation implies, in the most radical sense, intuiting the whole energy.* The individual attempting to heal an illness is frequently operating from a narrowed perspective, or what I call "problem-level thinking." When we move toward specific problems we are on shaky footing. If we can change the perspective to a greater level of awareness, the result will tend to be integrative. Obviously we never see the whole picture completely, but we can strive toward that goal, and our behavior can carry qualities that recognize this unknowable potential. Words such as *reverence, trust* and *love* refer to the human state that arises when a larger sense exists coincidentally with our day-to-day experience.

Let me offer a story in which the holographic idea is contained in another way and shows a different kind of significance. A student seeking after the essential truth and harmony of existence had traveled throughout the world. He had mastered his body and become a witness of his own inner physical, mental and emotional states. Nevertheless he felt there was more to learn. He had experienced an incredible state of unity with a greater reality and the great rush of energy that he knew to be parts of the awakening process, but a great fear and emptiness kept coming back to him. Therefore he sought out a great master. The master welcomed him by asking him what had happened to the companion with whom he started on the journey. The student replied that he had had no companion. The master laughed and said "Surely, if you cannot remember who you left behind, I cannot help you." In that moment the student remembered who he had left behind and was united with the master.

What do we leave behind when we decide that there is something deeper to be experienced in life? Subtly we have said that what we are experiencing now is not enough. In fact, this very mode is exactly why we are driven continuously toward some deeper harmony even while we operate in the sequential, fragmented modes of experience. But eventually our search takes us full circle and we must embrace the apathy, boredom, limitations and fears and also the rage and power that underlie the original feeling that something else must be sought for. It is not until we move through all of these that we finally can draw the energy from them—the energy of our repression—and enter another state of being.

There are certain things we don't like, so we seek for something else, never realizing that the very energy that is our deeper thirst is born in the total acceptance of that for which we seek as well as that which we are rejecting. Even if what leads us on is a sense of inspiration and joy, eventually the awakening process leads us to recognize not only the inspired aspects that lead us forward, but also the simple, mundane self we left behind. This is why meditation loses its initial charge and becomes boring and inconvenient after awhile. It is the same mechanism in jobs and marriages that lose their initial magic.

There is a second anecdote that looks even more broadly at the unity of existence. A famous filmmaker goes traveling. He wants to find an ultimate theme because, although it is world-renowned, his work feels incomplete to him. He meets a wise old man who fascinates him in some inexplicable way, and he invites the old man home with him. The filmmaker asks the old man for the secret of the strange feeling he has when around him, but the old man remains silent. One day the filmmaker discovers the old man sitting with a scissors on the floor of the film library amidst a tangle of cut film. On the floor are all the individual frames, while the old man's pockets are bulging with the thin clear strips of the bordering celluloid.

In that moment the filmmaker understands the nature of the ultimate theme. While all his life he had been obsessed with each particular drama and looked for an ultimate reality at this level, he now sees that the space from which each drama emerges is of equal significance.

I do not believe it is ever possible to contain the energy of all of our dimensions simultaneously and still operate in the world physically and materially. However, we can—perhaps *must*— learn to stretch beyond our limiting addictions to personal pleasure and fulfillment, to embrace the intuition of a deeper sense. The limitation and perhaps danger of continuing to look at life only from our own point of view without sensing into a larger context is the arrogance of our blind egoism. This understanding is taught to me over and over again as I continue to fall into a narrow perspective. One of the most graphic experiences occurred with an infant.

The child, who was about eight months old, was a regular guest at my home. Usually the child was left in one of the bedrooms to sleep, but on this occasion I asked that he be left with me.

I had an idea that I could communicate with him through energy fields. (I had become very sensitive to energy flows, which will be described more fully later.) I thought I could use the same induction process of energy sharing that I was using in my work with individuals and groups. There we were on the bed together and the child was watching me. I shifted my internal focus and began to project a current of energy toward him. Immediately he began to cry. It was not at all what I expected. I tried to comfort him, but I felt inept and clumsy, and he just cried all the harder.

I stopped trying to do anything and noticed that he brought

his hand in front of his face. It seemed for an instant that all that existed for him was the hand. Without really thinking about it, I let my hand drift in front of my face and let myself exist for a moment as a hand. Precisely as I did this he giggled and the crying stopped. Thus began a fascinating play.

I understood through this child that *what he perceived, he was.* The moment I joined this reality I let the labeling process of my consciousness fall away and just began to experience. I followed his example.

We began to crawl around. I just *was* whatever was there: floors, corners, carpets, and so on. He found the coiled-spring doorstop that makes a thwanging sound if you flick it. Discovering this amusing sound, he thwanged a few times, giggled, and moved on. I thwanged, and felt the pleasure of a new experience. And so we shared an hour together. It felt like no time had passed. We were relating all the time, but the idea of control, or of a medley of personalized responses going between each other, was gone. We were simply *being* together, and at the same time *we were really the same thing,* not clearly two separate things. I was in an altered state of consciousness, one that has since become common for me.

I had thought that I could communicate with the baby by emanating a pleasant open energy, but this very idea was based in a me/him duality and had created separation and discomfort. In fact, we did end up in a more unified experience, but my initial idea of the world and our communication was gone.

Think about all the presumptions we each have about changing our world and each other. Perhaps every time we attempt to project our assumptions or our hopes to transform mankind, we may actually be creating more pain and more conflict. (Are those people who heighten the energy of their consciousness actually indirectly empowering Armageddon?) I believe our real task, as hard as it is, is to stop attempting to change the world in accordance with any image, and instead fall toward the center of ourselves so that we can see freshly what already is.

By becoming one with a child's reality of the unity of experience, I had discovered a whole different relationship. I realized how unbelievably conditioned I had become. There was nothing that I saw or experienced that was not filtered through one *me* or another. Everything was defined, locked into an appropriate way to know it, tied down tight. Just releasing this rigidity for a moment led to an immediate way to establish harmony and communion. Can you imagine what would happen to arguments between people in political crises if we simply removed the separating filters that are a degeneration of the greater potential that is *Now?* Such a possibility starts with the conscious choice to discern and release these filters.

❖

After several years of working together with groups of people, an extremely important issue is often raised by the individuals most closely associated with me. In essence it is "I can't tell anyone what this is about. How do we explain to people what this is like so they will be able to understand? Our lives are changing deeply but it is hard to tell people how this is happening or why they might want to join us."

My answer varies. Sometimes I laugh and say that this work is about learning to breathe underwater. One of my favorite descriptions for a while was that this work is concerned with *kundalinquency* (kundalini and delinquency) because of the challenges, both joyous and serious, of learning to master the expanded states of consciousness. Most of my answers are to let them find their own answers. Why do we really have to know? So that we can label ourselves unique?

Only gradually have I come to recognize the wisdom of having no clear handle to grab onto and no fixed syllabus. The experience of sharing must be fresh and real each time. *Learning to be* cannot be placed in a manual. I am leery of any fixed form, tool or technique for defining oneself in the higher states of consciousness, either for healing practices or for betterment of the world, or for any other reason.

Life is a continuous process of meditation, sometimes conscious and mostly unconscious, in a lot of people. But this conscious meditation of life is fluid—a constantly changing vortex in which every attempt to hold things fixed or absolute, or to stake out territory for oneself, eventually creates pain and distortion. It is as if, in our attempt to recreate an experience through a particular tool or process, we are saying "Hey, let me get a handle on existence . . . I want to know. I want it my way." We are grabbed over and over again by our need to understand and become fixed in position while the tide of change flows on. Eventually we are extended off balance like the weight of a pendulum. When cast loose again, we oscillate violently within this ever-changing current. Out of this unique personal quality of oscillation comes our particular range of experiencing life.

Well that's fine. It is how we learn. Maybe it is how we appear to be here, wherever "here" is in the first place. But in my own life and in the process of communication that is my work, I am interested in cutting loose the various anchors that stop our fluid dance in existence. Life has to be in the moment, spontaneous and vulnerable. There isn't any winning or any losing. Life itself, as it flowers in depth and subtlety, is the reward, and it isn't always an easy or fun process. We must learn to see that the issue of happiness is irrelevant. The relevant quest is the expansion of consciousness.

People can briefly envision a world that is constantly changing and are able to let go into being in the Now. It gets tricky when they later try to use the same cue to get back to that deeper sense of being present Now, and it doesn't work. Of course it doesn't work, *everything is changing*. The cue or technique was participating with a moment that doesn't really exist anymore. What is transforming us is not in the tool, it is in the energy of our communion together. I find it impossible to define my work or to formalize or rigidly apply any specific tools. It is being born anew every moment. It is alive. It is an energy.

Sometimes people have a wave of fear about this. Is this too much freedom? Can I handle knowing that so much is beyond the *me* I appreciate? We tend to turn the cues of our teachers into parenting values and our beliefs into happy families. The truth is that the fear is natural, and knowing that we are meant to explore our limits, and that at those limits love is there to be realized and to hold us integrated beyond any sense we could have known, can allay the apprehension. Needing to have a name for this work, or some specific tools for its ongoing manifestation, is a corner of that fear being subtly expressed: "Let's make the vastness of consciousness a little more knowable." I am learning to rest into the vastness of it and to find such space to be breath and life itself. I am moved beyond words by the eternal, boundless realm of self. I love the frontiers, and part of this love is to know fear.

The labels and the forms merely serve to tell us where we've been, like droplets in a cloud chamber that precipitate on the trail of passing cosmic particles. The tools serve to give us a context to appreciate our limits and the nature of the new territory we are entering. Still, we must understand that the tools become obstacles when we use them without understanding how we found them and in what context they serve us.

When I was a traditional physician I learned of so many drugs and tests that one day I had to clear the whole table to discover which ones were really of value and in what situation they were appropriate. I learned how often I used a drug or ordered a test because I couldn't say "I don't know." I learned how I needed to depend on a prescription until a certain force had matured within me, so that I could say with authority and true caring "You will be fine. Healing will unfold in such and such a way. There is no need to take any medications." I learned that I might consciously prescribe a drug for a certain person knowing that, in many ways far beyond the drug's effects, it would help him. But, equally as valid, I could consciously *not* prescribe, because I could infuse the confidence to heal through my presence and reassurance. The number of truly valuable and efficacious drugs was reduced to barely a dozen.

Similarly, as we search for ways to appreciate the frontiers of consciousness, it is the deeper integrity of our commitment that is of primary importance. We often consider the process of establishing our intention to be masculine and directive; it is this, but in a deeper sense it is also feminine. Upon our intention, our future unfolding is based. It becomes the matrix upon which the next discovery of our Self will be manifested. If our intention is to undo ourselves and discover the deeper principles of love and to live them, then, when the gate opens into a new reality, that reality will appear to have an intrinsic harmony that is loving. If our intention is to gain power and to win, then, when the gate opens to a new energy, we may suddenly discover that God is wrathful.

It is the love of the adventure and the tremendous intimacy of sharing and receiving at the very boundaries of our being that enlivens me. It is passionate. It is sensuous in ways I could have never imagined. It is this quality, and not some tool or patent approach to experience, that guides the relationship to each Now moment.

The inspired individuals I have met who are helping to foster a new understanding about our nature do not approach life mechanically. There is a discipline and way of being that they live that is necessitated by an enhanced sensitivity to deeper forces combined with a tremendous reverence for living, but it is not mechanical. Why should anyone be locked into rituals, dogmas and techniques? Even if you do nothing, every state of consciousness will eventually change into something else. It is in the illusion of our *doing* that we actually resist this natural changing process. When the necessity for *doing* characterizes our own participation with reality it leads us into the pattern of contraction and diminished sensitivity to the wholeness of life. As I have said, this is the subtle root of depression. What then do we need to learn, and why are there so many tools and techniques for consciousness-raising and for healing?

Part of the answer is that there are so many of us and each of us is unique. For this reason we communicate our truth in many ways. But another reason, and an important one for us to appreciate, is that we are also afraid—afraid of the adventure, afraid of the uncertainty, afraid to not know how we are to manifest ourselves in the new energies we have discovered. We want to create some outer change, some outer formula, that reflects and defines our new insights without really changing us inwardly. We are apprehensive about how to manifest our new sense of self in the world. We would like to create security, like mommies and daddies, out of our beliefs and the very forms of our self- expression, and then measure ourselves by the recognition and energy we receive through these forms. Out of this blossoms the search for, and the creation of, more and more tools and schools for transformation. Part of our challenge in this time, because of the plethora of experiences and ways, is to recognize that the ego can be fed infinite new perspectives and sensations that appear like growth but are just the continuing satiating of our need to experience. There comes a point when you realize that one way can be enough if you stay with it and let it undo you.

The fundamental barrier is the illusion of "ourselves." We forget that transformation is about *expanding* the inner territory in which our real communications happen. We are being sensitized, made psychic and telepathic, expanded in awareness and imbued with new potential, so that we can transcend the boundary between ourselves and each other. Our fear of being possessed by life is the negative root of our identification with the boundaries—of our home, our nation and our faith. The positive root is our intrinsic connectedness.

The key to transcending these boundaries is unconditional love. It is the *yes* that leads us to infinity. It will carry us beyond the boundary of our personal reality. All of the other tools, techniques and forms can be set aside if we would but appreciate this one basic principle and commit ourselves to it.

# 4 ❖ LIVING AT THE EDGE OF FORMLESSNESS

*It is impossible to communicate from one plane to another plane; it won't function at all. You have to rise up to another plane of being; only then suddenly, can you see. And when you see and experience, then the trust is fulfilled. But before you see, one has to have faith to have trust, just to allow the transformation.*

BHAGWAN SHREE RAJNEESH

IN THE HEIGHTENING OF CONSCIOUSNESS, the higher order of energy that becomes part of one's awareness is brought into the body and into the personal psyche. The result is that new facets and sensibilities of consciousness, formerly latent or nonexistent, can now begin to develop. If such a heightening manifests rapidly, the effects can be radical. Psychic events attached to such openings may seem both positive and negative.

On the positive side is the development of extrasensory capabilities, as well as a tremendous enhancement of personal presence, personal ethics, and a new kind of intelligence. On the negative side there is the potential for the morbid activation of latent intrapsychic tendencies that are either unique to the individual or part of the collective consciousness not formerly

45

appreciated by the individual. In relation to the latter, any psychophysical structure within the personal consciousness that is not capable of dealing with this new and tremendously enhanced energy can become the locus for disharmony. As this occurs, one begins to learn that any attachment to people, to defined life structures, to rigid ideals or to fixed needs can become a powerful focus for pain. People who are not aware of how much they control their lives and the lives of those around them will find themselves forced to re-evaluate these patterns at deeper and deeper levels, and it may not be easy.

Some of that which we label psychological or physical disease might more creatively be examined as stalled or overly rapid penetrations of higher energies. Perhaps all of human experience is an interaction between matter and consciousness, and these energies are mediating that. However, at our present level of development, it is only possible to say that some physical or psychological dynamics *are* related to shifts of energy and need to be examined from the broader perspective of the evolution of human consciousness.

Whereas in ordinary levels of consciousness an experience is first labeled or diagnosed and we need to figure out why it happened before we can deal with it, transformation begins from a different premise, one of formlessness. We perceive the Self as consciousness at many levels of development and expression. We see that our personal consciousness is responding to hidden forces and that it has the option to alter its stance in relation to these forces, thereby transforming our experience. The vocabulary of the transformative perspective reflects this. We speak more and more in terms of the *quality, intensity, amplitude,* the *fineness* or *coarseness,* and the *cycle* or *rhythm* of the forces involved, as opposed to any absolute statement of their nature. The vocabulary must deal with the way these forces are transduced by the individual (and collective) psyche. Thus, it speaks of *openness, transparency, fluidity* or *rigidity, balance* and *wisdom, strength* and *surrender,* all of which refer to an individual's innate capacity to participate with the multidimensional forces of life.

The psychology of formlessness deals essentially with transformation and change. It refers to the permeability or transparency of the ego structure through which consciousness is filtered and encourages a multidimensional sensitivity. It reaches out to acknowledge forces that at first seem beyond our understanding. Rather than trying-to-understand such processes, one begins to participate directly with reality in an unconditional sense, and allows understanding to occur as a consequence rather than as a prerequisite. It notes the physical and psychical processes that reflect various stages of relationship to this higher consciousness. But it does so without judgment. Honoring the content of reality at any level of consciousness, it simultaneously teaches methods for opening more deeply.

Essential to this opening is the concept of *transparency*, of releasing into dimensions that are broader than those reflected to us through the content of our experience. *Transparency describes the perspective from which the effect of an energetic process changes with the ability to be present in it.* It is the perspective from which we can see that *our individual behaviors describe not who we are but what we don't dissolve into* and how we thus separate ourselves from a greater sense of being. It prepares the individual for an experience of self as presence, for there is a growing radiance of one's being as we participate more with the Greater Self.

It takes energy to maintain the *me* that is separate, that must stay discrete in the sense of "my" world view and "my" life. How much energy do you suppose it requires of us to constitute time/space in a particular form and sequencing (9 A.M. TO to 5 P.M., or Monday to Friday)? What about the energy that maintains self-definition through jobs, schedules, or labels (male/female, married/single, Lutheran/Jew)? Each of these can be regarded as a boundary that has been created in the psychic structure. How much energy do you suppose each of these structures filters out of our awareness? I believe it is the rigidity with which we identify and are attached to these structures that steps down the overall energy of our consciousness, and perhaps makes us vulnerable to the high-energy diseases such as cancer.

Setting aside for the time being consideration of the causal or conditional forces that create these definitions or boundaries (and I believe that they are essential, for they create the context in which to develop self-consciousness), I have come to see that a self-realizing or awakening process implies a return to the more unbounded energetic existence. There is an old wisdom, one obviously born of an awakened awareness, that asks the question "How do you contain anything?" Our usual answer is to repress it—to build a fence or put it in a box of some sort. But the transformative answer is "Give it all the room it needs." The next time you are struggling with an issue of some kind, try this approach. Open your consciousness and find the space that can allow the process to go on without any containment on your part. The energy reclaimed can be impressive. However, the consequence of such a way of being is that old identity, which has been defined by the nature of the reaction, is also dissolved. We expand and retrieve energy, but something must be sacrificed.

Life has a tendency to do this naturally. This is why so much energy is released whenever any major reality-structuring pattern is disrupted—for instance, when a job terminates, a marriage ends, a loved one dies, or we find ourselves experiencing culture shock in a foreign land. We don't usually recognize this as a shift in energy dynamics or as an opportunity to work the configurating forces of awareness in a new way. Instead we experience only the intensification of physical, emotional and psychological areas that we term *stress* and *crisis*. Then we seek to interpret these changes and react against whatever situation or agent we feel is causing the stress.

If we would recognize this as an alteration in energy and disburse the energy in a creative manner, the intensity and duration of the stress might be significantly diminished. This is very clear in the example of grief. Consciousness has been defined so thoroughly through the interaction with the loved one that the absence of the person creates an enormous vacuum of experience and an abundance of energy. What we do with this superfluous energy determines how the grief process resolves and how long it will be experienced. The depression that surrounds grief is not a result of loss of energy but of conflict about how to handle that energy. We can begin to appreciate the wisdom in many cultures where the dying process is celebrated. The sooner an individual can release the old identity, defined as it was by the former relationship, and be creative with the energy made available to them through the loss, the quicker their sense of equanimity will return. Carl Jung notes in his autobiography that it was not until after the death of his wife that he was able to lift into his most fully realized levels of awareness.

What I am suggesting here is that there is a kind of compensatory process. The structures that provide us with identity at one level (marriage, family, job), as natural as they appear in the unfolding of our lives, are nonetheless binding the energy necessary to recognize another level of experience. I suspect that there is a natural progression and life expectancy for these structures which, without our interference, would naturally release and allow a far richer flow of experience than we presently permit. In a transformative process the mutability of all structures in consciousness is assumed and one gradually moves to set aside such limitations.

In contrast to this, our traditional analytic approaches to experience tend to present us with a fixed sense of reality. It is not until this mode of consciousness is temporarily set aside and we sense into a more vast and formless aspect of our being that we begin to perceive another encompassing and subtle dimension. In experience of this dimension, all the perspectives gained through ordinary levels of energy seem to be held in a new relationship and all of experience begins to transform in varying degrees.

At this point, a word of caution is important. No good/bad dichotomy or judgmental comparison is being made about these various levels of consciousness. The issue is not whether the expanded energy states of consciousness are better than the "ordinary" ones. Rather, we want to begin to examine the process by which we become sensitive multidimensionally, and gradually learn how to refine our capacity to carry and integrate the higher energies.

❖

The awakening into higher energies results in a major transformation, and it would be ludicrous to think that one can move from the third to the fourth floor of consciousness without profound bodily and psychic effects. Though we may hear philosophical and spiritual illumination expressed by transformed individuals, or meet them and be touched by their presence, rarely do we learn of the physical and psychological components of the process. For instance, at the age of twenty-eight Krishnamurti went through a powerful and quite painful psychophysical process that initiated his spiritual maturity. My own experience began on my thirtieth birthday; the initial event lasted about two weeks, tapered briefly, then continued fairly intensely for several months, with periods of significant physical and psychical strain. After that it continued in waves with less strain, but considerable discomfort at times. It still pays me regular visits and has become what I call my "atomic cell disruptor." Considering the gifts that have come with it, I now regard it as a wonderful friend. It is not a state of resolution, but more like a psychospiritual transition zone by which consciousness is empowered.

I differentiate between the kindling of new dimensions that occurs in the group work and the spontaneous opening that I have termed *awakening*. Yet they are unquestionably related. The former respresents the induction of a higher energy through the group process which aligns the awareness to a new potential. Awakening means an empowering that is seemingly distinct from any known context and has an autonomous nature of its own. They are aspects of the same realm of phenomena, and the former often seems to precede the latter and to accelerate its possibility.

The following description is based on both kinds of experience. Sense into it and be encouraged to trust your own transformation even when it is hard to know the way. I do not claim that this description is universal. Obviously different temperaments and constitutions will experience transformation in different ways and at varying depths. I have come to believe that, for those who wish to pursue higher development, the degree to which the energies can be evocative of a new consciousness is determined by the underlying mental and physical health and stamina as well as the force of the intention. There is also a large unknown factor. Surely the panorama of various psychophysical aspects of transformation extends far beyond these brief remarks. I can speak only from my own experience and level of development.

Initially a powerful energy seems to awaken within the body. Sometimes it is localized in the chest, the head, the lower abdomen, but often it is a diffuse activation. In this sense the word *body* is no longer accurate because there is the feeling of extending outward beyond the body surface, not only through the energy that seems to be radiating both within and without, but through one's thought. In an instant one begins to understand the words of spiritual teachers. The experience takes the vision of life far beyond the domain of one's former intellectual spirituality. This latter is seen to be reaching toward, rather than responding to, the direct experience of this profound transformation.

It is interesting that animals can respond quite strongly to this energetic presence. They become agitated or peaceful and generally hungry to be near it. People are also powerfully affected, though they rarely seem to respond as strongly to the presence as the animals. The energy causes agitation and discomfort in some, while others become peaceful and even euphoric. I believe this variance has to do with the fluidity and openness of the individual. The presence catalyzes psychoactive forces in people who come in close contact with it. Those who are receptive and open expand and feel good; those who unconsciously resist this force feel uncomfortable or threatened. In either case the next exposure may produce a very different response.

As this awakening process unfolds, the usual perception of time and space is radically altered and the apparent boundary between self and others begins to break down. The fundamentals of one's personal identity begin to change in ways not yet fully appreciated by our traditional psychology. Activities and events that formerly carried meaning and motivated the life of an individual may suddenly seem unimportant. This is particularly true of certain personal relationships, while others grow deeper and richer. Personal relating becomes substantially less important in terms of social interaction or entertainment. Relationships that have been unconsciously teneted on dependency-control needs may abruptly sour. Attempting to move the consciousness into areas of emotionality in general, and emotional dependency in particular, cuts the individual off from the ability to center in the new energy and results in a great loss of well-being. Relationships based on dependency or on a static image will fall before the liberating force of the awakening consciousness. Events or situations that formerly evoked a particular emotion may no longer do so.

In general, the awareness turns away from the significance of the external event and toward the nature of the perceiving consciousness. In many ways it is like being turned inside out. You must release the energy bound to the former patterns, relationships, and situations into an unconditional quality that allows these patterns to resolve and re-form in accordance with the new energy.

There is no way to anticipate fully the forces of the awakening and the new kind of reality that begins to surface within oneself. One can try to turn away from the process but then an amazing discovery is made. To turn away from it is even worse: It is like denying a profound lover. To turn away and embrace the old spiritual concepts of goodness or light requires great will, and then produces only a temporary feeling of peace. As soon as this willed process is relaxed, its opposite begins to be empowered. A new kind of balance that is neither light nor dark must be discovered. The fourth-floor consciousness is not either-or consciousness.

This new energy is an inexorable force demanding an entirely new kind of consciousness. Older values, even those we deemed highest, are seen to be operating in a lower dimension; it is now clear that they functioned to maintain the integrity of the ego. One does not have to believe in a loving reality. One is led, or perhaps one might say *forced*, to discover it by the urgent need to find harmony. For the first time there is the realization that the kind and quality of love formerly known has been narrow, self-serving and extremely limiting to oneself and others.

While the moral, philosophical and ethical consequences of this awakening consciousness are in the long run extraordinarily significant, still the fuller appreciation of this evolvement is gradual. It is the initial physical and psychical phenomena that capture the immediate attention; one may be overcome by the intensity of the process. Every cell can be alive and vibrating as if one were electrical or atomic. This can be frightening and uncomfortable or indescribably blissful, and it seems to fluctuate of its own accord until there is a gradual stabilization. Basic to this is an inner kind of balance that cannot be described and must just be learned moment by moment. Physical symptoms such as tremor, weakness, extreme sensitivity to heat and cold, muscle spasms and fasciculations may occur. Yet if one comes into harmony with the current, the sense of strength and vitality can be nearly superhuman. But, even when there is inner peace the initial energy can simply be too much for the body — something like putting too much current through a wire.

In my experience there is an inner wisdom to this process that halts it before there is significant physical damage. However, this can be overriden by personal inclinations, and there are some who, from a subconscious avarice, attempt to augment the energy with meditation and drugs. This can be extremely dangerous and is basically stupid. Others have trouble because they become fascinated with or addicted to the intensity and power that accompanies the heightened energy. Then, when the energy quiets, instead of taking advantage of the respite, they attempt to heighten once again. An eventual physical and psychical depletion with significant threat to health can result.

I believe it is emotional struggle that leads to much of the exhaustion. Those who utilize the energy to empower emotional intensity, whether positive or negative, will not get very far in transformation of any kind, for to empower an emotional process, particularly a contracting reaction, during the heightened state is to create a personal hell. Image your own moments of doubt, fear or ambivalence activated with an energy immeasurably greater, not only in potency but also in its capacity to link every facet of psyche into one unit, and I need say no more. Even positive experiences of emotional ecstacy, which frequently take on a religious character, are depleting and usually swing to the opposite pole. Indulging such states can result in severe physical and/or psychological disruption.

It is not my intention to frighten anyone, but rather to evoke a properly focused attitude. I empowered such spaces myself and finally learned that to survive and integrate I would simply have to go beyond them. There is kinetics of the psyche that keeps these old psycho-emotional spaces still seductive during the early phase of a transformative process. But, as the deeper consciousness emerges, its fullness and subtlety quickly eclipses old identities conferred by our emotional dramas.

The heightened energy carries with it the capacity to perceive with greatly heightened sensitivity. It is as if the world is alive and aglow with life and light. It is possible to feel oneself becoming united, to actually be sharing awareness with things that were before clearly recognized as external, such as the tree or the cow in the pasture. One becomes extraordinarily sensitive to the feelings of others, and frequently to their thoughts as well. In fact the link between thinking and feeling is tremendously increased, and it therefore becomes clear that what we feel and what we think is an interpenetrating realm of experience. You can laugh when someone else is laughing or cry when someone else is crying. Where there is a cacophony of psychic realities, the internal sense of confusion and turbulence can often seem overwhelming. It is partly for this reason that a harmonious group energy orchestrated around the theme of unconditional love is such a safe, and therefore nurturing, environment to begin such an opening. The cacophony is minimized and the feeling is rich and loving. Ths psychic overstimulation is quite disconcerting until one learns to rest into a deeper sense of Beingness. Then we come to realize the incredible unity of all beings and the love at this level is a feeling beyond words. (The actual separation that people at ordinary levels of consciousness see as real communication can be painful to observe until one learns to simply appreciate the beauty and naturalness of every level of human development.)

What we think about the experience of awakening is largely determined by the context in which it occurs. In an alive spiritual context one may quickly appreciate it and rest into a great sense of gratitude with trust in the unfolding. But somehow the actual experience seems to go beyond anything one can antici-pate even in spiritual settings and then one must be prepared to transcend the ensnaring process of the spiritual setting itself. This last remark is based on my intuition of what I witnessed in my travels and in work since then.

I am continually amazed at how few of the so-called spiritual schools are able to recognize the empowering of these energies and willing to support this potential in the individual. So much attention is given to spiritual ideas and spiritual roles that the direct experience of empowering grace and the creation of a more fully realized human being becomes lost. I think that most traditional religious organizations are actually afraid of this po-tential, because it may carry individuals way beyond the beliefs of the organization.

All too frequently, the negative reactions of the threatened personal ego structure are taken to indicate possession, or the invasion of dark forces, or they are examined too specifically as psychological or personality issues. Only a broad understanding of transformational psychology can appreciate that the empow-ering force is essentially neutral, and that what it evokes and how it is integrated depends on two things: the intrinsic nature of the individual (physical, emotional, psychological and spiri-tual) and the collective context; and the ability of the individual to consecrate the process to a new, albeit unknown, integrative center of being. Unconditional love is the energy that encom-passes and supports this process.

Our very thoughts about the process channel our perception of what is happening to us. We become, or at least powerfully participate in, what we think. Since thinking is based upon memory and linked to the ego structure, which inevitably resists transformation, most rational thinking about transformation leads to frightening ideas or unrealistic negation or aggrandize-ment. The mind must become quiet and rest into a new zone of function; this comes gradually through meditative skills accom-panied by a lot of trial-and-error and common sense. Probably the best advice I know for passing through the phase which I call "where thought has power" is to meditate and seek into the

Divine Self. Then gradually, in the periods of silence when efforts and struggles have been abandoned, a new level of realization begins to emerge.

❖

There are other wondrous new areas that open concurrent with heightened sensitivities. Certain electrical applicances can cause interesting, sometimes unpleasant, sensations within one's body. Food formerly eaten without thought now is discovered to be formidably potent in altering this perception of energy. Some foods result in a sense of tingling, humming and well- being; others in a sense of volcanic turbulence and discomfort. Some foods tend to lighten the consciousness and produce harmony; others are quickly perceived to weigh down and ground the consciousness. A pattern begins to emerge of utilizing food to participate in the balancing of this energetic current. Some days it is necessary to eat frequently and heavily, while other days it is important not to eat at all or very lightly. One quickly understands why most schools of spiritual yoga advocate light or vegetarian meals. It is this kind of diet that results in refining or lightening the energy and facilitates reaching into the higher states of consciousness. However, for someone who is learning to stabilize a powerfully awakened energetic current, such a diet may be counterproductive and even dangerous. Instead one employes the heavier foods to quiet the process and provide periods of relief and rest.

Both sexuality and exercise are perceived in a totally new way. Sexuality can be a saddeningly disruptive and dissipative experience when one moves toward it out of a sense of habit or performance needs. It is as if energy is syphoned off, causing a loss of balance and shrinking of consciousness. This can also occur when one has sex only to accommodate the needs of a partner. However, if the sexual interaction is riding in harmony with the energetic current, it becomes an almost unbelievably uplifting process of profound communion. In this way it is deeply healing and regenerative for the body and catalytic of rich creativity and profound personal love. In certain rare circumstances it can be a way to empower the higher consciousness. It soon becomes clear that, depending on the quality of consciousness one brings to the sexual act, sexuality can be augmenting and balancing or dissipative and destructive. In general, sexual interactions in which there is communion create a love that can eventually free the partners relative to each other, while sexuality that is dissipative creates binding and dependency.

The point is that, after awakening, every part of one's being is more directly experienced as a living dynamic within the totality of a larger Self. The energetic awakening abruptly gives this Self a sensate, palpable existence. No *single* quality, narrowed orientation of consciousness or definition of relationship is ever again appropriate in contrast to that which is naturally balanced and of deeper truth in the Now. Intimate relationships that are naturally harmonizing in one moment may be draining and unbalancing in another. They have no real substance unless consecrated to a higher dimension. No situation can define a norm for any process that is powerfully active at energetic levels. Having awakened, we see how contrived and destructive moralistic social norms can be and how, if a higher consciousness is to evolve collectively, these norms will have to give way to a far deeper integrity. This is what I hear in Christ's statement that those who hear the word of God and do it are his family (Luke 8:21). As a higher energy and a greater love genuinely empowers awareness, sexual relationships and family structures will have to change to allow more balance and less dependence and territorial awareness. The seeding of the new and the deterioration of the inflexible are hallmarks of the penetration of a higher energy. Yet, to the rigid structures of our psyche this can seem to be the greatest of evils.

❖

Just as sexuality is recognized in a new way to be a dimension of energy expression, likewise exercise is soon perceived as a way to dissipate or activate energy. Rather than exercising to stay in shape or because it is healthy, one begins to exercise the body as a delicate and responsive medium for altering and balancing consciousness. It becomes a throttle that can be opened or closed so that contained energy may be released and redistributed throughout the body and consciousness to varying degrees. This is the case with jogging. It can be a wonderful meditation, as is any regular physically stimulating activity. But to jog regularly and then stop abruptly may lead to discomfort, moodiness, irritabliity or disease unless one can transmute the energy so that it is radiated throughout one's being in a more universal manner: i.e., as *presence*. *Any regular use of energy through a particular mode of life becomes addictive of that mode.* What we must come to appreciate is that we are multidimensional energy transducers and no one particular area should unconsciously dominate the expression of our being. If it does, the reality we build from that unconsciousness will itself be unbalanced. Then if, like the jogger, this form of expression is curtailed, the result is a loss of equilibrium of greater or lesser degree depending on how fluid the consciousness has become.

With increasing sensitivity there is an enhanced ability to employ exercise subtly and to derive its benefits in terms of the overall balance of consciousness without having to reach the domain of assaultive training. One becomes less self-punishing, more graceful and more fluid, accomplishing this by consciously joining the energy rather than following some idea about how to exercise or condition. My overall physical stamina and strength maintains an unexpectedly high level despite significant reduction in the kind and degree of exercise I formerly believed was important. What we call strength is in large part the degree to which a deeper current of energy can be accessed in our activities. In the early phases of an awakening process, basic exercise is an effective method one can use to ground the energy or activate it; exercise represents a powerful tool in nearly every aspect of medicine because it is a basic channel for the energies of consciousness.

❖

Another interesting facet of the deepening transformation is a change in memory that begins to occur. Memory of recent events seems to fade away or lose importance because the sense of presence is so vital. There are phases in a transformative process that simply aren't convenient or practical if life has been organized linearly and efficiently—especially if one continues to insist that this must be the case. It seems as if one has lost the ability to call upon the mind to organize itself in clear, linear fashion. Life itself is more in the moment, more fluid, and the nonlinearity of mind is but a facet of the greater process. Yet, if there is a real need for the mind to function at linear levels, one is able to make the shift. It is not that the memory is gone, it is just that information has to be summoned in a different way. In fact, a mind that works from the memory and brings forth that which is memorized seems dead and lifeless unless it is immediately useful to convey that which has real and living presence in the moment. As one acquires the capacity to channel thought and words in this way, information and understanding emerge from a deeper strata of consciousness. There is a new intelligence and new knowledge.

As one learns to communicate from this new level it becomes apparent that an energy is carried through the voice. The flow of words, modulated by the voice quality of the speaker, creates an energetic experience for those who are listening. One begins to understand that this is happening all the time. Most of the time ordinary conversation comes from such mundane levels of consciousness that there is very little energy carried on it. Lazy personability of this sort is probably one of the most common ways in which individuals of minimal conscious development dissipate energy and fritter away their birthright to ascend into higher consciousness.

There are some people whose very words carry a great deal of energy. To a sensitive person, such energy can be felt as a rippling within, and one begins to watch carefully to see what the energy carried on these words is evoking. A less aware individual can be caught up in this energy and ascribe a reality to the speakers and their thoughts that may not have any basis in truth. If the energy is strong enough (we call it *charisma*), the accuracy of the information may be almost irrelevant to the effect. As this kind of power emerges, one is rightly concerned with the integrity and motivation of the speaker, and appreciates those who use their extraordinary energy with clarity and honesty. It is the same phenomena that makes a great performance on the part of an artist. As the consciousness of an action expands beyond the form utilized to communicate it, it creates an energetic presence that captivates the awareness of the observer. All the phenomena just mentioned show how the newly awakened consciousness begins to perceive reality and underscore the responsibility one has to bring this forward with great integrity.

An area of newness that is often quite disconcerting, particularly to men, is the diminished motivation to achieve, which they formerly expressed through competition. Competition is hardly compatible with the receptivity and concern for the Now moment fostered by the transformation of consciousness. Along with this there is an accompanying shift in physical body structure toward decreased muscle armoring. How lost a person can feel as the old motivating forces lose their substance and one must discover a new way to evoke and empower one's actions!

❖

The awakening consciousness, with its tremendous heightening of energetic sensitivity, has its own developmental integrity, which demands a new psychology. While at ordinary levels of consciousness we are dealing with the content of experience, defining ourselves through attitudes and labels of all sorts, the more realized individual is directly accessing a sense of presence. The relationship of harmony and balance within this new quality of being provides magnificent, highly sensitive feedback to the smallest contractions and resistances that continue to be fabricated from some personal prejudice or from developmentally valid but less expanded levels of self. We seldom appreciate how each aspect of our multi-faceted self operates with different attitudes, values, and psychological structures (strengths, defenses, etc.) and resonates with its own unique quality within the deeper energy. For example, relative to the more expansive energy, the energies manifested by entering survival or need oriented levels of consciousness (when not essentially appropriate in the moment) are recognized as a contraction or disharmony within the sense of presence. Old psychic patterns or bounded belief systems that limit the energy level and try to hold it to its former state will now stand out clearly. Now one can see that these are not wrong per se, but are merely ways in which consciousness selectively narrows or expands as we touch upon different levels of self. I believe that apparent contractions of energy relative to the larger sense of being reflect developmental sequences in the formulation of personality, i.e. boundaries formed within larger reality to arrive at a functional self-awareness. We are immediately freed and uplifted by the recognition that these patterns need not be judged. Instead, we can get on with the challenge of opening to our fullest potential, knowing that these patterns will gradually dissolve back into the larger energy of Beingness. In fact, there is a very basic shift in the way we look at our whole background and conditioning. For the first time one can begin to look with love at the forces that made each of us who we are, because now it is clear that our present awareness could never have come about without them. From the perspective of harmony, everything about oneself, past and present, is seen to be relevant to Beingness. The great wisdom of "Honor thy mother and father," for example, takes on its true significance as a signpost for a higher level of awareness instead of as a guilt-producing moral injunction.

In general, with the awakening of this deeper energy one begins to recognize presence. The intensity of the initial awakening may last only a short time (whether days, weeks, or months), but one is never the same again. The very meaning and identity that one has associated with certain beliefs and life orientations and even with one's body now begin to be released so that a new orientation can come forward. In that sense it is a dying process, for the old self begins to fade—and not always gracefully. Nevertheless, there is no returning to the old orientations, and so it is the awakening process that shows where a deeper inner truth must be sought. A wholly new spirituality, work ethic, and sense of relationship to oneself and to others is fostered naturally and sometimes unmercifully by this directly experienced energy current. When a belief structure—even one approved by society, religion, or science—is not complementary and refining of this current, such beliefs become obstacles to well-being and must be released or re-evaluated. All outer events, and any interpretation of ourselves, become irrelevant, save as they point to an energy-configurating pattern that creates turbulence or disharmony. We must learn to fine-tune this quality of energy despite what our personal preference has been in the past. Fine tuning occurs as one learns to recognize the distortional areas as superficial to the deeper Self and thus enters into the discovery process that transmutes the smaller area. The resolution may take moments or years depending on the depth to which the distorting pattern exists within the psyche but *there no longer is the sense that such a distortion has an absolute reality or cause.*

The heightened awareness bequeathed in the awakening process does not provide an instantaneous purity of being, but rather a new dimension of self that amplifies and thereby reveals patterns of lesser being. Once contrast against a larger potential is available transmutation is virtually automatic. The pace at which it occurs seems to be a consequence of the ability to witness the uncomfortable process without repression while simultaneously intuiting the deeper energy. Indulging the pattern without the witness state and without a portion of one's awareness (no matter how miniscule) intuiting the deeper energy (or sensing it directly) leads to being caught totally in the reality of the smaller process.

Gradually, one's Self becomes the locus of interpenetrating forces (or wavelengths, or vibrational frequencies) that seem to be coming from different dimensions. The sense of Self is in constant flux, changing in different environments and around different people. The so-called ego boundary is no longer *the* self-defining parameter. Rather, it becomes a semipermeable membrane receiving experience at subtle levels from previously obscured dimensions. Whereas communication formerly occurred through a personality, now it radiates as presence. After the initial shock of this enhanced sensitivity, the refinement of these energetic forces can be mastered consciously. Gradually there is absorption into a state of well-being and balance, with decreasing identification with and reaction to the stress of outer life. One begins to shift from the perspective of making absolute judgments requiring fixed and programmed responses to that of evaluating the qualities of responses, while intuiting the intensity or fineness of the current that is flowing through consciousness. It is a marvelous shift, for rather than being concerned now primarily with the external experience, a sense of disturbance or stress becomes a reference point by which to reflect the intrinsic nature of one's own consciousness (the balance, fluidity, rigidity, or unconditionality with which one is meeting such forces).

Most people simply do not know this level of experience because they remain so bounded. Things are right and things are wrong; things should be a certain way. But once an individual has realized the broader spectrum of the underlying energies that give rise to multidimensional life states and has experienced them as a transcendent force, this current must be adjusted to, integrated, and rebalanced. This quality of consciousness is more open and in a very real sense more loving. In fact, when people find themselves in this realm, they tend to refer to it as sensing that their "heart is opening." There is a sense of inspiration and an inclusiveness with which one can regard oneself and the world. There is, for the first time, a sense of freedom. Experience that formerly locked the consciousness into polarization or struggle can now be integrated and harmonized. We can find balance within this new level and ultimately radiate a finer and finer quality of consciousness throughout the whole spectrum of our activities.

❖

There are some common challenges that are encountered at certain points in a transformational process. Earlier I alluded to my own experience around the fear of creating cancer. By no means was this misery the preponderant quality of the transformational process. On the contrary, the whole process (and it is ongoing) is like being born into a new life. It is magnificent and uplifting. But there are also certain areas of pain and turbulence that are powerful and necessary teachers. It is not uncommon for individuals who enter a transformational process to go through difficult phases of existential fear and/or the fear of developing disease. I believe the latter is more likely in individuals who have a background in biological and health sciences; their imaginations are filled with grisly possibilities! I suspect that the controlling personality types have a more difficult time, and that those who are open and shift quickly have a more intense sense of being carried into the new dimensions.

These challenges are not to be underestimated. The physical discomfort of new energetic sensations and the consequent morbid ruminations these may provoke (as well as the real question about one's sanity) can come to dominate the awareness and keep people from being able to rest into the deepest level of the energy, or from being able to honor and rejoice in their transformation. How, for example, is a businessman who has gone off for a ten-day retreat supposed to interpret the myriad new sensations and waves of feeling he encounters when he returns home. How do the doctors who begin to emphathize with their patients and then take on their symptoms know that they themselves are not developing disease? In the context of a transformational process they are beginning to awaken. But from the context of their businesses they are discovering a deep psychic aversion, a push-pull conflict at survival levels. The fear of death or loss of control becomes the binding locus. With impeccable self-honesty, and through the development of genuine trust and surrender, a new level of authority over the awakening process must be mastered.

The very ideas of trust and surrender are in many ways antithetical to the linear mind. Herein lies the challenge. We in the West often naively approach tools and techniques that have the power to transform consciousness. We behave like a mechanic approaching a car or a doctor approaching a patient. We have an unspoken formula: We want these energies to give us what we desire.

In this sense we approach our own consciousness as if it were a disease that we will alter in order to gain more of something we want. Often, neither what we wish to gain nor the source from which the search originates is understood, and our motivation is egocentric and self-serving. "I am going to do this . . ." In such cases the consciousness opening the flood gate of transformation and human potential is frequently unprepared for what it finds. For some, the process itself can seem like, and even become, a disease.

The transformation of consciousness is inherently disruptive. This is because the sense of self when we begin to search is intrinsically limited and out of balance compared to the psychic system necessary to hold the higher energies. We start out thinking we are going from A to B, but we actually go from A to A'. Our own prejudices and imbalances, as well as our tremendously augmented latent strengths and gifts, are thrust back upon us as we awaken to a greater consciousness. At ordinary levels these are adequately compensated, or may even be functionally adaptive (for example, competitiveness and greediness) so that they are only troublesome in the most critical moments. This is why we learn so much through crisis. During crisis our energy state is temporarily heightened and we are most alert and sensitive; we see and appreciate things in a way we never did before. But in an energetic awakening everything is amplified and a minor imbalance can become a serious disturbance.

Balance at higher energies implies a much broader appreciation of the human condition, and what can be denied at ordinary levels cannot be denied at the higher levels. If our motivation for attaining higher dimensions is naive, or too heavily involved in a self-serving ego structure, and if there is a tendency to be judgmental, what we discover can seem like a punishment. When my energy awakened I recalled walking down hospital corridors past hundreds of patients without caring, even hoping that I would not be called to take care of them. In the heightened energy, my past selfishness and insensitivity was crushing. This is why it must be stressed over and over again that the underlying principle, the foundation for the exploration, be developed in *love* and in understanding of what it means to be *unconditional*. It is also why the expansion of consciousness and spirituality are essentially synonymous.

Most of the processes capable of precipitating a higher energy state grow out of insight from the nonrational, spiritual or mystical mind. But we scarcely comprehend the dimensions such a mind encompasses; in fact, we cannot know until we enter such spaces directly. There are religious and spiritual schools, particularly in the East, that are generally more familiar with the phenomena that accompany a transformation of consciousness. But the transformational phenomena are encountered there in an entirely different context. It is difficult for the Westerner, traditionally an activist and doer, to accept the essential need for a detached or unconditional state of consciousness. However, in my experience such a state is central to integrating all deeper experiences of our multidimensional nature. The relative attainment of this state of consciousness becomes imperative in an awakening process and goes beyond commitment to family, career, and any idea or system of analysis that is arbitrary or splitting of one's wholeness.

People who start on a journey of inner growth cannot really know how much of themselves they are actually bringing to the process, how deeply it will affect them and how radical the changes they may undergo will be. As the inner processes begin to activate, and before there is much conscious sense that a fundamental transformation is evolving, a strange sense of fear may begin to signal that a deeper process is underway. Obviously, well-being and even bliss can also be there, which is why we continue on the journey, but as we get closer to a fundamental change the fear often begins to dominate. Very few can meet the unknown without fear.

The qualities of trust and surrender must be regarded as essential for realizing the unconditional state. Yet all too often rational intelligence points at the stated need for trust as evidence of chicanery. After all, why can't rational skepticism and trust go together? They can, up to a point. But there comes a space where integration and growth are not a rational process requiring proof of wellness, logical answers or any such security. At this point, trust is no longer a word. It is an energy field organizer. It is like a formless gelatin mold providing an integrity for the Self at a critical time of instability where no dimension of rational consciousness can function. Trust and its sister, surrender, are like a womb in which all of consciousness can gestate and mature. In this womb rational faculties are not lost, but they become blended with a formless, numinous quality of self. There is nothing logical or rational about trust or surrender: If there is, it is not the quality of trust necessary to undergo a transformation. When we reemerge and the rational faculties are once more applied in life, they have acquired a new tone.

Although there is no particular formula for the resolution of the awakening energies—the process itself is the teacher—there are certain guidelines.

First of all, any structure in the psyche that you are unwilling to accept or afraid to examine in depth will become an area of pain or even madness. For example, one morning during a conference I awakened quite early and right at that vulnerable moment between sleep and wakefulness a voice boomed into my thoughts. It said "Your work is superficial and inadequate." Immediately I recognized the part of my psyche that felt that way and the perspective from which it was true. I answered "You're right." There was no contraction, no need to go any further. And, of course, I gave myself to the work as sincerely as possible. People who cannot accept criticism and are not honest with themselves, who must hide or protect a part of themselves from minute scrutiny, will inevitably suffer when this area is exposed. The ability to laugh at oneself is very helpful.

Any rigid beliefs will begin to erode if a genuine awakening energy has been activated. Probably the thought forms that most limit the development of the largest numbers of people are about God and the Devil. Evidence of this is the invoking of God by one people against another people. This is not the experience of awakening. During my transformational experience the unity of life became clear. Yet, there are different levels of human development and all must be honored. I am certain the people of judgmental religious persuasion or violent political affiliation have never tasted the higher state directly. When they do, these structures will begin to fall away. Love does not belong to any religious faith or political ideology.

Many people use the Devil as an excuse to reject parts of their own nature by giving the power of these parts to a supernatural force, as if being human isn't supernatural enough. All too often the Devil becomes a catch-all for everything the smaller consciousness cannot reconcile within itself. I am not saying that there aren't forces that behave malevolently when experienced at certain levels of self. But these energies ultimately must be mastered, and not by resisting them at the level at which they are first perceived or projecting repressed human qualities onto them (which only empowers them). As the light of a higher energy quickens within an individual, each will meet the Devil in her or his own way, and the resolution of this experience will not come through repression. Until we have appreciated how this force works within one's own consciousness to prepare a deeper union, we continue to exist with a split psyche and the deeper love cannot manifest.

In the transformational process it is the fear of God (in the sense of the overwhelmingly disorienting newness and vastness of what is encountered) that helps create the humility and wisdom to go forward in a balanced manner. The powerful forces one meets along the way must not be underestimated. But fundamental change cannot be attained unless we appreciate that our ideas of God and the Devil are arbitrary and conditioned. In transformation these ideas will create limiting and at times terrifying moments when one has a choice to release into an intuited wholeness or be the prisoner of the ego. Thought itself is the trap, and the *me* behind the ideas is the obstacle. Attachments, even to our idea of God, cause the greatest turmoil in an awakening process.

Though the personal consciousness attempts to evaluate its situation while undergoing transformation, it can never do so directly. Such evaluation must rely on memory, for there is no other source of rational input than comparisons drawn from memory. Consciousness at this level will always seek resolution by attempting to return to a former life pattern and energy level to explain its experience. It will try to focus the past and project it into the future, fabricating some fantasy of a "safe" life in order to resolve the feelings of fear and confusion that accompany the new shift of energies. But the resolution cannot be attained in this manner. This mode of awareness must eventually be seen as a recurring pattern that can be evoked infinitely to defer falling into the new state. A profound process of trust and surrender must be reached into over and over again before the emerging new reality can begin to bloom in awareness.

A profound paralysis of volition may occur in some people at a point in the awakening process where they have let go deeply. At this point counterbalancing forces begin to be evoked to urge the person back into creative evolvement with outer life. Frequently this expresses first as personality or health issues, but the deeper process is not truly of health or emotional or sexual imbalance but rather a force demanding deeper involvement with life. This reinvolvement is necessary to stabilize and integrate the present level of expansion. But when individuals attempt to take some definitive step, they encounter the awakening force that is expanding them toward formlessness. Thus one can be caught oscillating between a deep desire to become active and manifest a creative self-expression and the formless expansion that refuses to be configurated into substantial activity. At this point, despite tremendous uncertainty, if inner wisdom dictates the need to return to outward activity (work, teaching, whatever), one must gather the will and trust the commitment into form. For someone who has been carried deeply into the new consciousness, developing a form for creative expression of the process is profoundly challenging but it is equally fulfilling and life giving.

❖

Journeying along this path, encountering new sensations and new aspects of awareness, many people find themselves considering the traditional medical and psychological perspectives in order to find the answers that release their fears. The rational process will naturally try to consider all possibilities before letting go becomes logical. Ironically, it is rarely logic that allows this final release. Instead, we cannot seem to do so until by the search itself we are confronted with the fears we are trying to explain away. Having no rational alternative other than a medical or traditional psychological interpretation of the emerging new energy system, one becomes caught in tremendous anxiety. Is this a physical disease? Am I going mad? What will become of me? Out of this convergence of the personal and collective rational reality with a process that transcends our present rational understanding, a whole new level of discernment is being learned.

The personal process has at its heart the question: At what point do I trust that I am not somehow creating (or being the victim of) the very thing I most fear? Is this transformation, or is it disease or failure or loss of wholeness? I was doing so well, now what is happening to me? When is it safe to recognize and accept, amidst the unfamiliarity of these new perceptions, the transcendent process, and stop configurating the fear?

At what point do we call something physical, or mental, or energetic? We are not so well-developed yet that we can make these differentiations accurately. There can be no guarantees of a happy ending. Would we rather imagine the process occurring only at an energetic level than search honestly to discover a possible physical component that is also active and requires medical attention? We know there is a psychoactive transformation going on inside of us, but is it also disease? In trepidation we approach traditional medicine with our symptoms, only to be referred to a psychiatrist because the workup is negative. We thus try to use rational process to eliminate a facet of our fear. But this doesn't resolve the doubt and fear! It can be set aside for awhile, but it arises again each time the energy shifts to a new level or some situation cues the fear.

This sort of rationally unresolvable fear is one of the great gifts of life when it is used as fuel to empower the transformation. The same pattern, unresolved and projected outward, results in more and more need for security against more and more perceived threats. In medicine we see the ever-increasing medical workups and expenses. We want others to prove that there is no rational, definable (and therefore treatable) basis for our fears. We want to be told what to do. We want to be assured that our experience is not life threatening, that we can stay as we are. The alternative is to let go unconditionally into the wholeness of ourselves, into a new space in which life and death are the same process. Once again we see the fundamental schism in the human psyche that represses death or dissolution and this time we have arrived there, not from the threat of physical disease, but from the awesome incomprehensibility of an awakening potential.

This process of fear/contraction exists in one form or another as a kind of death space in every individual. It is the key pattern that, when released, somehow unlocks life as we live it Now. As the energy level increases, this pattern will solidify, and it will only dissolve when we finally release to the new level of being.

We may think that to awaken to higher consciousness is fulfilled through a romantic vision, self-conceived expansion of being, attainment of new powers, elimination of our presumed negatives, and the bringing forth of new values that will save us and perhaps save humanity. But the process itself simply *is*. It is not fundamentally right as against something fundamentally wrong, nor is it going anywhere. Where is the earth going in space? There are no ultimate answers to be found by following a better life as we conceive of it from our ordinary awareness. These are the conditions we would like to impose. But many such conditions are painful distortions when we realize an energy that operates in a dimension beyond them.

In the process of integrating such a dimension, there develops an appreciation of the relationship of all unfolding events to a greater continuum of energy that unites them. When we are committed to a transformational process, but are troubled by symptoms and fearful about our well-being, it is not so much that we turn toward or away from any particular situation or belief structure that seems to hold the answers. Rather, we have a growing awareness that through this very process of oscillation, acceptance, rejection and search we are coming to appreciate in gradually deepening subtlety and wisdom the relationship of consciousness to energy to form as a new quality of living presence that is beyond the content of our outer minds and limited bodies.

For this there is no end-point, no goal. And when we can allow just a little bit more of this understanding to enter our whole being, our thoughts, our feelings, and our very flesh, it is this that is the awakening process, that radiates from us as a quality of love and wisdom. Furthermore, the fulfillment of this blending of the rational and the nonrational awareness, of form and formless levels of Self, is not complete in any one of us alone. It is being expressed and realized continuously in the collective process occurring in all of us and in all of existence. When we finally relax or surrender into this understanding, it is not necessarily some result we hoped for that is granted us, but perhaps only a tiny bit more compassion and wisdom about the vast interlocking complexity of life.

# 5 ❖ BRIDGING PSYCHE AND SOMA

Moving toward a collective level of wisdom, we must study the people who have entered into the process of awakening consciousness. Their bodies, the refinement of their senses, and their special perceptions and perspectives—as well as their ethical and philosophical reorientation—begin to explain the interplay between forces of consciousness and the physical and psychological states of the ego-self. ,

From the perspective of a physician passing through such a process and later observing it kindled in others, I could not help noticing that the limits of our present consensual levels of thinking about human nature do not encompass this deeper phenomenon of a transformation of the fundamental energies of consciousness. Our lives are so one- or two-dimensional, we simply do not understand that a human being is a multidimensional receiver/transducer whose consciousness determines how these forces are recognized, how they are transmuted, and what range of phenomena will gradually surface in our lives.

One consequence of this is that we have functionally separated the psychosomatic and psychological disease processes from the predominantly somatic diseases. Traditionally, something is *somatic* if we can see a change in the tissue and can discover a biological mechanism. It may have psychic and psychological consequences (e.g., a brain tumor causing personality change) but these are secondary. Something is *psychic* if no particular physical process is recognized, and *psychosomatic* if no somatic cause can be discovered to explain physically perceived symptoms. However, and this is extraordinarily important, as we experience awakening consciousness, we begin to merge into dimensions of awareness with sufficient subtlety and power to bridge the interface of psyche and soma. Now there is an energy body, a self-as-presence, which is directly experienced as a reflection of the level and quality of consciousness in any moment. At the same time this energy body is a subtle manifestation of the physical self, so that shifts in the energy correspond to bodily transformation and vice versa. Thus energetic dimensions are clearly seen to bridge between the body and the consciousness, where before nothing but an intellectual relationship was possible.

With this comes a further realization. As we enhance our understanding of the body energy processes, we begin to appreciate more the universal components of transformation and the consciousness (as subtlety of awareness) of the individual becomes of preeminent concern. Simultaneously, the individual "body" begins to be appreciated as a dynamic state of being that reflects the balance of collective human forces. This is leading us toward a new medicine. It is no longer a medicine based on disease (or even on creativity, change or peak experience), but one rooted in a radical and fundamental shift in consciousness—an awakening.

In practical terms, if we begin to focus on the development of the multidimensional awareness of all individuals—and especially our medical personnel—a new medicine will emerge naturally. In fact this is already happening as we blend the concepts of theoretical physics with Eastern mysticism and medicine into our Western culture. Transformation, of course, is an inalienable component of human nature that need not be identified with any religion or system. It simply is. All human beings can find a free and nondogmatic relationship to this process in themselves. In this medicine there can be no real separation between the therapist and the patient.

The experiences inherent in entering these new dimensions have much to say about the similar but hidden (to ordinary awareness) energetic phenomena underlying disease. For one thing, what may unfold unconsciously at one level of consciousness and finally present as disease may now be perceived as an energetic shift which, supported in a context of transformation, becomes an unfolding process of refined psychophysical subtlety and not physical illness. It is as if the personal self-consciousness and the physical sensations and interpretations available at its level of awareness have a very limited capacity to respond to the infinitely subtle forces impinging on awareness. What we call symptoms, or disease itself, have other interpretations dependent on the level of consciousness. Perhaps we need not interpret an interfacing of energies, or an interference pattern that yields a perception, as disease if our level of sensitivity is such that alternative interpretations and relationships are possible.

Most people in the early phases of expanding awareness can begin to perceive the approach of simple illness such as a cold. They can then take necessary steps in terms of rest and nourishment, but they can also work directly with the deeper balance within consciousness so that the cold never manifests. As one gets more sensitive, it becomes apparent that a cold, the flu, allergies and even asthma are part of a dynamic in which one's personal energetic equilibrium is being altered (usually excited in some way) by the energetic milieu. In my own development, I found that every Friday as I drove to Berkeley to work with the staff of the St. Georges Homes (an institution that is working very creatively with schizophrenic and autistic children) I would feel flu-like achiness, tightening in the lungs and watery nasal discharge. At first I thought I was getting sick and then I realized that these symptoms always occurred when I was centering my consciousness and gathering the energy (an activation of awareness and presence) for the group work. Later, as I brought the energy forth in the work, the symptoms would vanish. Somehow during this activation process I was directly influencing the autonomic nervous system as I prepared my consciousness for the work. The physical symptoms were signposts to center the energetic process more deeply.

The radiance of consciousness is a process in which the whole body is involved. In carrying the energies, the body is placed in a state of dynamic strain which probably does become illness in many who are not aware of a larger context for their experience. In fact many healers and teachers who do not totally accept the challenge to maintain such delicate balance within themselves, endanger their health or burn out. They then must seek help from someone of higher energy to establish balance once again.

The energy body does not operate in linear time. Thus we can experience an energetic state—with its concurrent physical, mental and emotional components—that appears to have no relation to "present" time and is later seen as having fostered the necessary refinement of consciousness required to meet a current situation. At a much less conscious level of awareness this state might be called anticipatory anxiety, but it is in fact subtly different, and from expanded awareness is seen to be an empowering process. The finer the energetic state, the broader the time frame to which one's being is responding. Translating the experience of a refined consciousness into linear time sometimes results in what has been called prophecy.

In varying degrees, I note the premonitory heightening process before any important piece of work. However, a similar phenomenon also occurs in response to other forces which have no apparent relationship to my personal activities. These forces can also be psychoactive in terms of influencing mood and behavior. It is easy to get caught up in these secondary responses and plug in the content of one's personal life without the deeper sensitivity that allows one to just center in the energetic process. When you are centered, the energy can pass through without your getting caught up in the feelings. This level of sensitivity is a fairly common aspect that accompanies the refinement of awareness. The ability to center within these forces is mandatory for all those who would explore the refinement of consciousness deeply. Both the sensitivity and the centering ability are at least temporarily ignited in nearly all participants of the group work and it becomes quite refined in a few. It demon-

76    THE I THAT IS WE

strates the natural ability to recognize and thus consciously attune to and master cycles and rhythms that formerly were unconscious.

This leads to a very important consideration—the idea of stress. The mitigation of stress has become a paramount concern of humankind. It has at its core a rigid over-identification with the personal *me*. Individuals of expanded consciousness are no longer exclusively concerned with *me*. They perceive issues differently and thus behave differently.

The nature of stress must be examined more closely. It is not merely the intensity of the force that comes at us that determines how stressful it is; it is also the degree of fluidity and transparency with which we meet that force that determines whether it knocks us over or merely passes through. The development of a more fluid nature, a more transparent quality of consciousness, that can allow many energies to pass through with less and less attachment to interpretations that narrow experience is a mark of heightening consciousness. Life is immediately de-stressed when we let go of personal control.

It is one thing to be able to release energy from structures and begin to become transparent to new levels, but another to be able to radiate that energy outward into life. One of the great challenges of our time, as people come into meditation and other deepening processes, is that they find the world in which they reimmerse seems to have no room for them to express the new level of energy. If we gain energy by the release of conditioned structures in psyche, as happens during meditation or spontaneous awakening, but then are addicted to redirecting that energy back into compartmentalized areas of consciousness, the result can be very painful. This is one of the reasons people who begin transformation tend to get off the path. They don't know how to integrate the new energy into their former life because it is too big for the old compartments. The energy of an awakened person radiates out *unconditionally* as a presence which subtly transforms everything it touches. Until this is appreciated and we stop demanding resolutions to personally perceived problems, the transformational process is very stressful.

From a transformational perspective on stress, the consciousness of the individual is more significant in nearly every sense than the source of the stress. In fact, it is the person's consciousness (or society's) that defines what is stressful. The things we are struggling with reflect to us the level of our own consciousness. Of course, in the medical sense there may be a toxin of such extreme power as to be beyond the transmutative capacity of nearly all human beings, and in this case removal of the toxin (stressor) is of primary concern. But there are always a few examples of individuals whose consciousness can respond to forces of such potency without being damaged. Take for example a yogi who remains in a small box without asphyxiating; or a story Ram Dass tells about his guru, who ate a handful of LSD without appearing to be affected by it; or the man in Kenya who walked barefoot to the top of Kilimanjaro and spent the night on the icy summit clothed only in a cotton jacket while he made prayers to his God. Research has been done to substantiate stories of this kind, so that there is no need for skepticism.

For an example closer to home, take the response of the ordinary individual coming across a horribly maimed person. Cringing, panic, withdrawal and general emotional crisis results involuntarily, whereas a trained physician or nurse enters this same situation with much less emotion. A trained consciousness or, more aptly, an expanded awareness, can experience stressors in a context in which they no longer have the same disruptive potential.

Obviously, the consciousness of each individual must be given as much attention as we give to the stressor (whether physical, psychological, or psychical in nature). It is consciousness that ultimately mitigates or aggravates the psychophysical response of the individual to any so-called stress. In medical language, the host resistance is more important than the inherent toxic nature of the toxic insult. That an even minimally expanded consciousness can transmute and alter the response to radiation has been suggested by the work of O. Carl Simonton M.D. and Stephanie Simonton. In my own work it has been clear that many individuals prepared for surgery by a transfer of heightening energy from a group seem to do better in surgery and recovery than they or their physicians had expected.

There are other forces impinging on the experience of human Beingness: cosmic, galactic, solar, lunar and collective human energies (a collective human energy would be the feeling you get in an angry town meeting). The ordinary human response is to oscillate uncomfortably within these or be controlled by them. Periodically, there is an unusual collective psychic response to a particular lunar cycle with an increase in suicides and erratic behavior. Lunar cycles are also known to cause alterations in human blood-clotting capacity. Solar spots are suspected of causing disturbances in human psychical and physical behavior. We even suspect that major evolutionary shifts have occurred on earth as a result of intensified solar and supernova activity.

Periodically one notices a wavefront of dissatisfaction, paranoia and divisiveness, or one of well-being, openness and creativity, that seems to capture many people. I will have noted this wavefront moving through me and usually have rebalanced within it by the time my associates are beginning to report personal responses to it. As I am in contact with people all over the country who have developed heightened awareness and are working with an extended family of people, it soon becomes clear that this wavefront is happening on a broad human scale.

The point is that the less aware individual is the victim of these forces and plugs human content into a surge of transhuman energy. The content becomes the way to recognize the energetic evocation, but, and this cannot be emphasized enough, the content is secondary and could be irrelevant. It is not irrelevant, however, because what the human content succeeds in doing is to increase the length of time and the depth and intensity of activation of the energetic wavefront, thus carrying it far beyond its own timing. This sets up a rebound of collective response. Then, though the original causal energetic impress has passed, the psyche of the less conscious individual rebounds with it in secondary and tertiary levels. The more conscious individuals recognized the energy, shifted to a state of consciousness that could allow the wavefront to pass through with minimal disruptive reactions, and then utilized the energy in the most creative way available. They then have very little if any residual reaction to work through when the impress has passed.

This is no insignificant insight. Ordinary consciousness could easily manufacture grounds for warfare during one of the intense energetic incursions. We might then find ourselves at war, and the original impulse—which was quite indifferent to the content we attached to it—has long since passed. Now, however, we must unravel wave after wave of energy that emanates from our own responses and reactions. This is another way to think about the concept of karma. The storm has passed but, noting the turbulence still on the waters, we are continuing to prepare for more trouble.

One of the ways people block the flow of these energies coming from beyond their awareness is to manifest them as physical illness or periods of intense emotional activity. Vast numbers of people with minimally developed sensitivity to these deeper forces seek the resolution of stresses in diseases that might not even exist (or exist in a much smaller degree or with different significance in individuals of higher consciousness). The treatment of the supposed stressor, whether it be psychic, toxic or organismic, is often just a conditioned response to the content evoked by this stressor. Medicine is doomed to frequent failure and enormous wastefulness so long as it extrapolates more and more treatments around the content of human reaction (which is infinitely proliferating), whereas a small refinement of consciousness may eliminate or significantly alter the whole stress/response pattern.

Today there is a near-epidemic in nonspecific allergies, a so-called hyperallergic syndrome, that traditional medicine is poorly equipped to deal with. People are unconsciously becoming more sensitive to vague and subtle forces and at the same time the congestion of human forces grows greater each day. Our interconnectedness at sensate, perceptual and cognitive levels grows tighter and tighter. The world itself enters our living rooms, but this is only the visible aspect of our growing human connectedness. The carrier waves of our technology bathe us all the time, whether we tune in our receivers or not, and with this there is a collectivizing of energies in deeper dimensions. We broadcast everywhere our anger, fear and hate, as well as our beauty and achievement. We empower ourselves with the violence and melodrama of our lives, but we do not ask how to transmute these forces, yet they are evolving the human psychophysical entity. We are becoming more sensitive, in a multidimensional way, to our intrinsic connectedness. But only those whose consciousness has bridged into the awakened states, or "the fourth floor," have the conscious authority to perceive and work with these forces rather than to be at their mercy.

Certain things that we now consider disease will melt before the expanded consciousness. At the same time many of our approaches to illness will be seen to require an understanding of how the energies of consciousness are balanced. Thus awakened people will begin to approach disease by applying principles that allow a conscious refinement of psychic energies to be coupled with our therapeutic regimens. Healers who can recognize the underlying phenomenon of a transformational process in any given presentation have access to a greater wisdom within which to apply their therapeutic tools.

To a large extent this is what is happening today in the holistic health and human potential movements. I refer particularly to our new appreciation of the dying process and various modes of preparation for death, as well as to many processes for working directly with body energies (acupuncture, polarity, breathing therapies, and so on). There is also extremely useful consideration of diet, exercise and stress reduction. Each of these procedures shifts the basic orientation of consciousness at least temporarily, and in this sense works (although indirectly) with the transparency and balance of consciousness itself. The trouble with the plethora of holistic regimens is that they often become competitive with each other instead of being recognized as operating within a larger, more universal perspective of transformation. (Western medicine has done the same thing within itself.) Each technique taps the consciousness at a particular level and creates an augmentation and focusing or a diffusing and diminution of psychic energies, thereby leading to a potential for new balance.

In my opinion none of these techniques are as significant as the overall consciousness and presence of the individual who employs them. Individuals who have undergone fundamental transformation can, through their direct presence, initiate a rebalancing process in those around them. In a similar way, they empower any technique they employ. Furthermore, a fuller awareness is capable of appreciating and accepting *all* the potential ways in which well-being can be supported without getting into competitive or defensive postures as to the validity or effectiveness of any of them. The awakened consciousness is concerned with the quality of presence with which individual's incorporate these modalities into their personal healing. Many of the so-called quack remedies gain the power they seem to possess because the way they are presented provides something the traditional establishment does not. While quackery exploits fear by providing unsubstantial hope, traditional medicine *creates* fear which it refuses to deal with; this is a shame, because to transmute the energy inherent in this fear would empower our healing even more. From the perspective of a more awakened awareness, the way in which Western medicine is practiced with so little deep sensitivity and love could equally be called quackery. However, higher awareness does not use these terms, because in the greater unfolding experiment of life none of us need be blamed or attacked for being less than our full potential. It is better that we all be encouraged to grow.

❖

As we explore expanding consciousness and consider its meaning and relationship to medicine, two areas of significance immediately come to mind. First, there is an array of physical, psychological and psychic symptoms that mimic actual disease—from nervous tremor and increased sensory sensitivity to inexplicable pains and sensations, to heart attacks to psychosis—that occur concurrent with shifts in the energy body. These experiences do not necessarily imply physical disease, but there is no other way to consider them prior to awakening. Thus if we seek orthodox medical and psychiatric evaluation in these instances, the interpretation and treatment can be wasteful or even disastrous.

How many times does a traditional physician do an expensive diagnostic workup, only to discover there is no evidence to confirm a diagnosis. There may very well be minor laboratory abnormalities, but they are nonspecific, and we are just not experienced enough at this time to begin to correlate such subtle physiological changes with transformations in consciousness. At this point the word *psychosomatic* is brought forth and the traditional physician will suggest psychiatric consultation. (This is not an argument against traditional medicine, but an invitation to take our medicine into a larger context of humanness.)

During the intense early phase of my own transformation I could not explain my physical symptoms and my imagination ran rampant. Twice I turned myself over to an internist, one of my former instructors, for a thorough workup. At the end of each he honestly told me that he didn't know what was wrong and sensitively suggested a psychiatric consultation. I knew, with sure intuition, that this would only confuse me. The medical consultation had been undertaken to rule out the possibility of a dynamic that could be more easily handled by traditional approaches. Having exhausted what traditional medicine could provide, I knew the resolution would have to come from within myself, which it did.

If the individual practitioners have begun to recognize their own transformation of consciousness, then they can help create a new model for understanding the patient's experience. This model must contain the basic concept that the human being is a multidimensional transducer of energy, and that experiences of personal, physical and psychical content are really reflecting a larger, interpenetrating relationship to life. These forces can be harmonized by beginning to balance and refine the energies through the direct therapeutic use of food, exercise, water immersion, massage, relaxation techniques and meditation, to mention but a few basic approaches.

Most important to this model is the ability to communicate the transformative context in such a way that we recognize the evolution of our being and our own power to find authority within the process. The tools employed within this context are merely methods for activating, quieting and balancing the energies of consciousness. Obviously, the application of energy-balancing techniques has validity, not only for those areas of symptomatology that we would say are concurrent with transformation, but for every disease process, especially those such as cancer (which I regard as a high-energy process).

The healer must have had some direct experience of the transformational process in order to recognize the subtle dimensions underlying the presenting symptoms. Psychoanalytic and psychological insight are important, but they do not necessarily convey, and frequently obscure, direct experience of energetic processes. One must be able to sense directly, and thus in varying degrees consciously interact with, the energetic state of the individual in order to recognize to what depth the process can be entered into and perhaps assisted. In this way the augmentation and refinement of the energy is undertaken as opposed to suppressed, the latter being the approach of traditional therapy to many of the higher energy psychical states. Healers can undertake the balancing of energies directly once they themselves have been initiated into the awakening process and learned to refine and transfer energies.

When we create an analytical or behavioral model, we are attempting to understand a phenomenon at the level of effect, rather than cause. Our traditional psychiatric therapies frequently slow or even obstruct what is a profoundly creative process (though it may be frightening and bizarre). To suppress an experience of multidimensional significance can result in permanently limiting the consciousness of the individual. The kind of energetic balance necessary to refine these processes is exquisite and requires wherever possible the creative integration of such experiences into a person's life without lowering his or her overall energy state too much. If this is not achieved the individual may be functional but the deeper mystical refinement of the consciousness may not emerge.

I am concerned that, if the energetic process itself is not allowed to mature and is never fully appreciated as a transformative potential, some disease process may then result. Consider that the incidence of cancer in the schizophrenic population is one-quarter that of the rest of the population. It is possible to consider the psychotic process to be a nonintegrated relationship to higher energetic potentials. It may be that the cancer process reflects the consequences of insufficient transparency to these higher forces, or an unconscious repression of the higher states of being. Recently I presented these thoughts at a conference of the Association of Transpersonal Psychology and a psychiatrist who attended told me that my ideas provided some insight concerning one of his patients. He said that he had treated a schizophrenic woman for a number of years and had "cured" her. She then went on to develop cancer. While she was schizophrenic they had had a very good relationship, but when she developed cancer she began to hate him. Unfortunately, what we call cure is sometimes the suppression of a higher process.

In general, schizophrenic disturbances are occurring at higher energy than the ordinary consciousness within which the therapist attempts to connect with the client. Thus our current therapeutic approach is suppression of symptoms through drugs. While it is true that many schizophrenics present a picture of apparent low activity, this is not be be confused with a low energy state. My experience with autistic children demonstrated that while they are often behaviorally withdrawn their energy field is rather expanded and they are unusually sensitive at subtle levels. In my own experience, and in experiences I have observed at ashrams, it sometimes happens that a person deeply disoriented in a high energy state can stabilize and become balanced and functional merely by being in the presence of an individual whose consciousness has heightened. This larger consciousness is like a container or womb in which the disturbed space can safely resolve or decompress. It is this very process that the high energy teachers bring to the people around them.

Our present day medical science does not recognize an interceding energetic dimension that unites consciousness and form—a dimension that becomes a living presence in heightened states of consciousness. This is not to say that all psychiatric problems will be resolved in the presence of a higher energy. In fact the opposite can occur, and the so-called psychosis becomes intensified. High energy amplifies everything. Frequently the intensification of physical and psychical content during transformation is at its most intense just before the shift to a new level of equilibrium. The point is that any force that can either calm or intensify the "disease" is obviously acting directly within the causal dimensions and thus ultimately can help resolve it.

We must be willing to release individuals to their own destiny as well as to make a primary commitment to our own transformative process. Some healers and therapists are so involved with helping others that they somehow find it extraneous to perfect their own being. The reason conventional therapy has not gone very far with sensing the energetics of illness is that very few individuals have gone through a transformative passage of sufficient depth to carry the energy to be a psychoactive presence in the face of major psychical disturbance. However, human beings can *collectively* evoke an energetic force field that is finer and far more powerful than the presence of any one individual. This is why we naturally turned to group and milieu therapeutic methods instead of one-to-one therapy for treatment of major psychic disturbance. With further knowledge about focusing and refining a group energy, the group processes can be taken to levels not yet envisioned by traditional therapy.

It is at this point that consideration of the consciousness of the healer becomes vitally important. As long as the illusion of a self that is separate continues within such individuals, their approach as healers will always be predominantly mechanistic and linear. Their action will thus have validity and effectiveness only within a narrow dynamic of experience, and may even obstruct deeper integrative potential. As the consciousness begins to transform into a subtler realm, this I-am-separate- from-you approach is finally seen as illusory. Now the interaction may be mechanistic at one level (e.g., the surgeon places a plate in a leg to repair a fracture), but there is a far deeper blending and interpenetration of energetic forces. When these forces are consciously attuned by the healer, a new and finer energy is attained in the interaction. Thus surgery by one surgeon may be incredibly effective for a particular patient in a particular situation because there is attunement, and the exact procedure can go sour with another patient if the attunement is lacking. A person whose consciousness has awakened can effectively suggest a doctor-patient match or, even more important, teach the individuals to attune to each other and to the deeper forces in such a way as to maximize the potential of the interaction. It is almost impossible to describe the difference that an attuned and unified quality of consciousness makes, even during the most mundane of therapeutic actions. A temperature can be taken and a person can feel loved. (In this discussion we are not even beginning to consider what this understanding could mean in any educational, political or business setting.)

It is the energetic context in which something is undertaken that must be examined, and not merely the outer attributes of the most gifted healers. It is their consciousness that refines and empowers the technique we observe. They are able consciously to bridge into realms of simultaneity with "another" individual who is the "object" of their study. Many good healers have this capacity to a high degree, but it is veiled from their consciousness. Thus they rely on their technique and, as teachers, extol their technique. They rarely appreciate the state of consciousness they are in as the techniques bear fruit before them. An awakened consciousness observing such a healer or teacher experiences an activated force field that is kindled as they work and that clearly is the deeper medium through which their work is communicated. Interestingly, if you try to share this with many such healers and show them ways they can become sensitive to this dimension they are often quite resistant, even afraid. There are, I thus conjecture, some souls who function better in their role through the self-imposed narrowing of their consciousness. But the point is made that there *is* an energetic presence that is evoked in any ritual of healing or in any human interaction. The ultimate effect of this presence (whether it is creative or destructive) seems to be related to the level of consciousness and wisdom as well as the motivation from which it is evoked.

There is a wonderful story in Richard Seltzer's book *Mortal*

*Lessons* about the master Tibetan physician Yeshi Donden. Dr. Donden is described as he correctly diagnosed a patient during grand rounds. According to the story, two hours before rounds he prepared by fasting and prayer. (Remember my earlier remarks about gathering the energy for a particular kind of work. Temporary abstinence from food and the turning inward of awareness are key aspects of this preparation.) In his examination Dr. Donden never spoke to the patient. He observed her and the space above her. He took her pulse for thirty minutes while absorbed in deep concentration (entering the dimension of energetic communion in ever-more-refined and heightened consciousness). He sniffed her urine (another facet of the deep ritual by which he accessed necessary information). Not only did Dr. Donden obtain subtle information in a manner quite foreign to the West, but (equally as important to me) while this was going on the patient was also visibly calmed and moved into a state of thankfulness. That the author was moved by Dr. Donden's presence is quite clear in his description of the process.

An individual of multidimensional sensitivity observing the room during Dr. Donden's examination would have undoubtedly experienced the activation of a powerful energetic presence and with it a sense of love. I do not think we can discover the power of acupuncture and other Eastern healing modes by a Western cookbook approach. We cannot separate the process from the refinement of consciousness in which it is undertaken. In many ways those deeply connected to acupuncture will understand what I am saying, and we have much to learn from the specifics of their energetic subtlety.

Of greater significance to me is the exploration of the consciousness out of which acupuncture might have been derived. I have no doubt it was the cumulative wisdom of many individuals who awakened to multidimensional awareness and studied the human experience afterward. The same is probably true for the modern healing approaches that come from an intuitive base. With any of these latter methods that are not based in the power of collective wisdom and science, in my opinion their greatest validity lies in the fullness of consciousness of the individual that empowers them. Where traditional science has tended to narrow its outlook, they thus provide vital contrast and the essential of growth through paradoxical insights.

Obviously Western medicine can make the same diagnosis as Dr. Donden did, although it takes longer and is tremendously more expensive. (It is probably not more expensive if we attribute a dollar value to the years of discipline and commitment it takes to refine consciousness to the degree demonstrated by Dr. Donden.) Compared to the quality of Dr. Donden's being, the Western approach rightly appears clumsy and unillumined. Yet by virtue of the way Western medicine comes to its answers, there is also a much greater understanding of the physiology of disease and likewise a technology to utilize for treatment. For many processes Western medicine represents by far the greatest healing capacity. But what we have sacrificed along the way is equally great. It is the impersonal force of love and compassion that is lacking. This is because these qualities are not something "other," they are intrinsic to and radiate from the refined levels of consciousness. Western physicians and scientists are trained as highly skilled and disciplined technicians, but not as multidimensional human beings. Thus we neglect our presence, which is subtly empowering everything we do. Thus we go about with the illusion that diagnosis is separate from treatment, or that the healer is discrete from the patient. Not caring to know ourselves, we lack appreciation for the multidimensional human energy system that unites body and psyche. We are ignorant of transformational states of consciousness and rely on technical knowledge when a moment of being genuinely present might offer a whole other perspective.

We must begin to examine the level of consciousness within which we explore our medicine. The physician's level of consciousness exists as the radiant quality of energy that interpenetrates every act and defines what is conceivable. This is also true of the patient. When the two are together it is the quality of consciousness that is their relationship, as well as the collective consciousness from which their beliefs and techniques emerge, that ultimately defines the potential for healing within the interaction.

This energetic continuum is far more than a theoretical context. For, as we have seen, it is this very dimension that begins to present itself as natural in heightened states of consciousness. If we refine the energy that is the context in which the doctor and patient are interacting, we automatically note a change in their perception of the experience. Even the so-called fixed physical manifestations of disease become mutable. Tissue structure changes, and so-called healings become more common. For those who can enter a surgical procedure at a higher energy state, common experiences include less bleeding, less pain and faster recovery. If the consciousness of any one individual is genuinely heightened, then every potential interaction with that individual is forever subtly different.

It might seem that all we have to do is heighten energy and all our problems will begin to evaporate. Not quite, for even as we explore this process our perspective and the center of our motivation is likewise changing. We *can* consciously evoke a higher energy state once such a dimension has become part of the awareness (or through the help of a trained healer or teacher). But the result is not some magic panacea to fulfill our personal desires. It would be a mistake to try to manipulate the powers of consciousness to avert our fears. The result, as I have said earlier, is to empower these fears in other dimensions.

We can, to a large degree, determine the quality of our energy, but what its ultimate effect will be must be released into a true sense of unconditionality. There is a deeper wisdom that acknowledges living and dying to be the same process. This is difficult for people to accept when they desire transformation in order to change something about their lives. Thus, while higher consciousness can bestow some amazing powers and does result in directly altering the so-called natural expression of certain phenomena (and these abilities are relatively simple to attain), there is also a deeper realization of the importance of remaining unconditional. This quality radiates as the healing presence, or the love, in even the most mundane of actions and is quite uninvolved with our personal goals.

# 6 ❖ TRAVEL: A TRANSFORMATION

WITH EACH PASSING DAY the world grows smaller. The media, travel and global commerce are gradually uniting mankind in increasingly complex patterns of interrelatedness. The ability to awaken to and respond to fundamental levels of human experience is more and more urgently needed.

After the energetic opening in 1977 I went on a pilgrimage. I felt compelled to discover a deeper understanding of what was happening to me through the contrast of new places, new peoples and the forces that I intuited were underlying these differences. Recognizing a process of rebirth, I knew somehow that the whole of the Earth was my new mother and through her I would discover a truer sense of being. I found my boundaries being stretched in ways I could not have anticipated. My energy levels, senses of vitality or anxiety, the very way I formulated words or wrote poetry, and the content and quality of dreams and fantasies would change from place to place.

The milieu of energies that surround the human experience varies greatly in different parts of the world. In foreign lands humankind displays itself in many different ways which are quite alien to one's own conditioning. For example, in India I watched the body of a child cremated on a platform along the crowded shores of the Ganges. The ashes were then swept into the river not more than twenty yards from haggling merchants. In the shrines of Benares one is continuously accosted by beggar/priests. In Nepal our possessive monogamies sound like cruel insanity to a Sherpa.

The rational mind attributes the familiarity or strangeness, the comfort or discomfort one encounters during world travel to the various new and unfamiliar impressions of foreign lands and languages. We make value and preference judgments based on our reactions to externals which we pretend to comprehend. But in my experience the phenomena is much deeper than this. Carl Jung wrote of the case of Richard Wilhelm, the translator of the *I Ching*. Jung felt that Wilhelm's prolonged time in the Orient resulted in his very soul becoming possessed by the East. Wilhelm had great difficulty later when he returned to Europe; his health and mental well-being began failing.

The force of the collective psyche of a foreign people and of the earth itself is something to be reckoned with seriously. Most travelers buffer against this by attempting to maintain some of the familiar rituals of their home life; for instance, through the timing and style of meals. But, as you release deeply into another culture, a force enters that begins to transform the fundamental energy of your own basic identity and this can be quite stressful unless there is an appreciation and a desire to allow the deeper process. Fundamental to this is the gradual refinement of those powerful qualifiers of our sense of self that we call meaning and purpose.

Meaning and purpose attribute substance to our lives. It is doubtful we could live without them. They are inherent in how we formulate our living. But there are deeper levels of meaning and purpose.

Usually we know ourselves through the meaning derived in our work and from the purpose we attribute to our actions. But out in the world, receptive to the moment, a stranger in strange lands, these old identity-creating molds begin to melt. The pilgrim who goes beyond travel as meaningful per se begins to realize another level. It is as though more of life plays through you and begins to show that your self is again deeper, beyond any personal content that may come from upbringing, no matter which *you* we look at anywhere in the world. However, it is largely how one inwardly travels that determines the varying degrees to which this realization can be born. The "doctor" or "teacher," the "American" or even the "seeker" who maintains this self-identity while traveling is limiting herself or himself unknowingly and in turn sees a limited reality. One who is willing to travel as a true student of Beingness is a pilgrim in the truest sense. For the latter, it is consciousness itself that receives its full earthly human inheritance.

As I traveled I began to recognize a part of my awareness that is masterfully gifted at diverting away from the transformative potential. For the first several months of travel I did everything I could to establish myself in familiar and self-rewarding activities. At Findhorn, a community in Northern Scotland, I lectured about dreams and the transformational process. On the island of Iona I organized a few evening sessions with the small group with whom I stayed. By so doing I could orchestrate a group process and tap into a higher level of energy, and this would give me a sense of balance and personal power. Even when group energies were unavailable to me I found other activities. In Egypt and in India I would take opportunities to become the doctor and provide medical advice. Gradually I realized that through this behavior I actually was blocking the deeper process I had come to set free.

It is easy for a person who has opened to a higher energy to continue to draw others into this process and in so doing be maintained in an identity. It is often a quite positive and compelling one. But by so doing there is an element of control. One never has to be ordinary, unimbued, and accept the world on its terms. I started to have invitations to travel and lecture all over the world but I recognized that a deeper step had to be made first. It was time to become invisible; to drop my old identity, to lose myself as utterly as possible. To do this I knew intuitively that I had to just be with experience on its terms and not manipulate to create self-esteem and meaning to redefine myself. I knew also that in order to accomplish this an environment with a strongly amplified energy was required.

This phase of the transformative process was anguishing almost beyond my ability to stay with it. But finally in India at an ashram I was visiting I reached a point that configured in the deepest dichotomy of mind that I had yet consciously touched. Already exquisitely sensitive, I now placed myself in a situation of tremendous physical and psychic intensity and not only did I have to deal with my own discomfort, but I was also surrounded by the energetic vortex of hundreds of people struggling to open to higher consciousness. If I stay in this experience, cried one part, I am just torturing myself needlessly and perhaps destructively, and I deny every shred of self-love and self-respect that offers me the freedom to choose and create a life of my own meaning. If I leave, it is because of fear and rejection and I deny the basic trust in the momentum of conscious opening that has brought me to this very moment. I knew somehow that resolution was not in leaving in order to sustain and perhaps even express my self-love, nor was it in staying in the experience at the apparent destructive level. Finally I let go of any struggle.

It was as though the fundamental ambivalence of my nature (and perhaps all of human nature—the personal self vs. the Self that is part of all existence) was crystalized in that very moment at a level of energy that could not allow that split to continue. Letting go was like choosing to sacrifice my sanity and my whole human history. I felt as if I were passing backward in time and simultaneously forward—but not in time, into another dimension. The energy was similar in quality and intensity to the original opening. But whereas the original experience had come spontaneously with no warning and a part of me had never truly recovered from a sense of uneasiness, this time I could recognize the conscious progression that had brought me to this moment. With each wave of energy I surrendered a little more and finally there was no more resistance. With a feeling almost of indifference I simply entered another level of reality. It was not ecstatic or dramatic, just a sense of quiet and clarity and an inconceivable ordinariness and freedom. While words cannot convey the experience the sense was of formless existence as a feminine principle—an ultimate mother—that bequeathed *life*

by the fact of existence itself. I felt in direct relationship, inseparable from this great feminine consciousness. As existence expresses through experience, so the very coherence implied by
any kind of experience is evidence of the Divine Creator.

I had to rest for several days (in terms of psychic stimuli) so I
retired to my hotel room. Then dreams and fantasies began to
indicate that it was time to resume traveling and in particular to
exercise the body. This I did by spending several weeks trekking
in Nepal. The fear of annihilation and disease that had at times
haunted me since the initial opening and which had motivated
my release of home and friends and the early group work in
order to find resolution, now passed from my life. A new flow
that continues to evolve in my present work began taking form
at that time.

❖

Maintaining one's health is one of the challenges travelers
usually find in their ramblings around the world. Prior to the
shift in my own consciousness I frequently became ill during my
travels. Afterwards this was not the case. I became able to maintain my health in my subsequent travels because I could sense
the energetic shift in each locale and maintain balance at this
more subtle level. It is all right to be shifted and deeply affected
by other milieus.

Maintaining balance means that one is not fighting these
forces as they begin to alter perception and the sense of self; instead one is consciously harmonizing with them. I found that
the key was to agree within myself to open slowly, to explore the
food, the water, the people and their ways gradually. I was not
there to maintain the old me, but neither was I there to devalue
or be disrespecting of my physical and psychic roots.

Of course, this means that at times one will have to allow
periods of vulnerability, doubt, perhaps some fear, and often an
inexplicable sense of loss or sadness. It is as if being inducted
into a new energetic is like taking oneself away from home or
separating from an old lover. But as this transition is allowed,

the energy eventually opens and a new level of expansiveness and freedom is obtained.

I believe this inward openness averted the disease processes that I saw many other people being involved with. It is not merely contaminated food and unfamiliar organisms that produce disease, but these in conjunction with the stretching and occasional rupturing of the energetic integrity. It might be called psychic exhaustion as the old identity mechanisms work over-time to bulwark against the subliminal assault on one's energetic nature. As one learns to open, the assault becomes a caress.

Sometimes, and this is particularly true of what I observed of Westerners in India, people seem to need illness to help them move deeper into themselves. In a sense it is a way to gather their own power in order to sustain their own identity. Some-times illness would force them to leave and return to a more ap-propriate or safer psychosphere. When the psyche is impinged upon by a force it does not yet know how to recognize con-sciously, then illness can become one mechanism or response. It may function to close one off from this impinging force or it may serve to help open to it by building a kind of protective co-coon in which to integrate the new energies. For some I felt that illness was unquestionably reflecting a process of opening. Per-haps it was just too much, too fast. Perhaps for their particular nature it was the best way. However I believe that, as con-sciousness expands and we gain multidimensional sensitivity, more and more of these deeper forces can be met and responded to without illness.

❖

There is an important counterbalancing understanding that must be clearly brought forward. For those who are to discover the deeper forces, openness, transparency, and a growing ability to release conditioned perspectives are essential. However, at every state of such opening an equivalent power to center with-in one's being and move forward with a kind of inner authority is also essential. This inner authority is not a rigidity that rebukes the energetic effect of a foreign environment or a new experience whenever it occurs. Rather it is the inner authority to carry oneself in a balanced way even while being shifted and changed by the deeper forces.

The most essential aspect of this inner authority is, in my opinion, the commitment to realize the highest potential within oneself. Armed with this and a deep belief that we are each responsible for our own unfolding, we must learn to evoke the power necessary to function in life in whatever way we are called upon to do so. To lack this inner authority or to be suspicious of the power (and, as is often the case, to project it onto others) means that to grow more open whether one is conscious of it or not results in being blown meaninglessly and perhaps destructively in the winds of the deeper currents. Openness without a basic strength and wisdom can be disastrous, just as an inflexible need to maintain one's own identity without genuine openness is equally limiting.

To be stretched and reconfigurated in the powerful forces of foreign places and cultures is a great learning process. It prepares the consciousness for a broader realization of dimensions which I have called collective energies and shifts the identification of self from localized and personal points of reference to a perspective of the deeper and more universal forces that configurate humankind in all of our variety. But once such an initiation has been entered into there is no return to the old level of the personal self. Therefore, those who appreciate the potential of transformation inherent in transcultural experiences must be equally prepared for the new self that must be rediscovered moment by moment throughout such an adventure and afterwards.

If individuals have opened sufficiently during their travels, whether they have been aware of this opening process or not, they may be unprepared for the kind of intrapsychic challenge that is required to reintegrate themselves into their former world when they return. There is a culture shock in going to a new place that can be anticipated and responded to with some of the attitudes I have described. But very often people do not suspect that these very same attitudes—and perhaps a good deal more of the process of finding the deeper inner authority—will be required in order to begin to work and function in the world of their origins. If one has stayed away long enough and has immersed deeply enough in a foreign setting, the process of reintegration upon return may prove to be a greater challenge than the process of travel itself.

I have recently had related to me a story of six hundred former Peace Corps workers who were invited to Washington, D.C. to be honored at a state function. These individuals had been carefully selected and had represented some of the finest among our youth, but then something quite unexpected occurred. These former volunteers who had returned to the United States after several years abroad began denouncing the United States. The person telling this story attributed this reaction to idealistic disillusionment and anger over political and economic abuses that they perceived upon returning. The teller was himself identified with his own anger and disappointment and he therefore found it easy to identify with the reaction expressed by the volunteers. Undoubtedly there was some validity to their complaints. But I suggest the deeper issue is not at the level on which they reacted, but why they needed to react.

I think the phenomena of their anger was initiated at a deeper level. It is doubtful that these volunteers had been prepared for the profound psychic shock and energetic confrontation that they would discover upon returning to the U.S. Their natural defenses had been broken down by the period of foreign context, which imbued them with a different quality of energy. Upon returning they were, I believe, overwhelmed by the intensity of their new vulnerability to the basic energetic that exists in this country. To be so deeply vulnerable can lead to becoming profoundly ambivalent, despairing, resentful and angry. It is very hard to initiate meaningful participation when someone is so open and people frequently draw upon the intense emotions to precipitate a sense of self. Thus the anguish of vulnerability frequently leads to attack or an effort to find the flaws in a situation. Not knowing the real dimension that caused their vulnerability, they responded as if they were being threatened. It is a kind of identity crisis, and in such a crisis one can either empower the familar emotive mechanisms or one can intuit and await stabilization in a new level of consciousness.

Without a transformational level of insight they had no choice but to utilize their reactions at the power and emotional level to redefine themselves. But, with a realization of the deeper energetic forces, their anger could have been easily transmuted to a wonderful sense of acceptance and a radiant quality of love. The latter is a more creative state of consciousness with which to approach all the real issues that require our attention.

# 7 ❖ DISEASE: A TRANSFORMATION

THE PROCESS OF DISEASE—cancer in particular—is one of the places where humankind is being given the opportunity and the challenge of bridging the interface of consciousness and form. I make this remark and the ones that follow with all due respect for the person with disease; I am not without personal experience in this area. In 1972 I was biopsied for an enlarged lymph node. The very real possibility of a cancer process existed for several months prior to the biopsy. When the biopsy proved negative, I thought I was through with the process, but this was not to be the case. A deep and unresolved fear had been seeded or, more aptly, reawakened in my consciousness. Several years later, after the major shift in my own energy this suppressed fear blossomed into full potency. As I have described, the powerful psychoenergetic awakening produced such a sense of vulnerability and so many strange psychical and physical sensations that I could not help entertaining the possibility of serious disease.

I became convinced that I had a choice: I could manifest a cancer very quickly by allowing the transformational process to remain arrested at the level of my fear, or I would have to learn somehow to move beyond this level to a new consciousness. It was partially this dynamic that had motivated my travels and that guided me into a process of psychological undoing.

Through this process I learned that nothing ever resolves through denial or repression. As long as the familiar *me* existed, the disease-creating contraction process would have power. It was not the cancer, real or imagined, that had to go, but the *me* that could host it. The old consciousness had to be released if I were to survive and integrate the blessing bestowed in the awakening.

I have learned and continue to learn that I must not call on another soul to make the kind of transformation that I myself have not made. Thus I do not make these statements casually, nor do I invite others to look at this out of idealism. But it makes no difference how or where the shrinking from death or transformation occurs. It must be resolved, and it is resolved at higher and higher levels as the energies of expanding awareness become more generally integrated into the full spectrum of one's being. We must attain higher energy states to begin to transmute the reality that appears unchangeable at our present energy level. Whether this occurs through the spontaneous awakening of energies or through a disease process is of little importance. Until it occurs, maturing into the higher levels is impossible. Consciousness will continue to empower the old reality until there is sufficient energy and and one somehow releases/sacrifices it, through a kind of mystical death, and passes through to a new level.

I believe that, when the new level of energy is attained, the forces that might have configurated disease at the old level no longer need operate. If it is not attained, then the disease probably perseveres and physical death may become the transformative door. In either case, transformation of consciousness has occurred, and to a deeper level of our Beingness this may be all that really matters.

As I observe people with major disease, it is clear that they are being reduced at the personal level and coerced into entering a more expanded awareness to whatever degree they are capable. Consider the choices one confronts: possible maiming surgery, potent radiation and chemical agents with debilitating side effects, realization that one's life may be ending, temporary or permanent change in work and lifestyle, and profound effects upon one's key relationships. The very roots of one's being are shaken.

People with any degree of awareness and psychological maturity cannot face these issues without re-examining their most fundamental ideas about themselves and about life. Whether the disease progresses rapidly to death, goes into remission or is cured, one cannot help being struck by the transformation fostered by the process. I have been with individuals so powerfully eroded by the cancer process at the level of external power and control that profound energy and (formerly unexpressed) wisdom radiated from them. This is most often true of individuals whose lives have always been oriented toward wisdom, growth and their highest potential. It is as if the disease provides the final empowering through which they attain a new level of consciousness. I am reminded in particular of a well-known psychiatrist with whom I shared the last weeks of his life. He was deeply respected and loved for his openness and loving nature. In the last year of his life he rapidly succumbed to a brain tumor. In the early phase he had considered suicide to avoid the period of debility, but instead he allowed the disease process to unfold. At the end his speech returned briefly and he expressed and radiated the profound sense of love that he finally attained. He had reached the pinnacle of his conscious development.

In my involvement with him it was soon clear that he was involved in a deep transformational process for which nothing need be done. I observed that, although the energy I came to share was never taken in by him, with each visit his wife became more and more at peace and able to release him. This kind of dynamic where the energy is brought forward for the ostensible patient but in fact provides a medium for resolution of some other related dynamic is often the case in this work.

A public example of a transformation through disease was the case of former Vice President Hubert Humphrey. In the closing days of his life, when he was slowly succumbing to bladder cancer, he became deeply concerned that his work be a contribution to the genuine well-being of future generations. He was no longer obsessed with political consequences. When he addressed the United Nations shortly before his death, the power of love in the talk stunned the audience. My intuition is that it was a transformative energy that captured the hearts of that diversified group. The power of the talk was not in the words themselves, but in the presence of the man. I am sure that this same process is occurring in many individuals we shall never hear about. It is through this process that the soul of humankind grows more loving.

People faced with the challenge of major disease can heighten toward an experience of love to a degree that they probably never touched before in their life. The awful friction of the disease process helps to create the transformation. One might almost speculate that the missing ingredient all along has been love: love in the deepest and most unconditional sense; love, not as an emotional connection, but as a radiant current that intrinsically unifies the psyche and embraces within its transformative power the whole spectrum of human experience.

When people facing major illness intuit this possibility, they have already begun the transformation. At this point they can be helped to move toward this realization and guided to operate in the kind of intrapsychic balance that can encompass the potent energies inherent in their situation. For such people the experience around their illness may be exceptional. They frequently develop the ability to perceive energies and reach deep levels of intuitive communication. They begin to "see," to recognize the souls of others, often becoming teachers, living koans, even healers of the people around them. Their medical process is often enigmatic, for it is overlaid with the indefinable symptoms of a heightening energetic process. Frequently these people do very well in terms of their medical program. They may be highly responsive to treatment and recover well from surgery and chemotherapy. But whether or not this is the case, many feel they have been given the keys to a new and deeply fruitful way of life.

For those who allow themselves to be transformed in the

process, cancer, the modern day symbol of death, has become the greatest blessing, the grace that transforms their lives. It is a way of life never conceived of before. It is marked by less concern with self and more genuine caring about the well-being of those around them.

Some people, of course, are at first attracted to this potential reorientation but later contract away from the possibility of actual transformation. They inevitably retreat to a more traditional and nonunified orientation to the disease and to their health. It was not transformation they desired, nor heightening of awareness, just release from a situation they did not like. It is my observation that when this more limited goal is the primary motivation, people do relatively poorly in terms of their personal experience and of their health. Despite all protestations, one gets the deep sense that many individuals need to be involved with illness in traditional terms. Who is to say that this (given the various stages of developmental integrity in any individual) is not a necessary and appropriate part of their growth?

To allow oneself to be catalyzed into a transformation process through disease requires that one release the fear of death. Otherwise, the healing process becomes a negotiation: meditating in order to get well, dieting in order to cleanse and purify, and so on.

I'm convinced that problem-oriented approaches are too small. They activate energy, but not the full energies of one's being. Such processes never carry the power to undo the old consciousness. Our approaches must be more comprehensive. To turn towards life and live it more totally empowers the whole of one's being, and the specific challenges of the disease process just become moments where the letting go of contraction and the surrender to Beingness occurs at an even deeper level. But whether spontaneous or as a consequence to disease, I appreciate that a deeper transformation is a level of experience that takes a kind of courage and commitment that all human beings are not ready to undertake. And certainly this is so if they have not somehow come to a fairly high level of psychospiritual maturity.

It is my opinion that we have a latent memory of the kind of transformation an awakening process implies. It is possible that this intuition is far more frightening to the subconscious than the debilitation and death implied by the disease process. Certainly the energy necessary to move through such a process, at least in my experience, requires total abandonment into the process—it cannot be undertaken merely as an adjunct to one's usual life. Based on my own experience, I no longer advocate transformation to everyone. I have realized that there is a natural inner timing and that people can be helped to go only as far as that allows. All judgment or subtle coercion to go farther must be released. It is natural for me now to accept and honor people as they are. People who are not ready cannot be brought forward into the fuller transformative energies even if it is clear that doing so could possibly release them from the forces configuring their illness.

When people hear that there is a medical doctor who works with the energies of consciousness, there are a few who approach thinking I may give them an easy out. They are afraid of their doctors and suspicious of the traditional approaches. But what I offer has nothing to do with easy outs.

We human beings are funny creatures. We want to be given easy ways to get from here to there and we pay an enormous price for it in dollars and energy. We want to be given more for less. This is because we don't understand the balance of energy at all levels that is essential to integral functioning. If more energy is placed *into* the system we call an individual, or into humanity as a whole, then more energy must be radiated *out of* the system.

To move from one state of consciousness to a fuller one takes energy. Repressing the challenges or denying the necessary interdimensional friction by which the cauldron of transformation is brought to readiness abort this possibility. Western medicine and lifestyles have done this. We answer or wave off the deep questions, sedate the anguish, and in every way possible try to lower the energy state. We confuse the narcotized calmness of a doped individual (and there are many drugs— religious, social, and political as well as chemical) with the quiet centeredness of a heightened consciousness. I'd be willing to bet that pre-operative sedation will be proved to lead to greater surgical complication and risk. But pre-operative excitation of energy will prove to be advantageous, and all the more so when it is consciously balanced and attuned. For the average less-conscious person, the anxiety before a stressful or risky situation is how energy is gathered. We need to learn how to heighten this to increase it even more, not decrease it. But, of course, the heightening must also be a refining and this requires love and wisdom.

Rather than harnessing this energy that resides within consciousness, we harness greater and greater external energies and pour them into hospitals, technology, chemicals, and so on. Western medicine can frequently sustain the physical embodiment, but it does not foster, and may continue to obscure, inner transformation. I am reminded of the example of a man who had a heart attack. After he was patched up he returned to his old life and had another heart attack. He was patched up again. He again returned to his old way of life. He had another heart attack, this time complicated by a stroke. He reached the point where he could neither move nor talk before he began to let the transformational process awaken in his life.

At one level or another nearly every human being is doing this same thing until some force comes along to incite a new dynamic. There are people who have energy and money (which is a symbol for human energy) poured into them by doctors and hospitals so that they can sustain their old life because they are afraid or simply don't even know that they can begin to harness the current of their own being. It is not until we have a problem that traditional medicine simply cannot handle that we look around frantically to see if there is something else. But by that time it may be too late. And even here we fool ourselves.

It isn't only traditional medicine and technology that can be abused to avoid real change and growth. It is often very tempting to try to console ourselves with spiritual, metaphysical or holistic models. Many seek such models because they sense a fuller wisdom inherent in them. But no model ever conveys its inherent wisdom until people have done the appropriate inner work, so that the model merely reflects their own realizations.

Some people pursue the spiritual like others pursue medicine – to avoid themselves. (The last place we look is within ourselves.)

There is a basic imbalance of energy in this outer looking that will eventually rebound. When human beings are acted upon by any external authority without a concurrent thrust to develop complementary inner resources, the eventual rejection of that outer authority is inevitable. Rebellion becomes natural, even essential. The child must eventually reject the parent in order to become whole within itself. The child becomes the parent of its own being. Society is rejecting the parenting force of our medicine (and all of our institutions) for similar reasons. However, while rebellion may be a first step, it is not enough for the deepest healings. Rejecting or running away from something may eventually lead to a greater sense of oneself, but it is nonetheless a splitting process; what we reject is in a subtle way a part of ourselves. But when one is moving forward in the embrace of something greater, then the forces for growth and healing are unified.

Sometimes a person will approach me and say "Well I guess you're another one of those people who says that all there is is love." I get the feeling that this person thinks he has got me and love all figured out. I smile at how the mind, because it can say the words, beguiles itself into thinking it knows. The mind is a coward, and most of our approaches to life are cowardly. But to approach the process of health and disease from the perspective of conscious transformation and unconditional love is certainly not the experiment of cowards. One is no longer in the realm of simple answers, burying one's head in the sand, projecting magic powers on healers, or hiding behind spiritual dogma. One is in the cauldron through which the heart is opened, wisdom is learned and a whole new level of Beingness may be attained.

❖

I have worked with patients with all kinds of illnesses who tried unsuccessfully to heal themselves through psychic processes, energy transfer, nutritional regimens, meditation and prayer. But behind what appeared to be sincere efforts was often a process of rejection and pridefulness. They rejected or avoided traditional medicine. They said they did this because they equated it with insensitivity, a lack of respect for the miraculous healing capacities that reside in every person, a general lack of consciousness about the multidimensional nature of man, and so on. While this may be true at one level, what was equally true and of much greater significance was that their encounter with traditional medicine brought up fears of maiming surgery or powerful drugs, the confrontation with death, and even worse, the conviction of personal failure accompanying their recognition of themselves as diseased, especially when facing a traditional setting that feels so impersonal.

In working with them it became apparent to me that, unable to face this, they found that the efforts they had made could not work fully because the psychic milieu in which these efforts were undertaken was part of a repression process that split their psyche and separated them from the deeper energy they needed for healing. To reach that energy they would have to pass through their fears. The infusion of energies that transcend and can perhaps resolve the problem level never arises out of a denial process, no matter how outwardly praiseworthy it appears.

The inner work with illness from the perspective born of awakening consciousness is a moment-by-moment, individual affair. The higher perspective offers guidance to utilize to the maximum all energies brought forth for healing by engaging them in a balanced and unified consciousness. For example, surgery (when it seems the likely choice) can be looked at as the most effective and potent process *energetically* as well as mechanically. This is especially valid for those properly prepared. The energy influx during a surgical procedure can be most awesome and transformative if the psyche is not split about the validity of the experience. I am not advocating surgery over other more natural or spiritual pursuits. Rather I am saying that there is really no difference how energy is obtained and transmuted once awakening has occurred.

In a state of unconditional love there is no distinction as to the naturalness and efficacy of any method, whether it be nutritional, the laying on of hands, or chemotherapy. There is understanding that the individual who contemplates such choices is the product of highly complex personal and cultural determinants. To adhere to a belief structure that says that one thing is better or worse would be to flounder in the sea of ordinary consciousness from which most of our reality is judged. It is imperative that we recognize the limitations of this level and develop the ability to discern more wisely than through the arbitrary preferences that usually arise from fear and ignorance. Interestingly, we have lost the original understanding that the word fear means "to pass through."

All healing experiences, whether laying on of hands, penicillin injection or surgical procedure, are essentially energy-modifying. They reach into this experience we call Self and interact at various levels, modifying the hologram of consciousness in various ways. If the individual Self were likened to a television set or a holographic projection, every adjustment within the mechanism would result in some shift in the image. Penicillin might be compared to a small focusing adjustment that makes the whole image clearer, while prayer might change the incoming signal and produce a different quality of image altogether. But whether the interaction appears to be happening within the organism or in some dimension beyond it, it is really happening in all dimensions. The nature and quality of this alteration is an expression of its relative intensity and vibrational frequency, as well as the depth within self at which the energetic interaction is allowed. Thus it becomes a question of the level of consciousness that must be reached into to release a disease pattern, and a matter of recognizing which experience carries the most appropriate energy for this process in a given individual. It is this understanding that brings the wisdom of higher consciousness into the experience we call medicine.

But what is this wisdom? Simply stated, it is the capacity to allow the psyche to unify by recognizing the whole within every part. This can be particularly difficult when faced with experiences that exceed our understanding, or when the implications of the disease and the treatment are unacceptable or just plain frightening. It takes enormous personal commitment that few are even capable of recognizing, let alone undertaking on their own. But I believe it is this process that heightens and refines consciousness in a genuine sense. The challenge is to open ourselves enough to tap the level of consciousness where the energy bound in the disease reality may be released into a more unified dimension.

For this to be possible the energy must have reached a sufficient peak, and we subconsciously fear this peak more than our diseases. This must be so, or why would we avoid the difficult questions, the ones that undo our lives? Who am I? What am I? What do I do? If I don't do this I may die very soon, but if I do do it, then I may be tremendously weakened and debilitated: What kind of life is that? Am I suppressing my feelings or reclaiming the energy that is in them for the empowerment of healing? If I keep thinking this way will I make myself sick? But how do I stop thinking when a time bomb is ticking away inside of me? Beyond these questions there may be a glimpse of what needs to be temporarily released in order to find the answers, real peace and a new center of being: family, husband, wife, job, self-image, even life itself. Yet it is these very structures that become so precious when we sense that illness will take us away from them. How few can step forward into the next moment of being and experience the self as transcendental, collective, the one that is many. The energy of this latter state is enormous. The compartments are released.

Everywhere we look, every question we ask, the problem is the same. It is the *me* that is asking, the *me* that is sick, the *me* that must do something—and there are so many *mes*. The energy is dissipated throughout a myriad of subselves. When there is only One (which is really no *me*) then the energy is ready for the jump. And it is through this awful challenge, these terrible questions, that the energy can be found. Why do we want others to answer for us, or drug us, or console us, when this dynamism can give us more complete lives? To work with the forces inherent in these questions leads to a deeper center, a more unified Beingness.

It is this unified center that can draw the deeper energy from any experience, making even surgery part of the journey toward awakening. A new sense of reality emerges as a refinement of energy. It is this very center that is bestowed by the contemplation of unconditional love. Unconditional love allows deeper and deeper penetration through these questions. It becomes the last context we can create for ourselves before we must finally let go and just be.

Do not let the word *allowing* persuade you that this is easy. If it were easy we would not repeatedly fall for the next miracle cure, the next "right" way, the next great answer, or the next "truth" of science. I write not of panacea, but of opening the heart of one's being to *every* facet or experience. It is in this process that energy of the higher reality finds its partner in matter, in our bodies, and in a maturing level of awareness. I believe that once this sense of wholeness is realized, any route for healing will prove more fruitful or perhaps be irrelevant.

Once this is appreciated we can utilize any therapeutic form as a source of energy in a *process of being* rather than a process with defined goals. Uncomfortable as it may be to contemplate, when we hold to the need for healing we hold equally to the presence of disease. This is another example of how empowering one side of the polar expression automatically empowers the opposite. The awakening levels of consciousness not only experience the Self as a dance of energetic interactions transcending our ideas and beliefs, but recognize that the process of life far transcends our relative goals. Thus, the perspective shifts from recovery to the fullest potential of being.

A basic discernment that is being asked of all of us as we enter into transformation is to learn the difference between two distinct dynamics. The first is transmutation. This is a process that frees the energy inherent in a disease or a psychological pattern and thus allows a new and finer perspective and energetic balance. Such a process is intrinsically unifying and results in a heightening of energy. It inevitably involves a deepening sense of love. The other is a process that is a subtle denial/repression mechanism that maintains a low-vibrational state of awareness, despite the outward magnitude of the rituals and technology to which we submit.

# 8 ❖ THE SPECIAL ENERGY OF GROUPS

IT IS IMPORTANT to any understanding of human awareness to examine the basic principles of group interactions that result in heightened energetic potentials. For example, the ashram is a very special kind of community. The quality and intensity with which individuals interact there potentiates the unique experiences encountered in such a setting. Likewise, a monastery houses a group of individuals consecrating themselves to a life of prayer and thereby creating a unique psychosphere. These cloistered environments create intensity of a very specific kind. Awareness is turned back on itself to seek the roots of ideas and attitudes. Simultaneously there is the embrace of a relationship to something beyond, something *other*.

As this process is going on in many people at once, the sum of such actions potentiates the process in each, and perhaps gives rise to sufficient energy to allow penetration into new levels of reality. The individuals fostering these environments are not only personal examples of higher human potential and wisdom who have created teaching regimens involving diet, exercise, meditation and work, but they are also gifted in orchestrating their communities into highly unified functional units. The Tibetan Buddhists are wonderful at bringing a community into a fever pitch around such a project as preparing for the visit of an inspirational guest or a prayer retreat. The deadline, the special moment of the arrival of the guest, the specialness of "our" work, become external motivations for the intentionality through which a group of individuals mobilize themselves to the same purpose. Acting as a group with a shared goal, and adding the element of urgency or crisis, we have one of the oldest and most powerful tools for focusing and intensifying human energies.

The ashram or monastery is not the only place where this occurs. It is a universal process. It happens at universities during final exams, in armies during war. It is the essence of every team sport to mobilize nearly superhuman effort from the players; outside the context of the team, few individual players could mobilize this kind of energy. Heros are made when the power of a unified context compels them to a singular focus where all thought ceases and pure being takes over. It takes over, but is defined by the context. The soldier fights ferociously, the athlete plays with amazing skill. In this state, so-called paranormal abilities become natural. Athletes report being able to influence the trajectory of the ball, people lift cars, and so on. Each of us has our own memory of a particular time when, for whatever conjunction of personal motive and outer situation, we have been lifted beyond ourselves.

There are war veterans today who still cannot free themselves of the power over their consciousness that was initiated by the sheer intensity of their heightened energy state during war. It becomes the pinnacle of their life. During war the intensity of camaraderie can be so deep that by comparison little else seems real. Veterans will be drawn to recall it over and over again, just as spiritual seekers are drawn back to those moments of realization until they finally comprehend the principles that fostered the experience in the first place. Then, they can begin to apply those principles in the Now and become free. To harness such energy without profound outer crisis and stress may be the challenge of our time. Toward this potential, the transformational process, and particularly the power of group energies orchestrated around the simple exploration of Beingness, opens new vistas.

For the vast majority of people the empowering of awareness occurs most effectively in groups. In one form or another meditation is the key to expanding awareness. By practicing meditation one learns the focusing and gathering of awareness and thus of energy as well; but, meditation is rarely effective taught alone. Most meditation is done in groups, because there is a power in the group process to induct and accelerate the experience, especially for those who are new to it. Prayer in congregations is more potent than alone. In the Jewish tradition a quorum, called a *minyan*, is considered a requirement for initiating the group prayer.

At other levels that may parallel this observation, some interesting research showed that retarded children tested better when their teacher sat next to them and worse when they were alone. People perform better to an attentive audience; the audience heightens the performer, and vice versa. In my work with autistic and schizophrenic children, the children did much better after the staff had been trained to enter, as a group, into a more unified state of consciousness. At still another level of observation, I have sensed that team sports in which large groups move as units are better attended, more addictive and somehow more powerful than individual sports. All of this suggests to me that there is a dynamic of human interaction that is rarely appreciated consciously but is universal nonetheless. Augmenting this group dynamic is the basis for the transformational force catalyzed in my own conference work.

In my opinion, the difference between the power of religious ritual and the ritual of a sporting event such as football lies in the nature of what is being evoked or called upon. In the former it is the highest spiritual principle and in the latter it is the highest human capacity. Religion deals with man's transcendent nature, while football explores the realm of emotional and physical mastery.

In both cases there is a heightened presence. To the aware individual this living presence is an energy field that is perceivable whether at a church or ashram or football game. It is energy, potent and sometimes even palpable, and it can be transmuted to empower multiple levels of awareness. For instance, in the awakened person the energy of either of these settings might potentiate heightened psychical powers such as telepathy or clairvoyance. The less-aware individual will feel a compelling sense of vitality and of belonging to something greater than self; when separated from it, there will be a sense of loss and of being cut off from life.

Once one has become accustomed to operating in an intensified energetic, to be removed from the setting causes great unrest. This is the basis, I believe, for the addiction that occurs around spiritual schools, cults, teams, the army—in fact, any setting in which human activity is undertaken with sufficient unity of purpose to create a heightened energy state. A common problem in performers is that they only feel whole during the heightened energy of the performance. Later some may turn to drugs and alcohol to quiet or activate the intensities to which they have been accustomed.

While most human situations are experienced without enough subtlety of awareness to reveal that the energetic context is more important then the event, one hopes that at least in spiritual matters individuals can recognize the deeper force catalyzing their sense of unity and participation. Unfortunately, until awakening this is not the case. People become addicted to the setting in which their energetic sense is heightened without developing the awareness to recognize the forces affecting them or the principles of existence necessary to attain to a deeper freedom within these forces. Even where there is little or no awareness, the process of human interaction by itself catalyzes some degree of energetic presence. Although usually it is minimal and unconscious (compared to that realized by the adept in the ashram, the consummate entertainer or the great athlete, each of whom evoke these forces with conscious intention), it is still participating within the universal principal of collective energy or presence in which our lives are undertaken.

Thus we become initiated into various levels of energy systems, and must gradually discern the dynamics within them and free ourselves into higher orders of interaction. In a sense we can speak of an energetic addiction to systems we call family (parents in particular), to schools, to patterns of behavior, to jobs, and even to struggle with disease, as long as each represents a level of activation (the receiving and giving out of energy) of an ever-expanding potential of consciousness. (Simultaneously there is a profound but subtle yearning/apprehension to be free of these systems, as if another part of us recognizes a call to a higher level.) As one enters a more unified context of human interaction, this energetic potential can be heightened (more is received and more is given out and with this there is an expansion of consciousness). At each new level the addiction process can occur again, until one finally has moved up and down energy levels and in and out of enough contexts to recognize a deeper or more fundamental level of awareness—the Greater Self that occupies all these spaces but is defined by none. At this point one has awakened sufficiently and is free at least of the blind power of most lesser human systems—the "illusion of the world" referred to in so many spiritual cosmologies.

❖

Until now the exploration of group energies has not been part of our educational processes, except minimally in the context of warfare or athletics. Instead, the movement into the expanded states has been the special province of ashrams or so-called religious schools. In these settings the basic phenomenon is understood and exploited. Wherever human endeavor becomes a collective effort, a phenomenon occurs that amplifies the energies available to any individual to move from ordinary to expanded consciousness. The whole is greater than the sum of the parts; or, as it says in the Bible, "Where two or three or more are gathered in my name there am I in the midst of them." (John 18:20)

I believe this biblical quote refers to a natural principle by which man becomes aware of a larger energetic dimension, to some degree evoked by and encompassing his experience. If we are gathered in anger and righteousness we can become a lynch mob. If we are gathered to foster a sense of greater awareness and love we may feel a "holy" presence. When a group forms to convey energy for healing, it can become a powerful therapeutic entity. However, the mere gathering together of humans does not by any means insure that they will transcend the basic energetic milieu and create a heightened energetic potential. Not all angry groups become mobs, and not all congregations enjoin the higher presence. By openmindedly exploring the principles of group energy we can free ouselves of limiting contexts (the group, team, church, religion).

I would suggest, for example, that we begin consciously to explore focused group energy in medical and educational settings. Since physical and psychological realities are functions of energetic states, heightening the collective energies could provide an accelerating and augmenting force field of human consciousness into which new sensibilities and faculties can be born. It will be seen that, as we operate in a heightened energetic milieu, the seemingly fixed biological processes become relative and behave in new ways.

The sense of other dimensions and profound sense of love and well-being that occurs repeatedly in my conference work inspires me to imagine that these phenomena *can* be more universally employed, particularly in education. There is an enormous unknown factor in human consciousness that exists dormant in every moment. To discover it and free it is a marvelous adventure. Having come through a highly technical, traditional Western education, I cannot overstress the importance of unveiling realms of human experience that come alive in heightened awareness. Until this happens we can have no idea how closed we are. Experience is the key, for there is at present a gap between what we can experience and what can be conveyed in words (or even understood). Thus in my conference work direct experience of higher levels is the teacher, and for this to come about it is crucial to appreciate the refinement of group energetics.

*Focused group energy* refers to the *conscious* orchestration of a natural phenomenon whereby human energy joins and amplifies when it is gathered around a unifying principle. This

process is the single most powerful way, except for the direct experience of Grace, through which the energies available to the
ordinary individual are amplified. When the boundaries of personal self-consciousness are set aside and one's identity swings
toward its collective aspect, the self loses fixed configuration
and flows into a greater continuum.

The heart of my own work is the volitional attempt at group
heightening around the state of unconditional love. I believe
unconditional love is essential for two reasons. First of all, for
the purpose of transformation, contrast must be created with
our ordinary levels of consciousness. The nature and quality of
this contrast is extremely important. Unless the contrast is set
against an unconditional state that transcends personal perspectives and moves toward the all-inclusive quality of love, we are
forever stuck in the sphere of the personal without seeing its relativity to some greater phenomenon. (A good image for this is
the cartoon in which two fish are seen leaping from the ocean.
One fish is indicating to the other the water below them. The
caption reads "That stuff, Stupid! That stuff!") Until we move
into a higher energy and a higher premise for human relating,
we will not understand the principles and forces that determine
our reality at a lower energy level. We will be like the fish that,
having never leapt in the air, does not know what water is.

The state of unconditional love becomes the "air" into which
conditional consciousness leaps in order to behold a new dimension. The state itself is an experience that transcends and
therefore ultimately disturbs the boundary-creating
mechanisms of our personal consciousness. Just being willing to
attempt to realize this state begins a major shift in consciousness. As we open toward this new experience the very intuition
of it subtly generates an atmosphere which inspires the potential within the individual. It is absolutely essential that, as we
encourage consciousness to lift into this new potential, the energetic milieu be of the finest consistency and quality. While this
potential is automatically set into motion by the commitment to
an unconditional quality of love, the new areas of experience
will come forward so long as the energy isn't repolarized into the
familiar domains of intensity such as the sexual and emotive
levels of experience.

I do not mean to exclude or negate these areas of human experience. In the sphere of my personal life, feeling and sensuality have been very full and rich. But there is something inherent in the sexual dance of attraction and in the emotional and power configurations—like anger, possessiveness, self-pity, competition—that simply obscures the more subtle potential. It is like always listening to the tympani and not hearing the nuances of the harp. Therefore, although much good work is being done to help people clear patterns of emotional reaction, such work often becomes a closed system that represses the direct knowing of a larger milieu of experience. We end up trying to explain feelings by looking at the reality in which they occur instead of beyond it to a higher level of order. But feeling and explanations for them are infinite, so the process at this level is never ending—a closed system. Many people even feel they should push for a certain peak of intensity and then cathart the energy in a powerful emotional outburst which they equate with realness or with healing. But this merely serves to dissipate the energy and then the pattern begins all over again. Rarely does this intense catharsis catapult us to a new level.

Encouraging the sexual or emotional/power area in the exploration of higher potentials continues to obscure the as-yet-unexperienced areas of Beingness. The emotive interpersonal processes must be set aside for awhile, with powerful emotion witnessed nonjudgmentally (not repressed) and lifted to a higher potential. The importance in my own life of spending a number of years learning to control emotional response cannot be overstated. I could never have appreciated the energetic phenomena underlying the emotional plane had I not intentionally set it aside long enough to sense another dimension.

To set it aside allows the gathering of energy for a potential quantum leap of awareness. The emotive dimension is a high-intensity realm, but it is of relatively low and unrefined energy marked by strong oscillations of feeling. Someone who has not developed some emotional mastery could be swept into incredible intensity and potential danger if they empower this facet of their psyche at a higher energy. This is the significance to me of the words of the prophets: "Make straight in the desert a high way for our God" (Isaiah 40: 1–3); and "Every valley shall be exalted and every mountain and hill made low, the crooked straight and the rough places plain" (Isaiah 40: 4). It refers not only to stabilizing the high and low swings of mood but also suggests a straightening out of the various side trips by which we continuously dissipate our present energy state. One need not feel intimidated by such a challenge, because it is remarkable how easily one can learn a new mode when it is intelligently placed before consciousness as an option to be explored.

In addition to the indulgence of emotional patterns, the other significant process that hinders entering a higher level of awareness is the incessant need to intellectualize and figure things out. While this process has validity in making things work in outer reality it is a veil to entering a different kind of consciousness in which (as I said earlier) understanding must be allowed as a consequence and not as a prerequisite.

There is a second important aspect to focusing the group dynamic around the sense of unconditional love. Although the initial intimations of unconditional love can be shared as presence (and thus you can be guided toward it by a person who has realized this state), the realization in oneself is powerfully expedited and deepened by group energy. And, once you touch the unconditional quality, its exploration transcends any context. When unconditional love is finally born as a new dimension in an individual, it is not contingent upon an object, a person, a philosophy or a goal that can be construed as external to or separate from self. When the potential in this state becomes conscious, it can be made available all the time in any context.

I explain this to conference participants by saying that we will create an energy field through our interaction that will lead us to a new realization of our nature as human beings. It is not that this new level will be sustained indefinitely, but that the insight and actual transformation derived from the experience becomes the core out of which to evolve into other levels of Beingness.

By contrast, the collective energy in situations such as social crises, political conventions, movies, sports events, performances, love affairs and traditional religious rituals never really makes conscious the deeper process that causes the sense of heightening. One is swept up in the energy instead of being the refiner-transducer of it, in addition to which the context is a conditional and limiting one. In these situations people become stimulated and even addicted to the heightened intensity of amplified human group energy, but they also become identified with the context. The whole of the person is never involved. For instance, one can have the stimulation and arousal of sex without really caring for a person, or one can be emotionally involved in a situation like an athletic event without its having any real relevance to the rest of one's life. We can let parts of ourself merge with complementary parts in another person and thus experience a tentative heightening. But is is limited and, as I mentioned earlier, fosters push-pull dependency or addiction to the intensity itself.

The love, found in experiences of *conditional* unification and heightening (even when it is evoked in the so-called worship of God) is a love that might later go to war, or riot, or murder, to protect the context of its addiction. Truly to touch unconditional love is a radical experience—it changes the very foundation of self. It provides direct experience, not only of the many latent powers of consciousness, but also (perhaps most importantly) the sense of the collective Self.


Just stop reading for a moment.

> *Agreement, disagreement . . .*
> *The effort to understand can fall away.*
> *Here is a piece of paper . . .*
> *trees lumbered, timeless evolution,*
> *machinery, metals, refinement,*
> *millions of entwined lives,*
> *the evolution of language . . .*
> *The sense is Vastness,*
> *the Peace of incomprehensibility in which*
> *we all merely Are*
> *United.*

Frequently when I am giving a talk I use the following image. A group of forty people could fabricate a satisfactory home rather quickly. They could build a foundation, floors, walls, and a roof, insulate with natural elements, and incorporate fireplaces for heat and cooking. This could be relatively easy. But if all forty people were to work together for the rest of their lifetimes they could not collectively reproduce one disposable ballpoint pen. To do so would require the mining of ores and the refining and smelting of metals. It would mean drilling down through the ground to liberate the stored oil and understanding how to process it to synthesize plastics. It would require knowledge of dyes and fluids. Forty people, or even four hundred, are not sufficient to this task if they stand outside the industrial collective. A simple thing like a disposable ballpoint pen stands as a monument to our collective nature—a perhaps absurd symbol of our inseparability. And it points to this oneness in a single dimension, the material plane. We are, I have discovered, equally as one in the bodily, emotional, mental and energetic dimensions.

Group energy focused at the unconditional levels of Beingness can move the sense of Self into a direct realization that bridges our continuous tendency to split the part from the whole. It is difficult to describe the group process at one of my conferences, because the actual work is with the energies of consciousness. The form is only the scaffold upon which to build the energetic, and this form changes spontaneously so as to open a door into new spaces, spaces hidden between the obvious events. Someone looking through a window might see people sitting in a circle holding hands, listening to music played very loud, singing and dancing with abandon, or quietly sharing their experiences with each other. A typical day during a conference begins with morning meditation. There are two, and occasionally three, group sessions during the day with a lot of time for quiet relaxation or adventuring in the surrounding countryside. At this writing my work is centered at the Sky Hi Ranch in the high Mojave Desert of California. It is a space of great subtlety of color, vast expanses of mountains and sky, and great quiet that naturally augments the exploration of other dimensions of consciousness.

Energy is activated and awareness refined and expanded through various kinds of subtle contrast. For instance, energy is activated merely be being in a different environment or moving through the day in an unfamiliar time sequence. Even more energy is activated when one begins to explore the realms of human body energies and new and inspired ways of sharing and communicating one's Beingness. During the group process I emphasize to the participants the concept of building an energy charge. The group dynamic is a powerful amplifier and refiner of energy and each individual tends to be able to hold this energy differently. Awareness of how individuals open to a sense of fuller energies, as well as how they dissipate this energy charge, is crucial to each person's growth.

In general, the more receptive and open one becomes, the more creative and unconditional one must become in the expression of the energy so that balance is sustained. Opening to experiencing the energy is taught through various exercises, through the new context in which the process is taking place, and by my own example. People must be encouraged to release the linear, comparative and judgmental modes of self-definition. This allows a gradual merging into the larger energetic and the new sensitivity begins to develop. How the new energy can be expressed is suggested and exemplified, but it takes its own unique form through each individual. As people learn how they block openness (by competition, judgment, needing to understand, and the like) they begin to heighten the charge of energy they can sense within themselves. Equally important, as they learn how they have unconsciously dissipated energy (having sex that merely discharges, lazy socializing or talking to fill space, activating old emotional tapes, eating or exercising compulsively) they gain the freedom to hold more energy consciously and thereby enter new states of consciousness.

At this point we can explore subtle senses and direct energy from the hands or the eyes to relieve pain or as a simple gesture of love. At times this kind of exploration is humorous, as when participants are instructed to find a coin hidden under the clothing of their partner (such localization is possible because metal seems to create irregularities in the energy field that radiates from the body surface and this can be sensed by the hands). Once the required shift into a different perspective in consciousness is understood and practiced, such subtle perception is relatively simple to develop. Some people find the coin with nearly 100 percent accuracy. Later, without prior verbal exchange with the person being examined, this same subtle ability can be used to locate areas of trauma or to identify the presence of pain.

The exercise of scanning for hidden metal was the result of an experience I had while I was still in medical practice. I had been able to develop hand sensitivity so that I could sense fresh injuries and pinpoint them under triple thicknesses of hospital linen. At one point I thought I had discovered a strong abnormality, perhaps a tumor, in a woman's groin. Reaching down, I discovered there was a bunch of keys in her pocket. When these were removed the "tumor" field was gone! No doubt this kind of trial-and-error is common as people explore the subtle sensibilities. I have been able to teach similar sensitivity to hundreds of people, including health professionals who can then apply this dimension in their work.

While the coin exercise deals essentially with hand energies and hand sensitivity for exploring the body energy fields, there are other exercises that develop subtle skills. Some deal with learning how to sense the area around the body and interact with others while in this level of perception. Some are involved with the telepathy of emotions, with transmuting emotions, and with learning how to activate and center volitionally within various levels of consciousness. A large group of exercises deals with developing the sense of heart energy and of the unconditional state of awareness. All the exercises invite people into experiences that gradually extend the range of awareness.

Many of these exercises developed naturally out of my own awakening experience, while others are adapted from the work of other teachers in my earlier explorations and travels. (In particular I wish to credit Dr. William Brugh Joy, Dr. Claudio Naranjo, and the Rajneesh Ashram.) In general, the power and effectiveness of all such exercises is in accordance with the refinement of the consciousness of the person who offers them. When the leader's consciousness heightens and refines the energy generated by the exercise, there is no need to be violent or assaultive. The work has an element of stress, but this resides in the challenge to release into the process and then learn to carry and modulate the new energies that begin to be evoked.

What is particularly revealing about exploring some of the exercises, such as scanning for the coin, is that the sensitivity is readily available when one enters the process sincerely but *without trying* in the ordinary sense. Effort growing out of any idea about how to do it, or a feeling of competition, or needing to perform, obscures the capacity and the coin cannot be found. This kind of effort seems to close the gate to levels of consciousness where these abilities are natural and simple to develop. Happily, when one gives up the struggle and operates from a sense of openness, the coin is "miraculously" detectable. Such an experience acts as a simple, direct feedback mechanism to demonstrate that one is shifting levels of consciousness. But it serves another and perhaps even more important function: There is a part of consciousness that needs to touch into these seemingly magical dimensions in order to accept the possibiltiy that one's own perception of reality is in fact relative and mutable. There are certain essential experiences—such as the emergency-room experience I described at the beginning of the book or the conference experience of opening to a new dimension of well-being—that simultaneously give permission to begin the larger exploration of our nature. Later such experiences are there to help us to reconfirm our sense of newness and exploration when the dream of reality has closed in once again.

As a group unfolds in this kind of exploration, little attention is given to the content of the many personal states that come up. The personality is never attacked or focused on in any primary way. Instead personal reactions are reflected back to the individuals so they can examine how they are reality-configurating or boundary-making, relative to the larger context: the growing experience of unconditional love in which the deeper unity with experience just *is*. It is the sense of exploration, of opening to a new moment, of sensing toward that which is beyond the first level of response, that is the deeper focus.

To do this, people must be willing to set their personal process aside at least until the new level is reached; then the personal process begins again, but in a whole new dimension. This is the key to moving a group of people into a tremendously cohesive and powerful energetic. Obviously one of the first steps is to internalize trust, so that everyone is confident that postponing some initial reaction is making way for a higher dimension of herself or himself and not being swept into the leader's delusional system or power trip.

Gradually the more rigid personal areas that invariably activate to resist the expansion dissolve in the higher energy like a sugar cube in warm water. However, those areas of the psyche that open more slowly are not rejected or negated, but become the valid focus of the individual's personal work during quiet time apart from the group session. Such areas can be perceived by the individual from an unconditional sense, so that the energy within these patterns is finally released. When the group's attention is focused on someone's personal process it is usually to take a look at the universal qualities within their experience; this can be helpful to everyone and everyone is appreciative. There is almost no encountering. It is the responsibility of individuals to encounter their own personality patterns and then to let go to the best of their ability. If someone insists that these patterns are real or valid in an absolute sense, then they have chosen to live within them and the door of transformation is temporarily closed.

It is possible by working in this way to create a profound sense of well-being and love and to move in a matter of days into areas of insight never touched before and areas of experience never even conceived of. Once a group comes into harmony, the energetic presence is palpable and wondrous. Even after working in this way for five years it is a phenomenon that uplifts me every time I experience it. It is particularly exciting to watch individuals who thought they had thoroughly appreciated certain philosophical or theological areas as they begin to sense an entirely new level of significance.

Interestingly, the heightened energy allows buried trauma as well as buried wisdom to surface; also, forgotten or barely understood transcendent experiences come to light. I suspect these areas may have been forgotten because they occurred in a narrowed focus during brief or explosive states of heightened awareness and intensity. At the usual lower levels of energy they recede and become subconscious, sometimes being expressed through the body as symptoms or in behavior as neurosis. It is not until a similar or higher energy state is reached that one can again access these memories. At a balanced and openhearted level of keen awareness, the energy patterns formerly held in check can be released without ever having had to uncover them. They emerge naturally and are integrated in a deeper way. *What is subconscious at one level or vibration of energy enters conscious authority at a higher level of energy.*


A group of people in heightened consciousness creates a sea of experience that amplifies their capacity to explore the subtle forces that relate the individual's energy level to perceived reality. Thus it is seen that one's perceived reality is in a continuous dynamic with shifting currents—sensed as a kind of energy of flux within and surrounding one's "body." Interaction with this energy field results in sensations involving all the normal senses in new ways, as well as emotional shifts and qualitative changes in one's space/time orientation, feeling tone, and thought. (Only later does this experience begin to be translated into symbols, images and metaphors. Thus trying to understand or explain the process prematurely calls forth a more superficial level of consciousness which veils the deeper process.)

Dimensions we think of as reality in a psychological/ behavioral sense—behavior patterns, issues of security, pleasure, power and control, as well as attitudes, values, ideation, memory and even intelligence as we usually understand it— begin to appear as vibrational functions of consciousness. Components of personal reality can be evoked or evaporate in an instant with shifts in the energy field showing their relativity to a larger milieu of experience.

One of the great moments of awakening comes when we truly discover our multidimensional nature. Quickly one perceives that motivation and behavior from the unawakened level are relatively crude responses to being penetrated or perturbed by forces acting at subtle levels of our being.

It is as if we exist in sheaths of potential reality that open or close on various planes of experience dependent in some way on the level of energy (fineness, as opposed to intensity) animating our awareness. We are capable of multiple simultaneous and frequently incompatible, contradictory or paradoxical perceptions and responses depending on which level or quality of energy our awareness is centered in. At lower energy states the multidimensional awareness is constricted and the options for behavior and experience are limited. At this level self-identity requires greater intensity in order to define or recognize itself, and this conditions our experience toward intensity.

In a sense we can say that we *know* ourselves through the intensity generated by our personal stance in life (which is the expression of our level of awareness) as it creates its own unique interference pattern within the larger existence. There is a meditation that I use to help convey what I mean by saying that certain patterns and ranges of intensity form the hidden matrix for how we *know* ourselves. I call it the "the New York City cockroach meditation" because of a joke I heard while still a medical student in New York. According to the joke, if all the structures in the city were to disappear and only the cockroaches remained there would still be a faint but discernible image of the city. Likewise if only the plumbing or electrical circuitry remained the image would be there but with differing qualities.

I instruct participants to close their eyes and project a mental hologram of themselves. Consider that this image is configurated from psychic material such that various qualities define more or less of the total substantialness of the original image. I then suggest that they make believe that the cockroaches remaining are that part of themselves that they *know* through needing to be loved. How fuzzy or tangible is the image? Now let the defining ingredient be needing to love someone. How is the image? How much of the image is discernible when the "cockroaches" are the sense of wonderment and love, distrust of others, ambition, needing to understand, or the ability to allow life to unfold? These patterns and the intensity they evoke literally define how we *know* ourselves and the world we are capable of experiencing. Now that you understand the exercise, try it yourself and discover the patterns of intensity that you employ to configurate your psychological reality.

Our responses, interpretations and rationalizations, even the form of our so-called scientific description and discernment, are secondary to the overall energetic refinement of each individual and the the collective energetic milieu. At any level of Beingness the reality we participate in is entirely cohesive and compelling as long as we remain within its dimension. At finer vibrational states we recognize a broader reality, begin to appreciate our multilevel nature, and thus can opt to respond and create in new ways. There is less addiction to intensity in the old sense, and consciousness naturally begins to enter subtle realms. If we are defined by experience, then it is not experience itself but our addiction to levels of intensity that partially determines this.

❖

No individuals who have observed their own nature and seen how something can look one way in one state of consciousness (e.g., fatigue) and entirely different later (when well-rested) would argue with the statement that reality is relative. And if just a shift in energy from fatigued to well-rested can present a different reality, what happens when indivduals are heightened into energy levels they could never touch on their own? It was this very question that was being answered as I worked with the groups.

Groups became the context in which to explore and contrast the energy of the individual with the larger energy of the group. Trying to develop the subtle sensitivities alone is tedious, but in the group dynamic these areas can be brought forward quite rapidly. From the perspective of the individual, group energies represent a tremendous acceleration and amplification of the potential to enter into heightened states of consciousness. In traversing this range of energies a whole new understanding of consciousness becomes apparent. People realize that communication among themselves as well as within themselves is mediated through the quality of their consciousness in ways analogous to the experience of trying to locate the coin.

At this point an apt analogy to the laser and hologram phenomena can again be made. The principle of the holographic image requires that a coherent light source be developed. This "pure" source acts as a constant or reference against which to form the interference pattern from which the image is derived. The image is only possible because there is a pure reference; if the light is incoherent there is no fixed basis for interaction. (Think of the surface of a calm pool as the reference medium in which to observe the intersecting ripples made by pebbles thrown into the pool. If the pool surface is churning, the pattern created by the intersecting ripples is lost in the confusion.)

I have begun to sense that consciousness as we know it is the result of a wavefront of our personal vibration within an infinitely coherent other medium that is beyond our rational comprehension. The reality we see from an unfocused awareness gives us one level of experience, one kind of interference pattern. It may for instance show us a reality of territorial imperative, of immediate needs, of have and have not, or whatever. As the energy state of the individual heightens and refines, the resulting interaction with the eternal reference medium results in an interference image of a different quality. This may present a reality of intrinsic interrelatedness, of basic harmony, of vast sweeps of time and space, and even of dimensions only comprehensible within a structure beyond time and space. The less coherent or refined the vibration, the more personal the perceived reality; the more coherent it is, the more the perceived reality tends to be nonpersonal in nature.

My work with groups seems to suggest that the heightened energy state of the group dynamic functions as a coherent reference that allows more multidimensional clarity to personal realities. We may be standing on the threshold of an evolutionary experiment. The work shows through an experiential process how human consciousness represents a multipotential state that can project its identity outward into ever-expanding systems of refinement. It is what I refer to as the progressive collectivization of mind.

One way to understand what I mean by collectivization of mind is to look at the nature of human gathering as it occurs today. We come together in gigantic rituals of powerful intensity called athletic events, concerts and conferences. Through growing technology, our lives are becoming inexorably entwined in newer and more intricate permutations. Physically we are able to live in increasing proximity and density. We are resonating and vibrating in ever more complex and dynamic pools of social interaction. The world in all its myriad processes, from the most horrible to the most wondrous, is reaching into our bedrooms, our kitchens, our stomachs and our hearts.

Perhaps less obvious but even more fascinating to me is to contemplate how, through the media, we are tuning into the same input at the same time. Millions of minds are receiving the same signal and responding to the same input simultaneously. It is as if we are unconsciously fostering the same process that I attempt to catalyze in the groups. I consider the group explorations to be a kindergarten-level microcosm of the larger collective process, a microcosm that is somehow slightly more accessible to awareness. In this arbitrarily created context, in a manner that is uplifting instead of intimidating, we can begin to glimpse the nature of the sea we swim in all the time.

Certainly we can become concerned over the quality of what is being purveyed over media and concerned over the effect that TV overuse may have on learning. We can feel afraid of the incursion into our narrow system of belief of the beliefs and needs and feelings of others. We can resent the way things are done and find infinite things to be afraid of and angry about. But perhaps we are measuring from old standards and from a narrow dimensional viewpoint. I have no doubt this kind of splintering is part of the process that leads to a potential for refinement. But it is also a boundary-making mechanism of the existing ego structure that holds us back from a deeper sense of a more unified and collective mind.

Perhaps we ought to be looking at whether this simultaneous

broadcast and reception of identical signals to millions of human beings, this ever-growing interpenetrating condition of life, is fostering greater collective sensitivity. Are people as a result of this becoming more psychic—though with little awareness of the multidimensional transformation they are undergoing? Is there an increase in telepathy, in empathy, in the ability to share and respond to a common sense of subtle forces? Are we perhaps feeling and sensing each other more deeply and more of the time? I speculate that this is in part the basis for the so-called New Age, and maybe for the epidemic of diseases like hyperallergic syndrome and cancer.

If we unconsciously defend our existing psychic structure as we try to evaluate what may actually be a transformational potential, the evaluation is bound to miss the deeper process. We require new criteria that simultaneously embrace the ego structure and the higher consciousness processes that arise as we begin to dissolve it. This means a sense of the refinement of consciousness in which the full spectrum of human potential is regarded with wisdom. This requires teaching/learning processes that provide direct experience of the multidimensional states. Only experience in these areas can take us out of hypothesis and speculation and into meaningful knowing. For this to happen safely we need the "Open Sesame" of the heart, the beginning exploration of unconditional levels of awareness.

There are now many experiments involving focused group exergies springing up throughout the planet. In one ashram I visited in India the guru transfers energy to an individual in an overt ritual while hundreds of disciples simultaneously focus their awareness on him. The effect on the recipient of the energy can be quite dramatic. The laying on of hands by healing circles is another form of the same thing. Evangelical healers who catalyze an audience and then invite people for healing are also tapping the higher energy process.

In every one of these forms the people attribute magical power to the individual who focuses the process, and many believe that they have had a taste of God, who somehow ends up being peculiarly theirs. While the process can be regarded as sacred, it arises from a subtle level of what we already are, and is no excuse to regard ourselves as even more finite. The seduction to become identified with the form and allow the power of the experience and the form to become a part of one's identity is a universal facet of human consciousness. When I let a deeper part of my awareness look at the whole panorama of such experiments I cannot help being struck by how primitive we are. There are so many dimensions to explore, but we barely wet our feet before we are caught once again in a new form, a new system, a new scientific theory or a new religion. At another level of my awareness that requires structure and form I feel the constraint to join myself to some system of thinking, so I truly appreciate how difficult it is to try to hold the possibility of a simultaneous awareness. How difficult it is to move in and through these forms with freedom; to honor each of them but be open and free without having to relinquish the sense of our basic unbounded essence, and to begin to know each other through presence.

Perhaps the reason we become so easily identified with form is because we are continuously shifting levels of consciousness without even being aware of it. For instance, at one level of awareness I can feel completely at peace, yet at another on-going level I need to make decisions, feeling pushed and pulled toward one issue or another. In a single thought I can be moving among many of these levels. No wonder when we enter into a new experiment of expanded Beingness we quickly try to root ourselves into some structure or another. We continuously need to impose or create a dominant theme or relationship to concretize reality and eliminate the ambiguity and vulnerability inherent in multidimensionality.

❖

The work of Carl Jung and others that began to unveil the archetypal, astrological and alchemical symbology of Western man's collective psyche was an important building block for the work I have been describing. Through it we begin to appreciate some of the patterns and rhythms inherent in the dance of consciousness. Most important, we finally recognized the universal nature of these patterns.

Where Jungian psychology falls short, in my opinion, is in the idea of an unconscious that is essentially nonexperienceable except through inference from other structures (dreams, myths). This is the limitation of all the analytic psychologies; they are essentially intellectual and only minimally enter into working with the energies of consciousness at a bodily level. The one-to-one dynamic is itself primitive, smacking of the most basic parental dynamic. As long as the process of growth relies on language we are dealing with an ego-configurating process that is linear and only very slowly translates across dimensions to interact with the whole of Beingness. Processes capable of going deeper are less verbal, more experiential, and work moment by moment directly upon awareness and the energetic state. Simultaneous with the intellectual process they activate the energy body and the physical consciousness more directly.

Although Jung implied a continuum of consciousness in his concept of synchronicity, the inability to work directly with energy leads to an intellectual splitting process. Although I respect what has grown from psychoanalytic psychologies, this work can end up maneuvering ideas within an essentially imaginary unconscious. Transformation along such a route is slow indeed because the basic ego structure is maintained by the intellectual context. Once one begins to explore within the domain of energetic awareness it becomes more valid to examine the *conscious* awareness as a relative state governed by the energy level of the individual consciousness. The unconscious is thus seen as subtle levels of consciousness rather than an entity in itself. As we enter directly into the deeper levels of consciousness it becomes evident that the energies evoked are actually the levels of awareness out of which many of the archetypical Jungian images arise. The archetypes are, in my experience, energetic dynamics that are fairly universal to stages of the awakening process. They vary in content in each person and each culture. But the energetic experience is, a priori, the archetypical expression.

During and after a conference many people have the same or similar dream content. Recurring symbols marking phases of integration of the transformational process are common collectively. Earthquakes, tidal waves, movement of water over land, bridges, pursuit by powerful and frequently fearful forces, radiant beings and higher teachers in many forms are all part of common recurrent symbology presented in dreams and visions as individuals begin to break free of statebound levels of consciousness. The transformation process is impressed energetically and telepathically. There follows a process of translating this impress into linear awareness and this becomes the images and symbols of our dreams and a lot more. At this point dream analysis becomes a very valuable adjunct for appreciating the transformational process.

Perhaps the greatest significance of dream material is that it demonstrates how an unconditional and impersonal level of reality gets pulled down into relative experience by one's personal awareness. It tells something about the hidden filters within awareness that take a subtle impress and translate it down into the realms of sensation, intensity and symbol familiar to us.

I often remind individuals not to make the study of their dreams into another dream. The importance of analysis is that it open a way to embrace the process displayed in the dream. The interpretation should provide a twist in perspective that allows for a direct adjustment in life orientation and fine tuning one's awareness. This should come from within by taking the time to feel into the dream and from this making the appropriate qualitative commitment into living. Merely retranslating dream symbols into someone else's language or into the rationale of waking awareness does not imply that one has learned to directly adjust one's own awareness. Such dream work is just another kind of non-consciousness.

There are two other considerations that I often share about dreams. First of all, and this should be obvious, the interpretation is relative to the level from which we are looking. My own sense is that the dream process is an impersonal facet of human experience. Yet all too often people use their dreams to support a very personal self-image whether positive and hopeful or negative and frightening. My sense is that these are irrelevant stances in examining dreams and in life in general. The essence of the dream can be most closely appreciated by waking awareness when we take a very dispassionate and detached view of the dream content. Emotional identification with the content of the dream fixes the dream in one dimension. Dreams reflect many levels of reality but the symbols they use are often highly charged within a limited framework of the waking awareness. Unraveling the deeper level that has called upon the particular symbol and images requires entering a deeper meditative silence. Dreams then become another way, beside waking awareness, to notice how Beingness is expressed, and they allow us to choose how and in what spirit we wish to direct our return to an essential state.

The second point is that, as awareness grows, one notices the flickering imbalances and distortions with which one responds and participates in the moment by moment adventure of living. With this degree of alertness one can anticipate the way the dream reality will be displayed. If waking awareness is biased toward a particular expression (for example, quiet strength), and one notices the subtle background play of fantasies about power, the dream process will invert this. Power will become the dominant atmosphere and weakness or vulnerability will be the personal quality. Another way of saying this is that the subconscious waking process which is in itself another kind of dream reality becomes the dominant quality of the dream in many cases. When one is capable of noticing the subtle interplays in one's psyche and can immediately bring this into simple unbiased acknowledgment, dreams at this level cease or can be anticipated. Thus one can be dreaming and recognize the pattern in the dream as an extension of a process recalled from the waking state. As new levels of dream material come forward they then begin to reflect a new level of subtlety between realized and not-yet-realized levels of consciousness. I have found that when I am in a deep sense of balance (by which I mean physically, emotionally and spiritually in harmony), dreams cease entirely. If even one of these areas becomes imbalanced (e.g., I have been writing a lot and neglecting my body) or a new impress of energies begins to activate in my consciousness, the dreams start again. In making these comments I am only suggesting a way to approach the dream process, and am by no means claiming full understanding of this area of awareness.

❖

I regard the conference work as the beginning exploration of the possibility of an unconditional awareness and a process capable of activating the deeper energies in those who are ready. The various exercises and processes designed to teach energy sensitivity and the subtle nuances of shifting between many levels of consciousness, gradually open a chink in our linear and narrowed Beingness. Then, quite naturally, a deeper energy awakens and begins to radiate outward as presence. The process provides and demands a great deal of linear/rational stretching, but there is also a great emphasis on the feminine nonrational and intuitive modes of being. Individuals learn to sense into dimensions or areas of self-knowing that are ordinarily unrealized or repressed. Some move into major life-changing realizations. Some are "healed" of serious illness. Yet, and it must be emphasized clearly, the central work is always toward each participant's direct experience of shifts into a greater awareness and not on any particular personal problem or issue.

The exploration of the heart, of Beingness, and of the higher levels of consciousness is not a therapy process. It is not to be compared with conventional group therapy processes because the work is with the multidimensional phenomena of the higher planes of consciousness and in particular the human energy systems. No goal in any tangible or programmed sense is set and no outcome is conjectured beyond the capacity to engender experiences that by their very nature contrast with what we might call ordinary consciousness. It is then each individual's responsibility to allow this new opening to unfold and to take on meaning and form in accordance with her or his own nature.

This is a spiritual work that honors and incorporates psychological and scientific insight. It is a work that comes to teach balance and wisdom, for without balance and wisdom plus a deep love and reverence for the reality that contains our ordinary awareness, we would be foolhardy to attempt to loosen the psychic structures that maintain our ordinary consciousness. The individuals who have joined me in this adventure had to be fundamentally mature and sufficiently developed in the egoistic sense to recognize that the next step is the journey to a less differentiated nature.

Each person is a teacher in such a process, but ultimately it becomes clear that the real teacher is the energy vortex evoked by the group itself. The finer and deeper the energetic process a group is able to evoke, and the longer they are able to sustain it, the fuller the transformative process experienced by each.

In such a process everyone plays an important part, even those who carry the greatest scepticism or are initially angry at the process. Each is an "ingredient" that ultimately leads to the balance of forces in which the energy refines. Just as it is essential that individuals learning to integrate the awakening process not reject or repress any facet of their nature, it is also essential that the group dynamic include the disharmonious forces carried by certain individuals. There is an anchoring phenomenon inherent in the so-called negative forces that undergirds the building energetic process. This is not to say that antagonistic or irrational forces can be indulged; they cannot. But every effort must be made to allow the full spectrum of human experience and to encourage every individual finally to release into the process, even though the initial sluggishness of some may be difficult for those who are ready to move more quickly. A certain amount of patience pays great dividends, and once this is achieved an intrinsic harmony and communion happens among people. At this point there are few indeed who find their personal reactions so compelling that they would separate themselves from this incredibly inspiring and healing experience. Also at this point there is no single individual, no matter how evolved, that isn't lifted, heightened, and expanded in the group vortex.

While my primary focus for exploring the transformational process with others is the conference form, other processes have naturally grown from it. For one thing, there were enough people who participated in the conferences and who lived locally that ongoing work developed. Individuals can only gather together within the specifically intended structure of a conference process for so long before the very reality the work initiates must begin to be explored in other contexts. Gradually, all kinds of permutations and recombinations of individuals emerged naturally and were encouraged. People began to organize regular evening sessions to further develop their abilities with energy transfer. In so doing they began to focus their own transformation dynamic and take on the mantle of teaching. Other projects were entered into as well. The ability to sustain the sense of a group energetic in different kinds of actions (group meditations, landscaping homes, planning holiday rituals, creating a healing support group) evolved naturally for those who lived near each other.

To share in this way is predicated on the ability to sense and work in the energetic level of experience. No group can be focused to achieve a transformative potential through a committee process. Nor can the coalescing force emerge from a sense of idealism or from the need to find a new family. When emotional needs or intellectual constructs dominate the coalescing of individuals, the process, in my experience, is short-lived and doomed to failure. There is insufficient depth at this level of motivation to consciously attain to a transformational energetic. Such individuals rarely will stay through the roller coaster effect as the deeper process is evoked. But when a group of individuals come forward who recognize that working together to catalyze a heightened energy does in fact empower their individual transformation, then a deeper inspiration is touched and the process begins to grow. And it teaches everyone a great deal.

Individual opinions and ideas are not much discussed before the focusing and unification of the group energy. The latter cannot be faked. Only the direct experience of coalescing into a heightened energetic and then refining this energy is evidence that the group has achieved its deeper centering and that group action can now be undertaken. Often the ideas and needs with which one enters such a process will simply evaporate or lose meaning in the heightened group energetic, for those ideas were relative to the consciousness in which they were conceived.

In my experience, while the primary leadership in this kind of dynamic emerges in accordance with one's ability to sense and catalyze the energetic process, this leadership then shifts as the group process is taken into tangible activities where other individuals demonstrate greater know-how. At this point the leader capable of bringing through the initial catalyzing energetic can assume a more ordinary position as one of the participants in the manifestation phase. This kind of human interaction is different from the guru model, where one individual is seen as the embodiment of the higher consciousness and the community coalesces around his or her presence.

I have observed that the energetic force field of any awakened teacher grows exponentially in direct relationship to the interaction with those who come forward to study and learn. The teacher or guru almost literally extends power out through the collective energy body of the students. If a new form is to emerge, the key is to return the power to everyone, and this is only possible if all are brought forward enough to recognize the subtle dimensions, so that they can enter a heightening process consciously within themselves. Then, according to the discipline and inner motivation of each individual, they can develop the capacity to carry a growing quality of presence. This presence can be deepened and matured in the context of any sharing with another and particularly through the relationship with the transformational community. It is further refined by the natural koans and challenges of life's refining fire.

Thus the primary difference is the internalization of the guru principle, not as self in any personal sense, but as presence that is a shared and collective phenomenon. For the individual on a transformational path, attachment to the context of one's initial heightening and transformation, so that it is projected onto an individual or a specfic setting, while essential in one developmental phase, later begins to shut out the potential for change. I believe it is equally so for the individual who chooses to be the object for such projection, and thus chooses to carry powerful collective forces so that others can experience a touch of the transcendent. However, the latter is the free choice of an awakened soul, even if it is an old choice, one that has been made over and over again for thousands of years.

A new form is emerging and it does not need mystical systems and arcane relationships. But it does require a good deal of maturity and strength to be willing to explore the many levels of Beingness without hanging on someone else's spiritual coattails—and without rejecting them either. There is a profound vulnerability and consequently a great maturity required to take the gift of presence and to give the gift of receiving and then walk on into the next new moment, neither lingering too long nor rejecting the inspirational source.

The freedom to merge and coalesce into a transcendent (beyond the personal) energetic, whatever the focus of human interaction that presents itself moment by moment, is the natural birthright of every human being. And in this process we have much to learn. We need to learn about new types of leadership, about going beyond the law of diminishing returns whereby the initial capacity to coalesce and heighten is predicated on expectation and transference to a person or a goal. The release of goal and the attunement to the fineness of the energetic Now, in this moment, must be developed.

I have said that a new form is emerging. As one facet of this new form, the importance of the imbued teacher cannot be underestimated. One way to consider such a person is as a refined energetic or a larger context for Beingness. To enter into a relationship with such a presence allows an expansion or decompression of consciousness which can be marvelously freeing but also painful and disconcerting. But, in my opinion, once the grace of decompression is bestowed, to reconstruct a new identity while remaining in the presence of the teacher results in addiction and dependency of such magnitude that it can outrival the most powerful narcotic. This is one consequence of the old guru-disciple process or any situation that causes a heightening of energy. When out of this context, a rebound into depression and disorientation may occur which is also part of the overall integration process. An individual can become terrified or incapable of releasing dependency on the high energy source. It becomes a special situation where the person may be arro-

gantly defensive. Others must force themselves out of the interaction by a rejection process. They tend to become critical,
judgmental and disillusioned with the magical powers and wisdom they initially attributed to the teacher. They seek the flaw
by focusing on the personality level where everyone, no matter
how gifted, is limited, or on the teaching which no matter how
well-conceived is also potentially limiting. Neither rejection nor
attachment and adoration is the resolution state in which the
person can grow. It is an imbalance that binds people to their
present energetic configuration, so that they miss the gift which
is the new spectrum of sensitivity and awareness within their
own presence.

The key for me in these kinds of relationships is to stay with
the process until there is a sense of expansion and of deep love
and communion, and then to release the interaction with the
teacher until this phase has integrated. Unconditional love represents the state where the energetic transference goes the deepest. But, soon thereafter the need to integrate the impress of
energy leads to the calling forth of all the ego-sustaining forces
of the psyche. At this point one activates variations on a
theme—the idolization worship process or the disillusionment
rejection process. Rather than do either, one can walk on into
new experience and find the deep freedom, vulnerability and,
ultimately, strength that had been disguised by attachment to
people and systems.

The gift of presence has been received and will mature and integrate in its own timing. What traps many people, so that they
cannot sustain a sense of balance, is the underlying power issues
(inadequacy, selfishness, greed) that were hidden motives in
their seeking the teaching in the first place. Some teachers can
see this egotism and will play upon it, thereby creating anger
and distrust or dependency and paralysis in the student. But
since these weaknesses were there all along, to bring them out
may ultimately be creative and healing when one is finally ready
to accept the whole of oneself. The other ensnaring imbalance is
a presumption that there is an ultimate state that is other than
one's existing state. This is another subtle form of self-rejection
that allows the initial projection onto the teacher. It can seduce

one into the search, but later it must be faced and resolved. Even if one were never to touch such states, acceptance must begin now. Simple self-honesty can allow one to appreciate the opportunity offered by an expanded being without having to become lost in the process. We must in a sense become lost and die to ourselves, not someone else.

These remarks have relevance to any ongoing transformational community. There must initally be an awakened individual who can lead the energetic to a dimension beyond the ordinary and still honor the process of developing and releasing personality that will be ongoing within such a group. There must also be an ability to allow the community or the project to configurate around the consciousness inherent within it as a whole and not simply around the expression of the most evolved being. Balance between the two forces is delicate and ongoing. It cannot be written into rules or systematized or ritualized.

Although I neither set myself up as a guru, nor feel that way about myself, the responsibility to carry and focus the energy of the conference process inevitably leads to the presentation of only certain facets of my nature. This results in a particular kind of projection that tends to amplify the depth of my gifts (or limitations) and this is necessary for some people in order to begin to recognize the same potential within themselves. A sense of the sacred and mysterious is, as I have said, an important part of what allows some people to start on the journey of transformation. I try to offset this process by honestly representing as much of my personal nature as possible at all times without overly indulging a limited or expansive area. Since there are still plenty of areas asking for refinement in my nature, I have had awkward occasion to demonstrate my developing Beingness.

In a group of mature and committed individuals who can appreciate entering a refined energetic process, the energy evoked is comparable to that of the presence that surrounds any mature spiritual work. As I often say to my groups, the guru is the presence of our collective energy field. But there comes a point when one must move back and disengage for a while and this is particularly essential in the ongoing explorations. In the ongoing work that I facilitated, we met for about two-and-a-half to three months on a weekly basis and then stopped for two months. This allowed a time for integration, for re-appraisal, and for experiencing other teachers and other group dynamics. Thus there was a continuous turnover of people on the periphery of the process as well as a core that grew deeper and deeper in their sensitivity and ability to work in this way. This mixing of new and old blood with the freedom to disengage and then come back is healthy. At the same time, out of the core, new leadership emerged and I have been able to move on into other areas of work. I think this basic idea of balance—of going deeply and then releasing and allowing consciousness to explore other areas—is as natural as breathing and it pays dividends in maturity and in the establishment of individuals who can stand in their own light as independent, awakening beings.

❖

Having seen perhaps forty groups come into heightened states in hundreds of sessions over the past few years, and seeing the multidimensional maturity that develops, has led me to some exciting speculation. What if our greatest thinkers, scientists and philosophers could be brought together and, before beginning to share theories and papers, they would first consciously evoke the heightened group energetic? This would take several days of setting aside the problems and theories and using the skills that I and other explorers of transformational group energies could bring forward. In the heightened energy state the whole process of insight and cognition changes. Because various levels of reality are contrasted in such a process, new understanding would automatically emerge.

What would happen if already-functioning teams that exist in medicine, in education, in business and industry, could be shown how to use their collective presence for the betterment of each other? I cannot help thinking what would happen to government when Congressional sessions and committee processes began to operate with deeper sensitivity and awareness; when the errant egotism and self-serving personal motives would finally be seen as natural levels of individual development (realities built from particular addiction to intensity and processes of shielding), but nonetheless narrow and limiting relative to a greater development. What of consciously empowering the deeper thrust to serve humanity that also resides within the psyches of our government leaders? The present lack of awareness and of selfishness and separation that marks the ordinary human condition is remarkable and, unfortunately, it too is potentiated in any group process. *Where a greater understanding of focused group energy is not consciously considered, focusing on the problem empowers the problem.* But it does provide intensity, and we then move larger forces around (money or armies) to have a sense of doing something. The positive side is that this blindness may naturally lead to crisis of such a degree that transformational levels of energy will be fostered.

❖

The key elements necessary to working with a group to create a transformative experience can be summarized at my present level of understanding as follows:

1. *A multidimensionally awakened individual who can initially provide the presence, wisdom and experience to move the interaction safely into new dimensions.* Such individuals are capable of perceiving through one or more modes of subtle awareness, thus they are able to sense the energetic process that is moving within an individual or a group. They can volitionally activate and refine their own energy level and are capable of activating specific energy centers. They are able to transfer energy through their presence and thereby directly induce an altered state of consciousness in those who are open to them. They usually can transfer energy through the voice and may be gifted at articulating dimensions that are ordinarily beyond rational expression. They are capable of maintaining several levels of awareness simultaneously and can sustain extended periods of deep concentration. They are able to let go and refresh themselves thoroughly in a short length of time. They will be gifted in the use of

specific techniques and tools for moving energy in groups such as energy-activating exercises, high intensity sound, media processes, and ritual. Finally they must be capable of releasing any personal identification with what occurs in any individual or the group.

2. *The setting of the intention for the process.* This begins long before the group ever comes together and involves sensing into the highest potential inherent in the experience and consecrating oneself to this. This process initiates what I can only describe as a deeper guidance or energetic overview that envelops the whole undertaking. As the particulars necessary to the experience unfold, every detail, whether within the group process itself or in the surrounding environment (such as decor, food and housing) must be concordant in quality and intention with the larger overview. Activities that are out of phase must be somehow consciously integrated by the leader or if possible deleted.

3. *An especially inpiring location in which to undertake the exploration.* It becomes a holding place for the energy and heightens the potential for opening as well as providing a psychically secure milieu for the early and vulnerable stages of opening.

4. *Deep and mature commitment on the part of each participant to enter an open-ended exploration of Beingness and to be willing to release old patterns.* This includes the ability temporarily to release personal goals and to bring forward a sense of newness, spontaneity, and change. The willingness to master emotional reactions and the defusing of power issues is crucial. Each individual must be willing to internalize trust and to temporarily set aside philosophical debate and the need to understand intellectually.

5. *The infusion of a basic sense of well-being and a new sense of love*, without denying or relegating to the negative those painful aspects of reality that must eventually be embraced by this love.

6. *The X-factor.* The contact with higher dimensions of consciousness as a direct experience is an essential part of transformation. Each person must receive some direct experience in tapping into multidimensional reality.

7. *Grace.*

# 9 ❖ UTILIZING GROUP ENERGY FOR HEALING

For over a year I undertook an exploration of more advanced energy work with individuals who had gone through a conference with me. These individuals had achieved various degrees of subtle sensitivity and could at will join their consciousness in an amplified group energy around the theme of unconditional love. The nature of the exploration was to develop skill at utilizing a focused group energy field as the psychospiritual milieu in which to work with individuals suffering major illnesses.

The "patients," or more truly, guests, came forward through word-of-mouth or by referral from local physicians and therapists. I would invite a guest to visit when the explorational group had been meeting regularly for several consecutive weeks, was balanced in its internal dynamic and had built up to a refined charge of energy. The group would then move into a heightened receptive state and interview the guest.

The interview was directed most often by me, though some input from the whole group would occur. It was a kind of intuitive dance in which sensitivity to and honoring of the guest were combined with developing deeper psychic rapport. No guest was ever forced or pushed to share beyond what came forward spontaneously. The input from the group may not have always been helpful but it was rarely destructive or unwittingly irreverent. This was possible because each participant could sense the energetic note or quality that was set each session.

By "set" I am referring to the level at which the energy would be placed as the group entered the initial centering process. There is an experiential and subjective appreciation of the quality of the energy that seems to manifest around a particular focus or intention. To appreciate what "setting the energy" means, you have to look at the quality of intention with which you enter into an action. If someone brings forward a quality that is highly discordant, it could be said to be out of phase with the deeper level that was originally set into motion. On the other hand, positive or negative, it might be a valuable and integrative addition. The intention of the group in this exploration was to maintain an open and unconditional appreciation for the guest and, within this, to share an energy of unconditional love so as to support the highest potential of the individual.

In the second phase of the interaction the guests would lie on a table and the group would share energy with them. Sharing energy involves focusing at the heart center, consciously attuning to the highest sense of inspiration and love, and allowing this to flow to the guest from the hands and one's whole sense of being. Writing about it tends to trivialize the experience. In fact, it is a sacred action. In my experience, when the group has been properly readied, this sharing process becomes one of the most powerful teaching experiences. Even in those group participants who had been only minimally experiencing the energy during the earlier phase of exercises, the unified group action would provide a profound direct experience of a higher dimension.

In a regular durational conference I had always utilized the sacred ritual of group energy sharing as a capstone experience. It teaches reverence for the mystery and beauty of the human soul in ways impossible to describe. However, the durational conference permits working with only one guest. A single session with a guest usually lasts from two to four hours. Now I had the opportunity to work with a group in a longterm process in which literally dozens of guests participated.

The group became exquisitely refined in their energetic sensitivity and intuitive insight. Because the group always consisted of the same individuals, the guest became the new factor, and we began to learn the subtle differences in the energetic configuration of different individuals and to notice that there are certain subtle differences in the deeper patterns underlying various diseases. The energetic quality of the group was affected uniquely by each guest. I should emphasize, lest we get caught in a disease-healing model once again, that it was not our primary intention to analyze the disease process or heal it, but rather to enter the highest state of consciousness possible (as measured by the quality of the energetic presence during the action) and simply share this with our guest. Because of this, no guests were ever regarded as "patients," with disease processes that had to be resolved by them or us. Rather, they were seen as teachers who, by their very presence, provided an experience in which everyone was deepened.

When the group was properly prepared, a common image reported by guests was a sense of having entered a room where they nervously expected to meet twenty strangers and instead felt as if there were only one person present. Also, they almost always commented on the sense of love.

It became clear in these sharings that force was present that acts as an extraordinary balm to any apprehension in the guest, quite distinct from any obvious external interaction. This was nearly unanimously reported without solicitation from the guests. But even more interesting, as guests would begin to talk about themselves, they would find themselves conveying areas they hadn't realized were involved in the issue of their illness. Thus the guest was frequently surprised to find that many things that formerly seemed separate and confusing now seemed suddenly to clarify. This phenomenon of insight and self-appreciation that arises spontaneously merely by being in a higher energetic milieu is a common aspect of exploring the transformation process in groups.

Higher levels of consciousness carry healing potential. When the group energy was directed toward particular areas of physical pain, relief could usually be achieved in seconds to minutes for such pain as that of migraine, muscle tension or metastatic bone disease. After awhile, members of this exploratory group visited patients in the hospital. They could share an energy that released post-operative nausea and pain and the need for further analgesia in many cases. In pre-medicated patients, the energy-sharing process would usually induce sleep in a few minutes. In general, the pain relief achieved by the group sharing lasted for hours to days to even weeks. Occasionally, unusually rapid bone healing was noted on X-ray. Many episodes of disease amerlioration and/or remission were reported to us. But most responses were subjective, and no attempt was made to try to quantify the responses or differentiate which treatment caused which result (many of these people were involved concurrently with other health-care processes).

Nevertheless, the magnitude of response and the depth of the experiences—of opening to a sense of well-being and a feeling of being loved, and of suddenly "knowing" or "understanding" which happened so frequently during these sessions—goes beyond the power to describe. We physicians and therapists who were part of these groups had never seen, in our many cumulative years of traditional practice, experiences of such magnitude, or that conveyed such reverence for life.

Another dimension of experience that is quite common in this kind of exploration and in the transformational process as a whole are phenomena of altered perception. It was common for guests and participants to see brilliant light and colors, symbols, columns or vortexes of energy and auras, as well as to sense themselves floating or levitating, or hear unusual sounds, or smell unusual fragrances. When this occurs in a group my only response is to appreciate the reality of such experiences. These are real experiences and I have had them many times myself, although they were more frequent in the early stages of opening. Attributing significance to such experiences is a personal matter. I simply observe them as unconditionally as possible and move on.

Physical response on the part of the guest—apparently to the energy—encompasses a broad range. These include alteration in respiration, feelings of vibration or tingling, muscle trembling, large-scale muscular contractions, swallowing and intestial peristalsis, crying and emotional release, strongly perceived alterations in temperature, and more. There is no point in going into this very deeply since we already know that the energy is a bridge between psyche and soma. It is important to mention that the frequency of occurrence and the strength of these physical responses, and in particular the emotional releases, seem to diminish as the energy grows more refined.

Another important aspect that has direct practical implications is that some fairly subtle diagnostic information was available by interaction with the energy field, as in the process of locating the coin described earlier. This could be confirmed later by the patient's history. This information usually had to do with locating the areas of disease. While locating an unusual or abnormal energy configuration is a fairly easy skill to develop, an interpretation of disease process (old or new trauma, benign or malignant) is more difficult and requires deeper practice.

In one important example, I went to scan the energy field of a woman I had never met before. She was the guest of Dr. William Brugh Joy, who had introduced me to energy scanning and energy transfer some six months before. At the end of the silent process of scanning and sharing energy (which Dr. Joy describes beautifully in his book *Joy's Way*), we discussed the woman. I perceived abnormalities in the energy field and deduced that she had had a left radical mastectomy and abdominal surgery in two places. The latter I guessed represented oopherectomy (removal of the ovaries) and adrenalectomy (removal of the adrenal glands). The deduction was based on my medical knowledge that removal of these glands is sometimes an adjunct to the treatment of breast cancer. It gave me a nice package to hold the three primary areas of perceived energetic abnormality in a single diagnosis. However there was a fourth area of energetic abnormality, different in quality, that I perceived over the woman's left ankle. In order to tie this in, I thought it must be a metastatic process. In fact, it turned out that it was recurrent bursitis that the woman had had for over twenty years. My medical training, which had taught me to try to find a single diagnosis, had led me to an erroneous interpretation. My interpretation of the other areas of abnormality was correct. Incidentally, this experience occurred in late 1975 and I recently met the woman again; that single experience, in which nearly no words were shared, had created a warmth between us that continues across the years.

A point can be made here. I do not know whether the perception of the energy is the source for the interpretation, or whether the information is received in some other way (e.g., telepathically). Whatever the case, going to the level of awareness in which the energetic sensitivity is heightened and using the form of hand scanning leads to levels of subtle perception.

In addition to the physical diagnostic capacity, specific psychological information about thinking and behavior patterns and, more importantly, a clearer sense of the deeper soul patterns were also often directly obtainable. In a heightened state of consciousness it is possible to access information directly without secondary association to analytic or behavioral models or the need to translate such information from imagery. Granted, the development of this ability takes practice and deep self-knowing so that you aren't confusing your own patterns for those of the person being sensed into. But the fact that it *can* be refined, and that this kind of exploration heightens and accelerates the possibility, suggests something of deep import: that this is how we are interacting all the time. It suggests that the incoherent way in which most human interactions are undertaken relegates us to fairly slow, even primitive forms of communication.

Armed with new insight and refreshed and vitalized through the force of the energy transfer, some of the guests appeared to move forward into a new potential in their lives. Given the vulnerability one would expect in being so intimate with a large group, the depth of the sharing was remarkable—I'm tempted to say miraculous. But I can say from direct experience that it is possible for a life moving along a certain path to be tranformed virtually in an instant. We are, I believe, only on the threshold of demystifying the power of love and of collective human energies in the configuration and evolution of man.

❖

It soon became clear that the more that was known about the patient, the more difficult it was to keep the group focus in an unconditional state, and the power to convey the expansive energy was diminished. Any ideas other than those born directly in the moment were soon recognized as ways of veiling from a deeper knowing. Therapists and healers identified with particular medical, psychological or spiritual models were often the ones who had the most difficulty at first in entering into an unconditional sharing. If more attention was given to these preconceived ideas (such as therapeutic-prognostic concerns) than to the direct experience of communion, the overall sense of the energetic exchange was minimized. This was also true if there was any identification at the personal and emotional levels with the experiences related by the guest. Entering into the energetic dynamic in any way at the level of the guest's situation obstructed the ability to reach into an unconditional state and offer an energy of love. To enter the problem level is disaster in this kind of exploration. At the energy level in which the problem configurates in consciousness, problems dance in endless recombinations of interpretation without resolution. The same problem resolves automatically, or reveals its roots in a different dimension and thus is approached differently, when the energy level is heightened.

Not only does the group induct a higher energy into a guest, but also the guest influences the group with his or her energetic reality. By its very numbers, and because of the unified intention of the group, the group energy has a far greater impact upon the guest than the guest on the group. Nevertheless, even if no words were spoken between a particular guest and the group, some members of the group might then spend days working through a psychological-energetic dynamic kindled in them during the participation with the guest. For instance, they might find themselves dwelling on and having to work through feelings of inexplicable sadness, power struggle or fear of death. It is as if this were seeded or activated in their consciousness through the interaction. This may sound dangerous to those familiar with transference/counter-transference concepts in psychotherapy or with the idea of transfer of "negative" energy so prevalent in spiritualist thinking. From one perspective it is dangerous, but there is also a profound learning and wisdom potential.

Each of us has areas of immaturity where we recoil, whether consciously or not, from some aspect of life. To begin to explore higher states of consciousness and naively expect to be healers without resolving these areas is foolhardy. In the energetic enhancement of the group process, or in any energy heightening practice such as meditation, when such an area becomes activated it becomes a challenge to reach to a more encompassing state of awareness. But it is not as if such an area or space is sought for and thrust upon consciousness in order to be dealt with once and for all. In fact, it was because sufficient love and energy had been generated that the area could come forward.

While we remain in the heightened state of consciousness such areas are no problem. One can examine them without their dominating the psyche. Thus in a sense they are already resolved. But later, at one's more ordinary level of awareness, this same psychic area (fear of death, fear of other entities or realms, fear of one's own power or loss of control) can come forward, and all of a sudden it does have authority over our sense of self.

From the perspective of the overall exploration of consciousness, when such a force has activated in my own psyche and does not resolve easily I have come to recognize it as a slowdown sign. It is saying don't go deeper into the formless dimensions until this dynamic of recoil and the binding of one's energies has been resolved. No matter what one's ideas about reality are, such areas of contraction indicate that the vision of reality and in particular one's sense of an unconditional witness point in consciousness needs further maturing. And whether this maturing takes hours, months, or years is really irrelevant.

The transformational group process is one of the faster ways of opening the individual to whole new realms and, if undertaken with wisdom and love, simultaneously evokes resolution. The individual's task is to learn to access and integrate this higher level when operating independent of the resolving presence of the group (or of a high-energy teacher).

Heightened presence is the true mark of resolution, as compared to ego-defense processes such as denial and repression. The latter can allow the closing off of the unwanted, but only with the simultaneous down-throttling of Beingness. There are a clutter of spiritual and psychological cosmologies that fabricate structures that are no more than safe ways to label and exclude. Throughout history, spirituality has been one of the greatest ways to shield against genuine transformation.

❖

We are shielded naturally by our own unconsciousness and by ideas about reality that force us to operate in a relatively narrow dimension. For example, the technical orientation of Western physicians, and the huge body of memorized information necessary to practice medicine, also acts to insulate their awareness from levels of interaction in which reside the potential for multidimensional sensitivity. The Western psychotherapist is similarly shielded, although the high suicide rate among physicians may indicate that at a higher energy level an induction process is going on even though they are unconscious of it. It may well be that the kind of individual who is drawn toward a helping or healing profession already has a fairly semipermeable energetic nature, and is both more sensitive and more vulnerable to deep sharing with others.

Once we begin to open to unconditional states, the unconscious protective device that is intrinsic to our ego structure is automatically and intentionally weakened. Thus we can suddenly experience forces and activate areas of consciousness that we were entirely oblivious to before. Physicians or therapists who rely primarily on outer technique and who enter this kind of exploration may find their old buffers are no longer effective and begin to activate their own death/rebirth process. It can be quite disconcerting, because there is the very real sense of having been thrust back, as if reactivating a beginning stage. In the context of the transformational process, this newness and vulnerability is a sign of opening and healers can be guided to work creatively with it. Then they may begin to touch directly, through their own experience, the state of personal resolution where the shielding is no longer unconscious and they have gained mastery of subtler dimensions.

In my experience, to continue to avoid or block the potential of entering more subtle levels of experience, even though certain aspects of this can be unpleasant to encounter initially, means to refuse the full inheritance of one's humanity. This isn't to say that such openings cannot be done wisely and (generally) safely. They can and should be. There are areas that, in the very act of touching and allowing and moving beyond, empower us. In the group experiment when certain participants found themselves inexplicably forced to contemplate areas of their psyche they thought were resolved or new levels they never seriously believed existed, the overall result was an accelerated maturity and a deeper and genuine compassion and wisdom.

We can easily say that we want to develop psychic skills and be able to appreciate a larger reality. But this implies two things. First, you will see not only what you want to see, but also what you may *not* want to see. It is necessary to look at both with the same sense of balance. Second, in order to perceive something, you must enter the level of reality in which the perception is being created. Thus you are influencing what you perceive to a certain degree. Therefore, you may also be creating what you want as well as what you don't want. This often becomes the great fear in a transformational process—that you are creating the very thing you are most afraid of.

It is true that as consciousness expands those areas that are feared or rejected at first seem to grow larger and more real. Entering into the subtle realms of consciousness with conditioned ideas about what is right or wrong or about what is real may result in great misery until this dynamic is understood and no longer needs to be empowered. It is essential to develop the unconditional center of awareness out of which to view all experience, whether tangible or of subtle dimension, if one is to resolve fear and more deeply empower consciousness. Having exposed a so-called bogeyman of the exploration, let it be stated once again that the exploration of the transformational process and the opening of the heart is by far one of the richest and most rewarding experiences of life.

As I have said, there is a natural shielding process bestowed on us by our own unconsciousness. But, as the exploration deepens, the undertaking of a conscious shielding process becomes more and more important, at least during crucial early stages. I don't intend to say too much about conscious shielding. It is often our own misplaced motivation, such as an underlying greed for new and more extraordinary experience or impatience about the rate of our own development, that leads us into trouble. Therefore, a basic, no-nonsense self-honesty is an important part of shielding. Learning to modulate the speed of one's unfolding through the use of sex, food, exercise, meditation and sharing of energy with others (as discussed in Chapter 4) is also a part of shielding.

It doesn't matter how resourceful and balanced you are, there are certain energy levels that the physical and psychic mechanism cannot tolerate for very long. Transparency to perceived forces because of a deep and unperturbable sense of love—as opposed to the walling off of the consciousness, for instance, by visualizing white light surrounding oneself—is in my opinion a mature level of spiritual shielding. However, to image the wall of light is important in the beginning. Basically, just to wonder about shielding without paranoia is important. Meditate into it, think about it. What part of one's being is essentially pure and impregnable all the time? Who is the final arbiter of your experience? What are you consecrating your life to? Where does your sense of the universe and of God finally rest in your awareness? Is it loving or wrathful? There is basic wisdom in recognizing that different facets of our being evolve at different rates and can sustain different levels of intensity. Therefore, for what level of your being is the shield provided? Is there ever a part of you that isn't new and vulnerable and developing?

The concept of shielding evolves with spiritual maturity, which really means direct experience and growing awareness. There is one important thought, although I know how controversial it is with some people: I believe you will always need an excluding shield as long as the exploration is limited to the dualistic concept of good and bad forces. There is, in my experience, a higher level than this which is evolved with a maturing sense of nonduality, beyond time and space (linear or even Einsteinian), and crucial to this a growing sense of unconditional love.

❖

By its very nature the dynamics of group energy held in a unified focus at the highest possible quality of consciousness creates a force field that transcends the issues of individual human concern. Areas of the human psyche inaccessible to us through ordinary introspective modes (i.e., by ourselves or in a one-to-one dynamic), can be reached into much more rapidly and safely in the group dynamic. The heightened energy of the group provides a quality of resolution and healing that penetrates to a much greater depth than if such were attempted at a lower energy state in the more energetically balanced one-to-one modes of therapy.

The energy available in a dynamic of two is greater than that available to a solitary individual, but is far less than that of a larger group. Remember the concept that energy evoked by two or more is somewhat determined by what the interaction is consecrated to. If the therapy process focuses on the problem area, the higher energy may temporarily lift the patient out of the problem, but it empowers the problem in the therapist too. In my experience working with schizophrenic and autistic adolescents, the energy level natural to these disturbed children was generally greater (higher vibrational) than the people trying to help them. In a one-to-one context the children would disturb the therapist more than the therapist could balance and quiet the child. The children radiated a stronger induction effect on the therapists than the latter did for them.

The solution, or at least a possible place for exploration, is to heighten the energy of the therapists by taking them into a group dynamic orchestrated to accelerate their personal transformation. When we did this at the treatment center and the therapists then went back to work with the children, they reported remarkably increased ability to communicate with the children and to enjoy the work as well—where formerly they had been exhausted and barely getting by.

Similarly, the energy field of the individual with cancer is very difficult for a therapist to enter into directly without group support. One cannot touch deeply into the underlying pattern of the cancer process until one has gone very far toward resolving the death space (which is unique to each individual) within one's own consciousness. Also, to explore cancer deeply I believe we must begin by releasing the cancer-as-adversary process in our own psyches. What if it is a transformative mechanism of human evolution and not the enemy? In my growth as a healer I began to resolve the death space, as cancer, when I finally began to examine the idea "How do I say yes to cancer without empowering it?" Thus it became a koan in which I was transformed, rather than the enemy I had to vanquish. In my opinion, to approach this disease freshly, one must have awakened and activated the higher and collective levels of energy within one's psyche, and this is far beyond the energy levels available to the unawakened individual. The resolution may well come when we learn to heighten and refine the energy state in the so-called patient, but most significantly, on a collective level involving all of us.

What is possible in a group context that is working with the process of holding a heightened energy field is not possible in a one-to-one context unless the healer has already resolved the areas of problem carried by the client. The qualities of such a healer are: directly awakened into the higher energies (no longer requiring an augmenting context such as a group to be in contact with this dimension); an ever-maturing quality of unconditionality; a moment-by moment capacity to rebalance his or her energies; and the ability to release, at the first clues, any process of repression.

❖

The group experiment was carried into another octave. It became clear that unified group consciousness can produce a vortex of energy that accelerated healing and learning for the guest as well as a profound growth experience for the group members. It was also clear that the guest represented a particular dynamic in consciousness that would then challenge the psyches of the group members. What would happen if a guest, rather than being an individual with a major illness, was instead a well-recognized and gifted healer, therapist or educator? Calling this an experiment in "learning through energy induction," the group began to work with leaders in the field of consciousness. The guests included Jack Schwartz, Gay Luce, Hal Bailen, M.D., Ellen Margron, Lynn Lumbard, Helen Palmer, Franklin Merrell-Wolff, Justine and Michael Toms and others, each of whom is either locally or nationally recognized for their ability to work in the subtle realms.

The format for the interactions was essentially the same as that used with the other guests. The session began with a piece of music played at very high volume during which the whole group would lie down and let go into it together. This letting go begins the ritual of coalition or entrainment of individual energies into the more unified or cohesive dynamic. Then, the group would move into a neutral but highly receptive mode. By neutral I mean that it was each person's task to experience the guest as a presence. This is quite distinct from the usual way people listen where they are trying to plug the speaker into their belief structures or trying to have some question answered. The guest was free to share and soar into any area spontaneously. It was my hope that, given a highly attuned audience, they would find themselves able to share with great fluidity and perhaps tap new areas. After this the guest was asked to open to a nonverbal period where they would be on the table and the group, highly practiced in this capacity, would then share energy with them.

Thus, the evening placed the guest and the group into an alternating dance of active and receptive modes. This was part of the beauty of the exploration. It is amazing how rarely teachers will allow themselves to go into a completely receptive state with a group they have never worked with before. At the end of these sessions several of these guests stated they felt they had been able to do some deep healing in themselves—that some deeper patterns had been released. Many felt they had a new appreciation for the energies of consciousness.

From the perspective of the explorational group it seemed that such guests added a special and refined quality, frequently awesome and inspirational to the overall energetic. The energy sharing-process would have a broader, more open quality to it. These guests could also give feedback as to the quality of the energy they experienced at a much more sophisticated and subtle level than the other guests. Without trying to qualify too specifically the difference between the gifted teachers and the guests with major illnesses, the former were far more open, receptive and sensitive to the energetic communion. Their consciousness appeared to exist with significant awareness in dimensions beyond the physical body and personal self, whereas in the individuals with illness this was much less true.

As for the group members themselves, many are now teachers taking other groups on into subtle work in ways unique to their particular natures. I have no doubt that having had the opportunity to share so deeply with inspired people helped their own paths.

❖

The experience of energetic communion in a collective vortex is multidimensional and tends to discourage making an interpretation of what is happening. Such interactions involve one's whole Self. It is experienced in the body in powerful flows of energy and sensation, in alterations of all the senses and of time/ space orientation. It feels as if one enters into another dimension in which the personal observing consciousness becomes insignificant and is best left out of any interpretive role.

The deeper the commitment into an unconditional sense, the more profound and illuminating these experiences seem to be, and the more moving and rejuvenating to the person who is the participating guest.

Participants and guests alike were frequently precipitated into a whole new perspective about themselves and their situation, and for some this resulted in immediate life changes. You cannot leap from the sea of personal reality into the mystery and magnitude of collective forces and the interpenetrating aspect of our nature without being transformed. The enormous energy in these experiences makes the setting aside of personal perspective very easy, almost compelling. And out of the gap emerges the new understanding and the profound sense of love. The depth of insight, the understanding, the manner in which information becomes available, and the observed psychological and physical changes evoked through these processes, challenge our orthodox ideas about human nature. And the beauty of it is that this realm of experience is available to anyone who is willing to explore openheartedly.

# 10 ❖ THE ILLUSION OF OUR SEPARATENESS

*Every exaggeration has its revenge in human physiology.*

WALT WHITMAN

AN EMERGING VISION of humankind confirms that the human organism is multidimensional and that it is likely that different diseases evolve from different dimensions of human Beingness. As we have seen, the physical body exists in relationship to a less discrete but nevertheless tangible energy body. Throughout human history this energy body has provided a natural bridge of communication for diagnosis and treatment—as in acupuncture, polarity, and auric healing—and for deeper understanding of the processes that result in disease. Levels of this energy field continuously interpenetrate and seem to operate beyond ordinary time and space. Within this phenomenon all human beings can be seen to be united in a continuum of consciousness. This may account for such phenomena as telepathy, precognition, telekinesis, diagnosis and healing at a distance, and so on. Modern physics is drawing us toward an understanding of this. Clearly, while reality is discrete at one level, at another equally valid level it is an uninterrupted continuum.

At the turn of the century a series of experiments produced evidence of phenomena that could not be understood, and in fact could not be accepted, within the framework of the physics established by classical mechanics. It was not until Einstein's Theory of Relativity that these phenomena were integrated by a wholly new vision of the relationship of matter to energy; the essence of this was that as one approaches the speed of light, mass and energy begin to exchange qualities. Thus time and space, matter and energy are all different modes of a larger dynamic. None of these concepts has meaning independent of the others. When this relationship was placed into a technological context, the quantity of energy released was enormous and birthed our nuclear age.

Just as one kind of consciousness (Newtonian) worked for certain kinds of experiences (i.e., those at which velocity was very slow relative to the speed of light, and at a very low energy level), another kind of consciousness (Einsteinian) was required to deal with events in which the whole idea of space and time was changed, and in which the energies involved were of a whole new dimension.

Here is an important concept. Let us begin with a partial definition: From a certain viewpoint disease reflects a relationship within an energy-transducing system (or state of consciousness) at one particular level of equilibrium with a force (another state of consciousness) that either disturbs the existing equilibrium or is of sufficient energy to foster a shift of the existing equilibrium to an entirely new energy-transducing system. Once stabilized at a particular equilibrium, *disturbing* forces may be those that initially fostered the equilibrium, and we find that we can adopt a new posture or appropriately interfere with these forces. However, if the force is actually *shifting* (as opposed to simply disturbing) the basic equilibrium state, it is difficult to recognize its nature and we are, for a while, being redefined in it—or, seemingly, the victim of it.

Analogously there are certain diseases—many of the infectious diseases—that we understand and pursue scientifically through a Newtonian-like ideation. Within present biological conceptions, and noting the manner in which these disease agents interact with the human constitution, we now recognize their *disturbing* cause/effect relationship to human health. Take the case of *pneumococcus*, the agent creating pneumonia. We can watch it under the microscope, isolate its various biological aspects, and interrupt the growth of the organism because we sufficiently recognize its distinctions from us. The totality of our collective evolution reached a point where this discernment was possible. Earlier in our history these diseases were *shifting* us, and we saw only the results and not the cause. The cause, the consciousness giving rise to these diseases, was hidden to us. Our present understanding of infectious disease is much like Newtonian thinking, which was adequate for low-vibration, low-speed, low-energy phenomena. These diseases are low-energy diseases. They have a slow vibration. I am not talking about pathology: Because they are low-vibration diseases doesn't mean they are not destructive. Maybe it is the extreme contrast between the energies of *our* consciousness and those of these entities that allow them to be so rapidly destructive. Wherever there is great contrast there is also the possibility of great conflict. At the same time, by virtue of their low energy, our relatively primitive Newtonian mentality has been able to penetrate this differential and master the process.

On the other hand, there are diseases like the cancers, certain degenerative processes, and perhaps the autoimmune illnesses, that seem to have a different quality. We can say that they are moving very quickly, that they are of a high vibration and of much higher energies. By analogy we are now in the Einsteinian realm, approaching the speed of light, where so-called matter and so-called energy are really just different modes of the same experience. These high-vibration diseases exist in the dimension where the physical self and the higher (usually hidden) energies of consciousness are in a subtle relationship of exchange. These diseases appear to evolve out of our own consciousness, at least at the level at which we presently recognize ourselves. They are still *shifting* us, thus their distinction from us is not yet clear. This is why we do not yet understand their etiology and we may not until our definition of life itself expands. The exploration of these processes invites a shift in consciousness as great as that between classical mechanics and quantum physics.

At slow vibrations or lower energy states our separatist

human individuality appears as a reality to us; I-Thou duality dominates our awareness. As we explore our world at this level, our thinking naturally tends toward understanding the causation of disease in linear, mechanistic, and functional ways. We seek an agent carried on the breath by droplet, or by physical contact, or through water or food. Appropriately, our prevention is mechanical—to interrupt the chain at the level of the agent or its symptoms. By analogy with light, this is what I refer to as the "particle" mode of consciousness. Unquestionably it is valid for certain levels of experience. At a certain time we were forced to extend our appreciation of interrelatedness, both to ourselves in the sense of hygiene, and also to a larger biosphere.

At the faster vibration, the higher energy levels of consciousness, our apparent individuality becomes more and more an illusion. The interpenetrating fields of energy unite all life in a continuum—the wave aspect analogous to light as a continuum. The high-energy diseases are degenerative, malignant, to a large degree unpredictable, and seem to blend into the totality of life. They are incredibly systemic. They are teaching us things about inter- and intra-cellular communication that we never dreamed of. They seem to be part of us. They are directly interwoven in our consciousness, our feelings and our social and cultural activities to a profound degree. They seem to emerge from our very thought. Prevention and treatment are for the most part poorly understood, symptom-related, often relatively ineffective and dangerous. The energy and time demanded by these diseases is enormous.

When we did not understand the vectors and causality of infectious disease, the treatments were also less effective and often dangerous (as in the medieval techniques of bloodletting). Today we are trying to look at cancer with the same consciousness with which we pursued pneumonia. But the difference between these diseases and the consciousness underlying them is about as dramatic as that between the energy of penicillin and the energy of a linear accelerator, or the energy of dynamite and that of an atomic bomb. What these diseases demand is a high-energy consciousness that simultaneously recognizes both our particle and wave modes of existence.

Usually we are only able to examine one of these modes at a time, and so life appears paradoxical and we become narrow-minded. Consider how long it took for Einstein's thinking to emerge and resolve the conflicting data that was beginning to be obtained through certain experiments. Similarly, we usually attend to only one mode of our human experience at the exclusion, even denial, of the other. We look at the individual and build a discrete science or a discrete psychology based upon a narrow range of recognizable and conditioned phenomena, and as a result we see only a physical reality or a tangible personality. On the other side, we focus on the continuum aspect and consider such phenomena as spiritual forces, psi phenomena, telepathy, and so on. But even here we are the observer, focusing on a particular range of evidence. We are not the living embodiment of the simultaneous experience of a fuller conscious Beingness. That would be to awaken into a whole new dimension of Self.

At present our whole culture is caught in a schism. Our assessment of reality is made from fairly low energy states of consciousness. This isolates us in the particle mode of experiencing. However, we begin to resolve this compartmentalizing of our Beingness when we appreciate that individuality is only the dominant interpretation of experience at slow-vibration, low-energy states. Simultaneously we exist as a nonpersonal, nonphysical interpenetrating continuum of tremendously high energy and high vibration. This has profound ramifications for health and disease. The individual's disease may not be his or hers alone, but rather the manifestation of a process within the entity *humanity*. Another way of saying this is that the interpenetrating energetics of consciousness—the continuum uniting us all—may represent the matrix through which forces for healing or for the fabrication of disease can be seen as contagious.

❖

The basic phenomenon of our interpenetrating nature can no longer be separated from our concept of health care because it points to, and in fact represents, the new level of consciousness we must come to understand and work with if we are to meet the challenge of the upsurgent neoplastic (new growth, i.e., tumor) diseases.

We are brought to the realization that the ways of believing and living of large segments of humanity constellate forces in fields of interpenetrating consciousness that are capable of engendering, or at least potentiating, their analogy at tissue level in the individual. In other words, the higher vibrational diseases are in part a reflection of *energetic* patterns within the greater human context and are not simply questions of individual behavior, individual biology, exposure to toxins, or some as-yet-unrecognized virus. Rather, it is as if these diseases represent a confusion within the life-configurating forces. This confusion arises through the capacity of collective human consciousness to impede or accelerate a potential by constellating a field of belief or a way of life that is imbalancing. This prevents the attainment, not only of the indiviual's highest potential, but also of humanity's.

The high vibrational diseases have roots in the energetic matrix of unresolved, deep-level conflict between inculcated ideas about life and the deeper experience of living; between one's deepest relationship to the allowing and receiving of (God's) love and the collective dogmatic thinking of certain religions; between the natural, perhaps unavoidable, capacity to love all beings and the collective inhibitions around the age-old issues of incest, nationality, class and race; between the limitations of energy and material inherent within the environment and the seemingly unstoppable belief in More. Thus, the individual can seem to be in harmony with the outer reality at many levels but at a deeper, soul level may be in conflict. We can be imposing many tissue-configurating identities upon our own being through the various powerful energetics carried by each plane of consciousness. But the higher and more inclusive energy state is the ultimate empowerer of what will manifest. When we make choices that are not in harmony with this energetic, we exist in a state of dynamic confusion. These deeper conflicts are basic energy-field organizers that, when joined with the proliferation of toxic stressors acting directly at the cellular level, may result in cancers.

Yet the individual immersed in a carcinogenic conflict at subtle levels of consciousness is ordinarily as unaware of participation in this force as the city dweller is unaware of constant low-frequency rumble. We cannot perceive this rumble or carcinogenic force field without contrast with relative silence or the clarity of another level of consciousness. Thus ascension into higher awareness suddenly thrusts the individual into the experience of many forces formerly not directly perceivable: a living, vibrational, sensate discernment of the subtle healthful or disruptive quality of attitudes, thoughts and feelings. This is accompanied by a general orientation of understanding that is simply nonexistent to ordinary consciousness. Thus, the essence of all work in healing at the level I am discussing is to help initiate this kind of awakening within the individual who seeks help. The deeper-level conflict is not apparent at ordinary energy levels, and even if you could be told by a psychic or through your own intuition where the issue resides, you must still attain a higher energy level in order to resolve the conflict.

It is the role of an awakened individual to show others how to amplify and refine their energy state and temporarily to induce a level of energy in which they can see that this potential is real. As we have seen, higher energy states can in a matter of seconds relieve pain and anxiety and instill a profound sense of peace and compassion. They can, over more prolonged exposure, empower an amazing sense of health and strength, but this induction effect is usually temporary. Eventually individuals must make the same energetic transformation on their own. To do this is, in a sense, to die into a new consciousness faster than the disease leads to physical death. It is to empower a new flow of Beingness at a higher energy level so that it transmutes the disease-creating forces.

Forward strides in healing and health care will be made as we recognize and appreciate the general shift these awakening levels of consciousness represent. Primarily, this shift is in the release of time and space as functions of psychological needs based in the personal self. It is also the realization of an entirely different set of life-forming laws and imperatives that reside in the high-vibrational collective Self.

We can say that personal psychological needs sequester reality into separate compartments, thereby applying one moment to one part of the self and the next moment to another part. Any compartmentalization of perceived reality through our own personal needs has a mirror in the way we conceive of our own being, our own body and its functioning. The greater self-awareness that is actually a continuum of energies thus becomes split by personal consciousness into varying, perhaps opposing forces, repressing some and enhancing others. This very process by which each of us defines himself sends energies of highly varying quality and intensity to different organs, tissues and bodily functions moment-by-moment in a kind of energetic ambivalence. These tendencies of an individual's consciousness have their roots—each at a different vibrational rate—in survival, in pleasure, in procreative instincts, in emotional needs, in fears, in power, in our need for interpersonal communion and loss of separateness, in the impulse toward prayer, creative expression, and God. Any of these areas can become insanely exaggerated or repressed in our *collective* expression, constellating enormous forces that engender conflict and oscillation within the individual.

It is as though the deeper awareness is trying to evolve to a higher level that includes and balances all these dimensions, while the personal awareness, affected by the collective patterns, imposes a limited or exaggerated expression. Our tissue-level reality experiences these energetic double binds. Imagine the tissue as a reflection of these conflicting energies: At one level it attempts to individuate through personal or collective conditional patterns, while a force originating in a more unconditional level attempts to express more universal patterns.

As I discussed earlier, the cancer rate of schizophrenics is one-quarter the national average. Schizophrenia is a very high-energy disease in the sense that the ability to differentiate between personal and more universal levels breaks down. This disintegrating boundary mechanism somehow provides a relative immunity to cancer, whereas the so-called normal person, by rigidly maintaining personal/psychological boundaries, may be subconsciously enacting the deeper energetic conflict at tissue level. In many ways "normal" human awareness is a repression of the higher-energy Self—a repression that I believe is at the core of our malignant diseases and a lot more.

❖

We resist change because we fear it. Orthodox medicine likes to pretend there is no energy body—that the theories of high-energy physics pertain somewhere else, not here in man. We would like to make believe that a virus or a toxin is to blame, and that all we have to do is find out how it works to solve the problem. This is only a narrow corner of the truth. It overlooks such things as the ability of every world-class runner to break the four-minute mile. Most of us are not aware that a breed of mountaineer has developed today who can climb in one day that which required two weeks just a decade ago, and that peaks unscaleable then are now routinely climbed with only minimal improvement in equipment. How is this? The human body has not changed so much in ten years. In the consciousness lies the difference.

We would like to continue believing that the physical body is powered by the metabolism of food alone, that it is solid, absolute. Yet homo sapiens are also empowered by the consciousness in which endeavors are undertaken. The expression of our being occurs in the material and personal dimensions, and simultaneously is continuously influenced by that which is not material, that which is energetics of the individual and the larger continuum. Like the particle and the wave, the differentiation in these levels of self is an *illusion* of perspective, of awareness, of linear communication. It is an illusion relative to the refinement of our consciousness. Our tissue structure is also fabricated—*enlivened*—by energy flows that can only be called collective. The force that lifts the mountaineer into expertise beyond the human capability of only a few years ago is the force of a collective belief based on recent achievements.

We would like to continue believing that the human immune system, which according to one theory is always removing new cancer cells as they form, has all of a sudden stopped functioning and allowed the development of a tumor, and that what we must do is figure out why it is not working or how we can stimulate it. In fact, the human immune system may *not* be failing. Perhaps it is simply not subtle enough to recognize the force it is dealing with. Like the limbs and lungs of a runner only a few decades ago, it has not yet joined a greater state of consciousness in which power over the tumor process is like breaking the four-minute mile. At present, our very conception of the disease and our approach to it *empowers the consciousness of the disease;* at the treatment level, we engage in brinksmanship, seeing if the disease will die faster than the normal tissue. All of this derives from a contracted level of consciousness that perceives only a normal/diseased dichotomy. We have not considered that the cancer may not be resisted by the immune system because the tumor *is considered self.*

The essence of healthy immunity could be stated as a refined discernment, with a greater recognition of subtle contrasts and appropriate response to such information. We err if we separate the subtlety of our consciousness from the same function within the body. Hypothetically, as a greater sense of Self emerges with the expansion of awareness—a sense that is more refined in its recognition of the forces and energies that penetrate or interact within Beingness, a sense that inevitably changes our relationship to living—such a sense will also be participating with the evolution and refinement of the immune mechanism.

We are having trouble recognizing the nature of cancer because the consciousness organizing its development is too much like us, hidden within us. It is supported and augmented in the individual by exaggerations of our collective outer psyche that are mirrored in our consensual way of life. One man's pollution is innocuous. Collective pollution is devastating, and dramatically points to the equation between individual and collective consciousness in the area of health and disease.

Years ago I was struck by an aerial photograph of a large city. It showed chaotic veins of urbanization that had spread out into the surrounding environment and one could clearly recognize areas of devitalized vegetation, churned hillsides, and the obvious discoloration of nearby waters. It reminded me of a pathology slide of liver cancer. Perhaps such comparison is poetic license. Yet the nature of the tumor is hypermetabolic, consuming an unbalanced proportion of the available resources and demanding unrestrained growth, rather than integrating with the total organism through a realization of the greater whole. Is it merely coincidence that highly technological countries, particularly in the West, have a similar ethos and an epidemic upsurgence of cancer?

We cannot continue to proliferate solutions to individual illness when we are all swimming in a stress-creating, carcinogenic collective consciousness. It is not I, an individual, who puts the asbestos and petroleum products in the air and water that results in the increase in cancers and other disease. It is *the I that is We* that does this. It is the collective I of the ungoverned, unawakened personal self-consciousness that shouts from behind our diseases and our suffering world environment. It is the illusion of our separateness that is killing us.

❖

The existing epidemic of cancers and, to a lesser degree, stress-related diseases and chronic degenerative processes, as tragic as it may seem, must be regarded as a force in the evolution of man's deeper soul. These diseases are urging each of us to recognize and embody the energy of our collective nature, both in the outer sense by which we share the resources of our world, and in the inner sense by which we release the contracted dominion of relative states of being into the fluidity of a greater Beingness.

Acknowledging collective levels of consciousness is not merely recognizing that we are all united—that every piece of food, every thought, if followed back to its root, links us to everything. An intellectual appreciation carries important insight, but it lacks the transformative quality imbued by direct experience of higher levels of energy. From this experience it is not ideas of how to transform our world that we gain, but, much more simply, an understanding that our nearsightedness resides primarily in the very planes of consciousness by which we define our reality. When we can step beyond this myopia, we become something *other*, something experiential, alive and direct. The first contact with energy flows and heightening of subtle sensitivities becomes a vehicle to *suggest* this new potential. But awakening into the expanded levels of consciousness then goes beyond our ideas of what we think we have entered into and how we imagine we will heal ourselves and our world. It is radical. It is evolutionary. It goes beyond humankind as we know and live it now.

We persevere in a few relative levels of consciousness when by our very nature we are already involved with energies of other dimensions. The energy we now bring through the few zones we permit is greater than this narrowed consciousness can integrate. The reality we have been looking at was never intended to hold the full intensity of our Beingness. For this full intensity the spectrum of reality itself must broaden. Natural fleshly existence cannot hold this greater energy when directed into any narrowed developmental facet of the living Self.

The denied energy potential must have its reciprocal expression in matter. It must be expressed somewhere. The analogy, I suggest, is clear within the body. The tumor is new life. It is of us, but *not* of us. It grows faster, utilizes more, violates boundary. Likewise in our world: Our society, our technology, our culture cannot hold the energy inherent in a multidimensional consciousness within the narrowed laws and ideas of man.

The diseases I have focused on are, I believe, evoked from higher energies. They are enormously systemic, beyond our wildest imaginings, extending the human body into a living relationship involving us all and more. To understand and resolve them will require a higher level of realization and a heightening in energy.

Few forces in biological life are as powerfully creative as a cancer. The "becoming" of a gestating fetus has this potential naturally. But where later, in the spectrum of ordinary life, do we allow a quality of consciousness with similar power of becoming? We cannot develop or "become" at this rate along our present route of feeding the personal me, me, me component. The exhaustion of our environmental resources reveals the narrowness of our approach to the broader forces through which we might give expression to this becoming. We bring too much energy to only a few of the myriad relationships that could be the channel for our becoming, and we are burning out the world at this level like a cancer in one organ burns out the whole body. We have been living within the narrowed, possessive or narcissistic domain of a contracted spectrum of relative levels of consciousness.

From an evolutionary perspective, these diseases may be telling us to empower the totality of consciousness itself: to learn of another body of energy, knowledge of which automatically transmutes the relationship to matter and flesh and life itself. As the awareness can shift into a multidimensional and fluid perspective, why not also the flesh? Perhaps cancer is an early evolutionary experiment in learning to transmute the physical nature by an internal dynamic inherent in the very consciousness we are becoming. In fact, for those whose consciousness has entered into new levels of energy in a balanced manner, there is a fluid-like transformation of the body, with amazing softening and redistribution of tissue. But for most people, as some levels of self gather the energy sufficient for such a shift, others levels remain fixed. The heightening is not in harmony, and it becomes an aberrant expression within the whole: a delusional system, or a power struggle, or a tumor.

I am not saying that the way we are is wrong or bad. I am saying that we are a beginning—a changing, transient expression of life—not a pinnacle in evolution but, more humbly, a phase, a process, perhaps a catalyst. We are being drawn toward a Greater Self. Through the consequences of exaggerating our human propensities and the enormous crisis energies we are now capable of activating both individually and collectively, something greater is being slowly revealed to us. It is, in fact, an immensely creative process. A force such as cancer is but one of the vectors for growth that have enormous coercive power to shift the orientation of human awareness. And I am suggesting that the high-energy diseases are doing so in ways quite other than traditional medicine or current holistic philosophies are yet acknowledging.

At the level where this phenomenon is challenging us we might rightly feel that there are no healers and patients; we are none of us separate from the diseases of our time. Our healing is a process of the emergence of us all, and not some kind of technological warfare based on a static posture of victory or defeat over the enemy, disease. These diseases demand a new mode of being, of relating to life through a multidimensional awareness.

Having conceived of the challenge at this level, let us meet this challenge appropriately with great courage and great love. The hardship of these disease processes is not resolved in some external change conceived from a reactive or narrow personal awareness. We are beyond being able to resolve the challenge by migration, as in times of famine, or through some other reshuffling of outer events, or by the accruing of money or power. Our technology, our politics, our medical system and our very lifestyle are designed to somehow buffer our fears, parentally to protect us from the essential risk and paradox of existence. We have narrowed the channel of becoming and thereby given birth to our nightmares and our cancers. To see if this process has another intrinsic message for us we must begin to relax our conditions about life.

The ideas of holistic health and New Age consciousness are only beginning to reflect the radical nature of the shift in consciousness that is taking place. Much in these areas is still concerned with "migrating," but now it is at the level of mental energies; we call this "changing attitudes." We are still trying to accrue power over what we don't like. We call this the process of positive affirmations, but it is still a reshuffling process that has at its heart a denial of the radical truth of transformation. Who is deciding the "right" attitude and who is empowering the particular quality of our affirmations? We can take a first step through these modes, and even be lifted without pain into a new sense of the world, but this is a short-lived honeymoon. Soon, if real transformation is to occur, the very self that initiated the quest will come into question and begin to be undone. Then we are into a genuine transformation.

At this level the deeper issues of life carry far more genuine spiritual significance than the vast majority of so-called New Age concepts, lifestyles and processes, or the panorama of mind-control reprogramming techniques. I sense that the immense creative forces within our diseases—forces that can cause tissue to manifest at rates similar to that of the developing fetus—require and can engender a much more radical understanding. This understanding is beyond the bargaining, reshuffling mind. To be sure, there are genuine transformative disciplines, but these are processes requiring total life immersion and they engender a profound disheveling of the old psyche accompanied by an ultimate crisis. Such a process must entail an opening of the heart in the most unconditional sense to the totality of life.

We cannot play around with just the body, or just the emotions, or with interesting spiritual and metaphysical cosmologies, and be content to call this transformation—or even holistic medicine. A shift in attitude can be an important first step, but it is often just a platitude, and in my experience of working in this field it is rarely enough. People can be led to say what makes them and us believe that they have gotten the part right, have really grown and changed. But it is so often a performance-level intervention, a reshuffling of the furniture within the same structure, a redistribution of energy within the same pattern.

Rarely can such an approach reach to the roots of transformation to mature and stabilize the process. Nor can it reach the roots of the powerful invocation of the cancer process. These roots are in the deepest fibers of our psychic organization, individually and collectively. And they are not just in our past, but reach into our future, into the very reality toward which they lead us. As we approach their source we come to the moment where there can be no resolution for individuals unless they can leap into the abyss, out of self-identity into another level in which we seem temporarily to merge with everything. If I stay *me*, the disease or the old awareness has power. I must go beyond me to take that next step, where the experience I perceive and respond to transcends the reality of what I have stubbornly and blindly insisted is myself.

This is true for growth in general. The patterns we can live out at any particular level of consciousness are infinite. When we finally realize that we are repeating the same dynamic over and over again and that it is not truly necessary for our well- being; when it narrows the potential for our relationship to love others and our world; when it is time to witness this process and begin to withhold the energy that we would ordinarily express by activating the dynamic; then eventually a new potential is revealed. This may not have anything to do with right and wrong, or positive and negative. It may simply be the free choice to expand the horizon of our Beingness and thereby perhaps discover truly new levels of experience. From this perspective a "good" attitude is not necessarily feeling positive (if positive is defined in terms of rejecting something else that is "negative.") A real shift in attitude grows out of direct experience of areas that one formerly didn't know existed or had intuited but never fully embraced. It can be assisted by the willingness to put more of the totality of oneself into any moment and by the willingness to enter new experience, even though it may mean starting over rather than continuing to reshuffle the furniture of one's old psyche. Clearly this is not easy.

# 11 ❖ TRANSFORMING OUR MEDICINE

As we have seen, there is a reality that can be experienced between the events and attitudes that seem to compose our lives. To know this reality directly means to forever regard such attitudes and events in a very different manner. From the perspective of our traditional or holistic medical activities this other reality must be sensed into. It lies hidden between the moment of frozen awareness when we stop seeing a human being and start into the clinical evaluation. It underlies our science, information, training, and memory, and the attitude of knowing we base on these. It is there between our diagnosis or interpretation and our assumption about prognosis and timing. It waits between our sense of responsibility and the actual choice to act; between the perception of suffering and the need to do something about it. A single pause at the point when we are least aware of ourselves—because we are caught in a chain that seems so natural, so logical, so imperative and *right*—can expose a dimension so awesome and wondrous that we never again are the same.

The existence of hidden dimensions is suggested even in traditional medicine by such phenomena as placebos; by the way in which identically performed experiments produce a certain result in one institution and a different result somewhere else; by the phenomena of healing and spontaneous remission reported in respected literature; by the new evidence that so-called "good responders" do better with both drugs and placebos than do "poor responders" (this calls into question the double-blind studies upon which much of clinical medicine rests, where the question of drug response and personal attitude hadn't been considered); by the various responses to "identical" therapy among patients with the "same" disease.

The very real question arises: Have we distorted the basis of our medicine by the predelictions of our awareness? Does an institution that is enthusiastic about some new chemotherapeutic agent it has developed demonstrate better results than another institution that cautiously, and perhaps skeptically, tries to repeat those results? The collective psychic force field of enthusiasm may directly effect the responsiveness of an organism in ways quite different from the collective force field of cautious scepticism. Is the biology of an organism—and therefore its physiology and biochemistry—an energy- or state-dependent function? Is it variable with consciousness itself? I say yes.

We can study music for years and look only at the notes, but what we hear—what carries us off into reverie, imaging, relaxation or inspiration—is not the notes themselves, but equally the intervals between them. Perhaps the notes are merely resting points in an infinity of sound. As Einstein indicated, the interval is greater than the event. If the studies of state-bound conciousness (recall the example of the drunken medical students) have anything to tell us, they may be saying that people who learn in an atmosphere of competition, crisis and stress may later require (and unconsciously foster) the same atmosphere wherever they are in order to perform optimally or achieve the sense of personal completeness. This may color our whole approach to health and disease.

Is it possible that the reality of our diseases has a relative quality—that there is something we don't appreciate about the quality of human consciousness from which they emerge? Perhaps we need not experience them quite the way we do. And, if not, how has such a reality come to be and what is the necessary shift that can begin to offer us new options? What is the process by which what has seemed compelling and undeniable can be transmuted (changed in its essential nature) or appreciated as moving toward a new dynamic?

This perspective no longer sees disease as a manifestation of some physiological, emotional, mental process to be negated as efficiently as possible so that one can return to the former state of balance. With exquisite sensitivity, disease and stress indicate the lively interface between our present level of awareness and the effulgent forces surfacing from not-yet-realized levels of our being. This balance is interdimensional. It is not a midpoint between a right and wrong way of living, between things liked and not liked, between a good and a bad diet. We might call it a *balance* point that allows paradox. It is less reactive and self-protective. It is a mode of consciousness that honors both the rational nature that integrates the infinite proliferation of humankind's thinking and materiality at any one level of exploration, and the vertical movement of awareness that shows the relativity of all statements, stances and perspectives.

This level of consciousness is not a controlled neutrality or indifference, or some idea or philosophy about being aware or about being healthy. It is not a state available merely through conceptualizing or through the shifting of attitudes. It is a tremendously alive, charged, "energized" state of being, involving the whole of one's self as a new entity. This new entity is intrinsically and inseparably a part of everyone and everything around it. I believe that in the next ten years medicine will make a quantum leap. We will no longer be able to speak of the individual body and aim our efforts at the individual alone. We shall speak of a collective body, an *I that is We*, and at this level we will not be able to separate biology and medicine as science from collective thought, from the consensus of the political, religious and economic psyche of our time.

Rarely do we conceive the possibility of touching such a state, let alone the tremendous significance it may have in transforming the whole of our nature. Rarely do we leap above the sea of personal self-consciousness or, in the case of medicine, out of the water of diagnosis and treatment and the roles of doctor and patient. Some deeper process within consciousness continues to solidify and stabilize our reality. It is the unshackling of this core process that allows the awakening of a new quality of consciousness.

Who in conventional medicine would think that the reality we perceive might be very different if we were to work directly with energy instead of content? The moment we enter the usual problem-solving mode of consciousness, we are not only in that sea, but also fascinated by all the ways we can play in it. They become our reality, our cross to bear, our exultation and our misfortune. *We define ourselves through problems.*

Have you ever stopped to realize that solving problems may not be the work of a successful life, but rather a compulsive identity-creating mechanism of the ego? This ordinary mode of the ego is necessary in one sphere of experience, but is simultaneously an impediment to the perception of a larger reality.

Analysis and interpretation merely substantiate this situation. Frequently the analytic and other therapeutic modes aimed at explaining or relieving specific problems indirectly reinforce them by making them real instead of *relative*. It is this approach to life that mystics have referred to as being "asleep." Sooner or later we must take the leap to an assumption that problems are statements of contrasts, not absolutes, and to an unconditional perspective in which such events have but a transient reality. Once this is done, 90 percent of problems disappear. The rest are simply enticements to grow.

The intellectual mind cannot make this leap because it has no original perception of reality. It functions through memory, and wherever it looks it is still in the sea. So the leap out of the sea is not toward a more exalted philosophy, but into another dimension. The nature of this leap is an *awakening*, an aspect of which is the presentation to our awareness of a whole new realm of energies. It is the discovery of an individual and collective force field that far transcends the personal level. This is not to say that the personal level isn't valid. Obviously it is, but not in the way we thought.

Interacting within their own dimension, the personal levels of consciousness become an infinite and essentially unchanging continuum. They may appear to change, just as a room may appear to change as we reshuffle the furniture. Still, the essence of the room remains the same. To more fully understand this room we must ask the house of which it is part, about the weather in the area, and the proximity and friendliness of the neighbors. We have some idea of the functional significance of the room because of the larger context in which it exists.

The creative or original mind, if it truly wishes to change the basic nature of the room, must either go outside it to see the greater forces that give it relevance, or must transform the contents, for instance by dismantling the furniture and creating a piece of sculpture. It was through my patients' responses to this analogy that I could tell who would tend to recover quickly and who would thrash around chronically. Those who thought that shuffling furniture represented essential change had a more conventional experience of being sick and often recovered more slowly. Their lives tended to be unchanging and repetitive, and their illnesses were repetitive and chronic. Those who questioned why they were in the room, who could conceive of taking the walls down or playing differently with the whole process, seemed to recover faster and saw it as a process of multi-dimensional growth.

Much traditional and even holistic healing is a furniture-changing process aimed at reducing discomfort, rarely with intention of resolving causal patterns, and almost never with the sense that truly radical change is possible. But if we begin to peel back the levels of self and the assumptions about life that underlie any problem, we begin to see that they are universal, existing in one form or another in everyone. Then we realize that unless we are going to step into another kind of consciousness, the issues are going to recur in one form or another indefinitely. We are going to remain defined by our very efforts to juggle our endless reactions to every experience that isn't acceptable to us. Because of this, the whole therapeutic concept may condition a problem-response pattern that supports a closed "room" of the consciousness instead of taking down the walls or seeing them in a multidimensional context. In this way, therapy and even our sanctified medical interventions to cure illness and mitigate suffering may for some people create disease.The cumulative effect of interventions, even in the name of healing, can be disastrous to a person and ultimately to a society. It presumes that we know where we are going, what health is, and what is right for humanity – which we don't.

The penetration of this issue must lead us to an examination of reality itself. The underlying imperative with which we interact with life is a consciousness that can exist at many potential levels. All human consciousness creates a kind of external authority, a veil or curtain upon which reality must be precipitated in order to have a sufficient sense of contrast with itself. It is as though the way in which we experience reality is really the reference whereby we bring ourselves into being. This is essentially the same idea as that contained in the metaphysical precept that the reality we know is the mirror of the inner person. Obviously the veil is relative and shifts as we grow and refine our awareness. It can be dense and reflect back a very clearcut, absolute world, or it can be very transparent. The veil thins and becomes more transparent when we release modes of awareness that compulsively need to explain, analyze, compare, judge and understand everything we perceive. As each veil thins and eventually disappears, the human experience moves toward higher energy states. There one looks at existence and sees profound spaciousness and mystery.

In our society our political, governmental and medical activities act as a continuation of a very basic energetic – what I refer to as the *parental dynamic*. After watching hundreds of people work with the transformational process, it is clear that the parent-child energetic dominates most human activity and is the main veil circumscribing consciousness.

The parental dynamic filters reality in an unconscious parent-child fashion. This begins as the infant gradually develops a personal consciousness and distinguishes itself from the parents. Our very sense of reality carries a hidden authority over us, and the seemingly external situation we are in (the medical world, the therapeutic world, the religious world) is held in consciousness as a parent is looked to for safety, answers and self-substantiation. By so doing we define ourselves in a circumscribed pattern as a kind of child that by its very nature never has authority fully to be. The child vis-à-vis parent is always being defined, never genuinely defining, and thus will never really have authority over the so-called problem. It is the veil of parental energetics that medicine must pierce in order to begin to awaken.

One of the reasons I stopped practicing traditional medicine was that I began to realize I had found a very compelling role in which I was fundamentally safe and well-rewarded—a role in which I was playing the parent while the patient was playing the child. I had found a way to be safely defined in reality and, despite increases in skill and knowledge, in a subtle way I was no longer growing. Accumulation is one kind of growth, but it should not be confused with growth that is multidimensional. Yes, I was expanding and becoming dense and filled in terms of information, but if any experience or psychic force came along that threatened to change the integrity of my reality, then there was inexplicable anxiety, fear and defensiveness. I could withdraw into my role (or favorite problem) for security, but I realized with astonishment that if my work as a physician was predicated even minimally on a subtle defense against a broader truth and range of experience, then in fact I was indirectly and subconsciously supporting the reality of disease. *We reciprocally empower the very reality through which we know ourselves as real.* The collective expression of this and other subtle dynamics may constellate present Reality.

The moment I no longer wanted to shield my life from genuine growth, my whole sense of medicine and the role of the physician changed. I realized that I had been a doctor who was a furniture shuffler—that I was in fact afraid to leave the room. I made my choice and left the traditional setting. I made a commitment to explore life in a much broader sense and not to allow my work to draw me into the parental dynamic that medicine had become for me. If this is unavoidable in some circumstances, then at least I knew that I did not want to foster this dynamic unconsciously. Rather than trying to help someone sustain a particular situation or guide an individual toward some idealized way of being, the real challenge is any situation is to awaken to a more essential level of beingness.

I remember the first time, while driving down the road, I realized with both wonder and horror that my life was totally my own. I had to learn to recoordinate my senses and my body. My very perception and the motivation for every action—even those as mundane as grocery shopping—had somehow been predicated on my former relationship to existence (as configurated in my role, my habits, and the daily flow of time and space). Now, as if I were born into a new body, I had to seek a far larger relationship to existence upon which to let my new life unfold. I realized right then and there why human beings are so afraid of change and why we worship freedom. Genuine freedom is simply the most awesome thing to us. It is like God Himself, and rather than intuit the divine directly and wholeheartedly we are forever crystallizing this freedom into behavioral and psychological idols until we are petrified.

❖

To begin to be released from this we need to appreciate the structure of consciousness that defines the individual. We must look for the milieu of energies in which this particular individual manifestation takes form, and work in a truly original and creative way with the content of our experience. The original mind *shifts* energy levels, it does not merely react to the apparent reality at a given energy level.

The idea of a milieu of energies (a psychosphere) coalescing the individual, out of which the individual consciousness and the totality of its perceived reality emerges, is very different from behavioral, conditioned, psychological, social or cultural concepts. Our symbols, linguistic and otherwise, are one level of reality. But the energetic states out of which these symbols are born are a finer or more causal level of experience, for they involve not only mental faculties but also the body. Making this realm of experience alive in one's body, and not merely conceptual, is the key, is the awakening.

A philosophical comprehension of human energies and of the

radical possibilities of transformation inherent in touching into higher states of consciousness is not the same as the experience of such a process. To *say* there is an energy that awakens in the "heart" is not the same as the tornado of emotions, fears, questions, sensations, and changes of myriad kinds that begin to happen when the energy actually does awaken. But all too often we content ourselves with concepts and flee any potential to touch a new state directly.

What must be understood is that these new areas are not something we add on but something that alters the whole fabric of experience. These new explorations are born in a context of letting go or releasing the mechanisms in consciousness that need to define, to compare, to understand—in short, to defend one's psychological territory in the broadest sense. It could more aptly be termed a *process of relearning or of unlearning*. This is why the conference work can be one of the deepest experiences in one's life, but also can be one of the most difficult.

To bring a deepening potential forward in our traditional educational settings does not seem realistic to me at this time. The general inertia of the traditional world is still so strong in its resistance to fundamental change that it seduces us into a polarization or splitting of our psyche. Over and over we tell ourselves that these things are religious and spiritual and these things over here are scientific; these things are for the inner life and these others are for the world. As individuals begin to do intrapsychic battle to bring this split into a living unity, they quickly discover how subtle and profound is the challenge to move up even one level of consciousness. This kind of growth cannot be imposed. You can't fruitfully offer a higher reality to someone, unless they are ready, whether they are conscious of their own readiness or not. Even if we are well-meaning, when we try to impose the energy of a supposed higher consciousness on others, a subtle polarizing phenomenon is again provoked. "My way is better than yours" marks the proselytizing and unawakened awareness, even though it believes itself to have tasted a higher dimension and wants to give this gift to the world. This does not lead to transformation at the energetic level.

The awakened awareness recognizes itself as a presence continuously interpenetrating energetically throughout a multidimensional reality and, in this manner, naturally imbuing in others the potential for ascending to a higher energetic state. This level of interaction is universal, although very few have awakened sufficiently to participate in it with more than a miniscule degree of awareness. From this perspective, whether or not a new sense of education is possible within our existing institutions, it is nevertheless important to understand that we are biased and evolving within hidden universal forces, like the parental energetic, even though we are not conscious of them.

Our present way of examining life through our existing educational system is arrested in a sea of egoistic development that refuses to acknowledge awareness of self as a conscious process. This is particularly limiting, even disastrous, in medicine because of its unique place in human experience. Medicine stands at the intersection of life and death, of the rational and the non-rational, of control and loss of control, of form and formlessness. Medicine can and must be a natural forum for the blending of science and mysticism.

For ages science and spirituality have been at war. Because the claims of the mystics were seemingly unprovable, scientists resisted the deeper quality underlying their statements, even though mystical realization often gave birth to a new vector of scientific inquiry and development. On the other side, much spirituality is an escape from reason and responsibility. It is often built upon experiences and miracles that probably do not logically or inherently imply the reality then professed by the spiritualist. But in fact mystical experience and its spiritual and religious outgrowths are dealing in essence with the quality of consciousness.

Religiousness is the space between the notes. It is concerned with setting criteria for navigating dimensions beyond form. Science, on the other hand, studies the notes, the event itself. But as I have tried to show, study of such events requires simultaneously the awareness of the quality of consciousness in which such study is undertaken. Thus the mystical dimensions in their essential and finest sense, before they are encumbered with dogma and tradition and ridiculous cosmologies, can never be separated from science (as modern physics is now showing us more and more clearly). They are two sides of the same coin. A profound refinement of the cohering presence of our being cannot be separated from the scientific process. This to me is true spirituality.

What medicine lacks is a science of rapport, in its most basic and unconditional sense. Like the fable of the blind men and the elephant,* medical education and practice still pursues only the pieces they can touch and measure. Medicine continues to differentiate its technical personality but, from a perspective of higher wisdom, is quite immature. It has not yet appreciated a gestalt in which what is already known gains new meaning and significance through a shift in focus. It does not sufficiently examine its motives to begin to see the hidden forces driving us along our present path. It hasn't really stopped to consider that the most powerful placebo effect of all is the quality of awareness radiating from the individual practitioner himself.

A shift is necessary. This shift is a conscious weakening of the usual ego-sustaining intellectual and technical approaches to life, thus inviting the numinous forces that give humanness a far greater context. It is time we support the search for the deeper Self as an inseparable part of the maturing of the modern healer.

The fact that this potential can easily be brought forward under certain circumstances by an appropriate guide means that it is available at least to those who intuit that it is time to take this next step. In my work, the "scientific" reproducibility of the capacity to bring disparate groups of strangers into experiences that illumine a higher level of self-awareness is far more significant than the powers of perception and healing sometimes

---

*Six blind men wanted to "see" an elephant and were led to explore one. The first went to its side and said "Oh, an elephant is like a wall." Another felt a tusk and said "It is long and sharp like a spear." Another felt the trunk and said it was like a snake. Each man perceived something different about the elephant; none were able to "see" the whole.

demonstrated by groups or by gifted individuals. It strongly indicates that there is a whole other mode of learning, communicating, and knowing that is available to us. As we have seen, this has immediate clinical and therapeutic application and far-reaching implications about how we pursue the truth of human nature. It suggests that the overview in which we can integrate our examination of the phenomena of health and disease lies not exclusively in the individual experiences, but simultaneously in the collective consciousness and in the concomitant energy field in which examination is undertaken. Unless we are willing to contemplate what it means to change the energy level of our individual and collective consciousness, we will not perceive that the totality of our present ideas about scientific and social truths and particularly about health and disease are also relative and, in this sense, limited.

To participate in such a process of unlearning necessitates a temporary surrendering of the familiar modes of learning and knowing. It assumes that we recognize the limitations inherent in further accumulation of information along our present route of inquiry. It may seem contrary to the very way in which we measure and award achievement in the existing system. Indeed, one must relax these normal tendencies until we appreciate that they are, at another level, ego-maintaining mechanisms that hold our sense of time and space and Beingness in a particular fixation. We then risk entrance into areas of nonrationality, or what I prefer to call *new* rationality. An environment of trust, acceptance and inspiration facilitates this process. In fact, they can't be separated.

The disciplines involved are not the accumulation and storage of data but the preparation of a mind through which this data can take on liberal new meaning. It is finding a new kind of inner balance and then discovering and evoking formerly hidden energies of consciousness. It is the evocation of these energies that begin to transform the self as they mature in our awareness. What is needed is an environment that genuinely honors the multidimensionality of human nature, no matter what level of relative knowledge is being mastered. It is an environment formerly labeled *spiritual* or *religious*, but which I prefer to think of as an experiment in being more of one's whole potential.

❖

Being is holistic. Just to be—our very existence—is beyond our comprehension. From this perspective ordinary consciousness must be seen as contracted—like a horse with blinders on. But we can begin to feel into what it is like to be part of an enormous experiment. Look, for instance, at the limitations of our ordinary time frame. We think in terms of the immediate past or future. Historians, sages and wise men through the ages have commented upon a somewhat broader scale of time. In the body of every one of us there are systems whose frames of reference span hundreds and even thousands of generations. In seventy years there will be some two hundred new generations of red blood cells taking the intricate journey through our vascular roadways. If our bodies attempted to modulate the activities of these cells based upon information in the immediate generation, we would be in trouble. What if this generation looks diseased or seems different than before? Do we wipe it out?

Fortunately, in health, our bodies recognize a larger continuum and allow the modulation process to trust a greater perspective. Wisely, our bodies do not respond too strongly to any apparent changes during one generation of cells because eventually there will be a natural balance encompassing the full two hundred generations. But what about our medicine? Is it possible that there are diseases that are modulating humanity on a much broader time frame than the lifespan of one indiviudal? What happens when we interfere in this process because of some poorly reflected-upon inner compulsion, such as the belief that every disease is our adversary and should be cured or attenuated? I went through a whole medical training without a single moment being given to the examination of the *consciousness* of medicine.

Which forces must be compensated for immediately and which must be recognized in a broader context? For example, in the individual, the sensate and emotional time frames are very narrow. Something feels good or bad *now*, and we do or we don't like it *now*. This is not the time frame that would healthfully govern our attitudes and responses. The emotional volatility of the adolescent component of our consciousness gives way to a maturity in which the immediacy of our likes and dislikes are no longer dominant.

Different parts of the human psyche develop at different rates and make different demands on life. Physical mastery is being attained by teenagers (witness the average age of an Olympic athlete), while emotional mastery takes longer and is rare even in adults.

What of mental and intellectual maturity, as well as the mystery of power, not to mention the aesthetic and intuitive components of the psyche? We are not just one person. A trained individual can learn to listen to the voice quality of others and hear them shifting between several levels of their consciousness even within a single sentence. We are capable of very different perspectives and behaviors depending on which facet of consciousness is dominant in a given moment. Basic psychology appreciates that over-emphasizing a particular aspect of the psyche, such as intellectual and emotional control, by suppressing feeling and sensitivity results in an unbalanced individual prone to a variety of psychological and physical illnesses. But there is also a wisdom which recognizes that it is natural and healthy to be exploring one or another basic component to the apparent exclusion of others during the sequencing of natural development.

It is important that different facets of the developing consciousness be emphasized during various phases of the unfolding, as long as there is an eventual modulation of the matured conscious energies throughout the whole being. Ultimately this overall balance is the determiner of basic health. During the natural cycles by which one or another component is brought forward, we need an overview of the transformation: We must have a sense of the highest potential of the mature individual. We can allow the repetition of certain patterns when we understand that they are a necessary cycling that eventually leads to the fullest imbuing of the total Self. Similarly, cycles that do not allow development and expression of the fullest potential can be pointed out and thereby automatically made referrent to a greater potential. One can envision that with each cycle the process of unfoldment is integrated more deeply, so that an area of consciousness that might previously have been too immature to handle the heightening energies of the transforming consciousness can thus be brought forward, enriched and perfected. Thus, although we appear to grow in stages, and can become crystallized in certain stages, we nonetheless grow as a whole. Any forced or sustained splitting within this whole will ultimately lead to a breach of integrity and thus to disease.

What if we step back from our personal fears and concerns about health and disease and consider that humanity as a whole may have a developmental pattern analogous to that of any person? This perspective can be helpful as we regard the unique expressions of various cultures, societies and races on our planet today. Some may appear backward, while others appear far advanced. Some respond to natural stress with an incredible stoicism while others are emotional and passionate. We see the adolescent idealism of young countries, the cautious traditionalism of older countries. We see the Third World countries attempting to "catch up" by imitating the materialism of the technologically developed nations. We see the same patterns being repeated over and over again, century after century, as one national or ascendant culture attempts to impose its values on the others— as if power and domination at a particular moment of time had anything at all to do with intrinsic value. There simply is no overview that respects the natural and highly variable developmental sequencing of humanity as a whole. But we had better start thinking about it, and more than thinking about it. We must find the overview in ourselves. This is the path of the heart.

From the perspective of health this opens up some intriguing new considerations. For one thing, our present appreciation of disease epidemiology is myopic. We record rates of occurrence of diseases that differ demographically and geographically across nations and the globe, but we rarely look at this phenomena from an overview of evolving human consciousness. We have pretty much fixed our minds on discovering cause-and-effect physical and psychological agents like germs and stress. But what if the individual's integrity is not to be regarded as separate from every facet of the total human experience?

Too many things are unexplainable through limited cause-and-effect models. For instance, in the United States, the rates of most cancers in young children are greater in whites than in blacks. The overall incidence of cancer is lower in blacks than in whites, but when blacks get cancer they generally have a statistically poorer remission and survival rate. The reason is not clear. We could think of it as genetic, but when we compare the rates of accidental deaths in young blacks and whites we see that again the latter is higher. Perhaps we must reach into an energetic or transformational overview. I suggest that there are natural balancing forces (as there are in an individual) that prune any developmental facet as it expresses through a particular population strata or aspect of a culture or nation. Is it possible that different disease processes reflect the imbalance of each developmental component, say a socio-economic group or a race, relative to the *whole* — and thus acts to either slow down or accelerate some strata of humanity in the thrust of its expression? Here we have a perspective about disease that is evolutionary, that encompasses social, economic, political, spiritual, and larger cultural forces all embraced within an overview that relates to a developing energetic transformation of the total humanity.

Is there any facet of human expression that can be suppressed, or another facet overly cultivated, without a wavefront of imbalance that communicates throughout the whole and gradually seeks to foster an evolving balance? Might not such a wavefront be the increasing incidence of cancers and auto-immune processes and other modern diseases? After all, in the body, what happens when any cell type ceases to maintain its natural boundaries as governed by the deeper wisdom referrent to the whole? What if one cell type is being stressed to become a different cell or to handle forces that it does not yet know how to work with? The answer to these questions could be seen as a metaphorical statement of cancer creation. Can we say that there is an equation of the forces of individual health and the forces of collective human expression?

If we begin to consider that the pattern of health and disease of any given generation of human beings is a tremendously integrated phenomenon within the whole of humanity, and that medicine's attention to immediate reactions and concerns may need to be modulated by, say, a two-hundred-generation perspective—the mind simply shuts off at the awesomeness of this. We begin to have to seek for a different quality of awareness beyond that which sustains our own personal needs if we are to unravel the challenge of health for our times. Each one of us becomes responsible for a statement of wholeness, not only in the sphere of our most immediate activities, but also in the totality of our Beingness. But such a statement must respect the unique perspective that others will bring to the same issues. Thus, wholeness cannot exist as anything other than a deep commitment to unconditional love.

Medicine could not entertain this very real possibility and continue on its present path, and neither could society as a whole. What if cancer is one of the diseases helping to foster this shift and is at the same time a force that must be seen as extending across a multigenerational span? Cancer forces us to examine multigenerational human activity as, for instance, when DES* use results in cancer in the next generation. If we want to understand and ultimately cure the DES-induced cancer, we must not merely stop using DES. We must ask what was the nature of the consciousness that motivated the use of this chemical. What were the fundamental assumptions about reality that led to the seeking and eventual application of this drug?

It isn't only the medical establishment that needs to ask these questions. It is everyone who used the drug as well. If we don't think in this way, what is to stop us from repeating the same pattern with hundreds of other chemicals and other technological "advances?" Our narrow feel-good-now, self-serving per-

---

*DES stands for diethyl stilbesterol which used to be given to women to decrease some of the symptoms of pregnancy such as morning sickness.

spectives, and even it's-good-to-be-helpful attitudes, need to be questioned more deeply. Human health is the balance of many subtle but nonetheless profound forces emanating from many levels of consciousness, and each may be operating over differing time frames spanning patterns that are both individual and collective in their expression.

Thus we are all invited into direct experience, into a vibration, a quality, a poetry that is a continuum that helps us abandon our relative viewpoint. Where it is leading us we cannot know. The rules for wise discernment must be learned anew and not projected from old levels. This is why genuine transformation is slow indeed, even from the perspective of multiple generations. We have to be willing to start all over. To our ordinary awareness this is scary, paradoxical, or maybe even dangerous. Where, after all, can we put our foot down and say "This is real?" All of a sudden we recognize the larger continuum, the two-hundred-generation perspective, and everything becomes subjective, ambiguous and transitory. It is like the paradox of light, which seems to exist in or to obey a dual reality: In one reality we discuss discrete quanta, a unit of particles; in the other it is a wave—uninterrupted—a continuum. *The paradox is only in our perception.* It is resolved by consciousness itself, in our very being and experience, as we lift to a higher level.

# 12 ❖ HEIGHTENING TOWARD COLLECTIVE TRANSFORMATION

THROUGHOUT TIME men and women of great spiritual and energetic development have stressed the need to discipline the basic personal impulses expressed in our desires for food, pleasure, power, and so on. They realized that energy expressed by the dimensions in which these desires find dominion is of relatively low vibration. It assumes a reality in which there is distinct separation between self and other, between that which is *me* and that which is *other*. At these low energies time is very narrow, and the future is a projection from these basic needs. The past is merely a way to justify how we feel and think today. In this sense, humankind in ordinary consciousness is said to be asleep. The future is rarely more than transposed memory. People cannot conceive of a new future directly, for it is not in their memory, and therefore from a certain point on the wheel of life it circles continuously like a recurrent dream.

Think about it for a moment. When a friend has not arrived on time, when a child is late from school, when someone doesn't behave as we expect, we begin to run the list of fears through our awareness. When the economy fluctuates down-ward and discomfort rather than comfort is anticipated, it is never considered "natural." Discomfort is not right! The linear mind does not comprehend the natural rhythms and cycles that permeate all of existence. It displays reality from memory in ac-cordance with the dominant level of its consciousness (basic sur-vival, psychosexual, psychoemotional). The tardy friend has been caught in traffic, has had an accident, doesn't want to see you, or worse. The friend has never found a wonderful book and been swept into a deep insight, a magnificient reverie, or a benediction of energy that made time irrelevant. We don't have a future, we have a dead past leering menacingly in front of us, appearing on a screen of our own fabrication. And with this re-current unconscious mechanism of the ego we build our lives. Collectively, we build our institutions, our medical health-care system or our military and political system. Now these cultural forms become monster resonance-entraining devices that effect the energy system, the perception, the thought, the flow of life force, and the health of every living thing.

And, who is innocent? Who is not involved in this? I ask my-self "What part of me wants to loft missiles at some enemy over there?" Even if we never go to war, do we ever ask what we are consecrating our lives to, and what are the consequences? At first it seems totally insane, some atavistic behavior from our dinosaur past. But no, I realize: Did I not build model tanks and throw toy missiles at houses made of cards or plastic bricks? Did I not want to outdo those guys at the other school? Wasn't there a time when it was important to be better than they, to gain recognition for my prowess, my courage, my intelligence, my rightness? Yes, I too have participated, and at one level always will, in our seeming madness. But I was only a child, barely a teenager when this ethos dominated how I perceived reality and lived my life. Yes, and most of us are arrested still at this level of development and are building our world from it.

It is as if the body and the ego, as they naturally mature, do so at the expense of a larger vision. At a certain point the con-sciousness ceases to remember its source in a vast, numinous, undifferentiated state of being. Having achieved personal self-consciousness, it could turn and, in a profoundly meaningful way, reunite with its spiritual roots. But instead it continues to try to pour more and more energy through one plane of being. In a multidimensional sense, it ceases to grow.

A well-educated and technologically sophisticated individual led by a psyche that is fundamentally contracted—that is rooted in *me*, in basic desires, in adolescent power needs, and in a sense of separation—can be a dangerous and tragic thing indeed. Such individuals do not see their world as only two-or three-dimensional in an evolving sequence that has further dimensions through which to realize Beingness. They do not see that any and every state of consciousness can change into something else, that even our deepest prejudice can transmute to love.

In the human scene it is often those most compelled to evolve in the areas of power and emotional intensity who lead us, just as the coarser and harsher emotions have the greatest power over our sense of well-being and lead us around psychologically. In the vast majority of people fear is a greater mobilizer than love. At least this is so until we come directly into the benediction of a higher dimension and finally a new journey begins.

❖

From the perspective of a higher dimension our behavior, at any level we choose to examine it, reflects natural phases of the developmental process by which we evolve from the undifferentiated state of the infantile consciousness into a functional personality. As evolvement continues we must release this into an expanded personality, a cosmic ego that exhibits what I have termed *presence* and *love*. In the first phase, consciousness learns to inhabit the body, to master level upon level of operations from the simplest, like walking, to those of ascending complexity that reflect ever-increasing levels of order and interrelatedness far beyond the functions necessary to the individual. It is through this process that the ego comes to be formed. In the second phase, a transformation begins, and the energies of a greater and numinous Self become activated while the ordinary personal concerns begin to attenuate.

From this overview we can see that what we call ego and what we call the body are not separate. It dawned on me one day that the reason a human child cannot coordinate and walk at birth, though it clearly has the strength to do so, is that the ego is not sufficiently individuated. The human infant isn't born having mastered self-consciousness, and therefore cannot discern itself from the environment sufficiently to make the statement "this is *me* and this is *not me*" that is necessary to coordinate the self-conscious *me*. The ego evolves to what we call human as we learn to master the body, and continues to evolve through the higher human functions such as language. As self-consciousness inhabits the body, existence takes on personal reality. I believe we are looking at the usual unconscious or low-energy awareness of this dynamic when we discover that a psychological or emotional trauma leads to a particular ego bias which can then result in a physical disease. The phenomenally small amount we know about the body is probably proportional to the level of human awareness at this time. Those who demonstrate higher levels of consciousness also demonstrate far greater mastery of many bodily functions if they choose to do so. But their personal reality is multidimensional and less personal.

Later in the transformational process, especially after the awakening of higher energies, there begins the transcendence of ego as tangible body. With the release of this original energy pattern by which the personal ego developed, new levels of energy and new levels of perception occur and the body becomes vast, collective and energetic. At this level it is clear that any attempt to define that which is *me* versus that which is *not me* is illusion. This includes the body. Perhaps this is why all great mystical teachings emphasize that we must release the identity with the body to enter a transcendent state (beyond the ego). I would reverse this and say that having entered a higher consciousness the relativity of the body is obvious. We don't discard the body, but we recognize that it is a configuration of energies from which no facet of existence is separate.

Thus, as I have already said, the "individual" is a spectrum of energetic dynamics encompassing those that define particular personal qualities and those that are part of a greater continuum uniting all humankind and beyond. In this sense the body is never our own but belongs to all of us, and the same can be said for a disease. We each participate in the process by which a particular disease is templated and comes to be. The human body is a perfect mirror of the level of collective consciousness; our diseases are telling us about ourselves collectively.

If we could but realize this sense of profound sharing and unity, our way of relating to life and to each other would change tremendously. It should not be frightening to realize how our interpenetrating Beingness unites us even in disease. It should exalt us and fill us with mystery and wonder. We are our brother's keepers in the fullest sense. Everyone of us has a Cain, a personal ego-self that cannot hear the greater harmony, that slays the Abel of our numinous unity. We do so to develop and to master our world. Then later through the "Adam and Eve" of our deeper nature, a new Abel is brought forward. It may happen that through disease, through the powerful energy it evokes and its grinding of the personal self, this new Abel is glimpsed.

Let me give an example of how this understanding can be brought forward in the process of dying and how one woman in particular learned to see this for herself. She was telling me of her great sense of anger as she watched people in their cars, stopping at lights and going about their business completely oblivious to her. "Don't they know that I am dying," she would shout inwardly. This caused her to contract into a knot of anger and it was difficult for her to gain perspective about her feelings. She sensed in some way that the anger was an inappropriate expression, an inner mistranslation. Although as a therapist herself she was wise enough not to repress it, still she did not know how to transmute it or to recognize its deeper significance. Certainly if the anger is not allowable, then the energy giving rise to it is repressed and may be utilized destructively. Even *expressed* anger is merely a catharsis of energy and, in a sense, a short-circuit or repression of a higher potential.

I suggested to her that the deeper evolving pattern of her energies (her soul) that had guided her to become a therapist knew exactly what it was trying to communicate. The disease had driven her deeper toward the inner current of her Beingness.

She was more open and sensitive than she had ever been, and from this level she was expressing a basic truth. Didn't they know that she was dying of a process that all humanity participates in? Didn't they know that she was in part an expression of all of us, not solely defective in herself, and that it would take all of us in concert to heal her, to heal ourselves? What were they doing, going about their business asleep? Wouldn't they get a little more aware and understand that we can be open to our wholeness every moment, right now?

If they had even momentarily touched the deeper energy, if they were aware of their own souls, it is possible they could have been sensitive to her, not necessarily knowing of her disease, but somehow sensing their mutual participation in a deeper call to realness. Resonating at a subliminal level with their common journey, their shared commitment, perhaps there would have been some acknowledgment. They might have found themselves glancing over from their driving, catching her eyes for a moment in silent recognition. Such brief but pregnant telepathic connections happen to many people who have grown more sensitive as they move through the world.

Her experience was far from inappropriate. It presaged a deeper understanding, although at the time it was not the fully matured expression of that understanding. Oh, how often we do this to ourselves: We believe that a particular reaction is to be regarded as real, rather than as the best we can do in that moment of translating into consciousness a deeper kind of appreciation. Her experience was part of a creative force trying to help her shift to a level of communion and simultaneously emanating an intensity of energy she recognized as anger.

It only took a moment for her to understand this, at which point her energy shifted. *It was only the sense of separation that kept the energy in the anger mode.* She connected deeply to a sense of her own eternal nature, and she knew more fully than ever what her life had been dedicated to all along. The anger shifted and became a presence and a strength through which she carried her family and friends into a deep teaching about dying. We each might well feel into the nature of the soul that can take on such patterns and brings such pain into the human dimension so that we can empower our consciousness and learn, even if momentarily, to more fully honor our divine nature.

It is possible that, when we all have evolved to a higher level of collective energetic balance, the compartmentalization of consciousness and separation from higher energies (which I believe is the root of the cancer-creating forces) will have been recognized and transcended. These processes that now seem such a challenge to us might be no more of a threat than a passing cold.

In the meantime we might consider that, at any developing level of evolving consciousness when balance is lost between forces that are self-defining and forces that are self-transcendent, the potential for disease development exists. The cancers, I believe, represent at a collective level an exaggeration of the self-defining potential, a kind of rigidness that becomes a contraction away from our divine nature. We may be unconsciously limiting higher levels of energy to a narrow range of expression and thereby forcing them to be expressed aberrantly.

There are some people who become genuinely spiritual in their life orientation, partly because other levels of life (e.g. the sexual) are difficult or unfulfilling for them. But as life naturally exposes them to higher levels of energy beyond that which they are aware of, the most balanced expression of these energies may be demonstrated, not only in true spiritual maturity, but also in the empowering of a high-energy disease at the very level (pelvic) at which they were the most rigid and me-dominated. (It is interesting to note that nuns have a high incidence of cancer of the breast and uterus.) It is this very level that is least capable of integrating the higher energies. It is the place in consciousness where the repressed no resides most strongly. As individuals attempt to resolve this process they are dealing, not only with their own particular energetic bias, but also with the collective exaggeration of these same inclinations and the ever-heightening collective energies. Perhaps at one level of energy the pattern could have been lived out fairly innocuously. But at higher energies we are forced to resolve it. This is how consciousness refines.

All this is meant to be food for thought; I do not conceive of it as an absolute formula. In fact, I am more interested in creating an energy that opens space within your own awareness that I am in developing a purely logical argument. If you wish to use this insight fruitfully, you could begin by making a list of behaviors, attitudes, and life-orientations that mark that part of the psyche that tends toward self-definition, security and predictability; then sense into that part of the self that is moving, growing, expanding, mysterious, unknowable and nonrational. However, if this turns into a mental exercise, it is of little value. Instead learn to identify the energetic quality of each of these tendencies and to integrate the two kinds of energetic dimensions directly within your own Beingness.

When insight does occur, one must be prepared to start living it. I recall the scary moment when I had the thought "Whoever said you are going to be a doctor forever?" That thought provided a glimpse of the formless background. I realized then how much I assumed about life and how much freedom we really have. All of a sudden I saw that being a doctor was just an arbitrary role and I knew that someday I'd have to release the role and open to freedom. A year and a half later I did. It is the unconditional quality that automatically facilitates this integration of the background and foreground of our Beingness and unconditional love which emerges when the fusion is realized with sufficient energy. Therefore, the focus must be on developing that unconditional quality of awareness which is capable of integrating the higher energies at all levels of self.

❖

We believe we know what we are about, but we cannot know the deeper forces that predicate behavior until the boundaries of energetic Beingness have been dissolved into a higher energy. Then for the first time we can truly appreciate how the ego becomes constellated, how it functions to serve us, and how, through it, we can become transcendent to a greater reality. There is nothing more humbling than this dissolution process. Once you have seen what it takes to unveil just one single step in the expansion of consciousness, you no longer desire to cast judgment on those who, for whatever reasons, have not yet seen this next potential and are therefore forced to live within the reality defined by a lesser level.

In the first phase of our life the biological parent represents survival, food, pleasure, warmth and a nearly infinite potential for fascination to the infant. This relationship is the first primary energy field dynamic through which we each begin to individuate our unique personality. Later, though we appear to have transcended our parents, we have not. Now by the same energetic dynamic by which we have developed vis-à-vis our parents we expand and extend our sense of self into the world. Thus, it is the lesser state of our basic energy reality that becomes the parent of our adult lives. We are invisibly parented, nourished, and oriented in time and space by the very patterns and ideas into which our life becomes set. And each level of this relationship within consciousness is energy-bound or energy-determined. To grow beyond it, to enter the energy of a higher consciousness, can seem as radical psychologically as it would be for the infant to be abandoned by its mother and await the embrace of another parent.

Although it is an important beginning, we do not enter this higher state merely by working through conflicts with parents. The same energy dynamic continues to define the self in relationship to experience, and it is the whole of reality in the way we hold it that is our real parent. It is this energy and this reality that must be transcended and not merely the ideas, reactions, fulfillments, conflicts or suffering consequent to it. Extending beyond the energy level of ordinary personal consciousness, we fear abandonment of our familar reality. We have not yet realized that existence itself is the new mother and that her embrace, although seeming to represent the end of the former consciousness, awakens us to a new and deeper love than any ordinary parent could give a child. It is a deeper relationship than any delusional involvement in a narrowed reality can possibly fulfill for the mundane ego. In its heart it is a mystical experience quite beyond words.

Why do we have this great fear of deeper change? Why are we unaware of the simplest of all understanding—that the future must remain essentially unknowable? Any actions taken to secure the future that becomes fixed and unchanging in a person or in a culture ultimately lead to destruction.

The answer lies in the great repression of death. Not the death of the physical body at the end of the journey. It is not this that we fear. It is much more the dissolution of our low-energy self, which has become the "body" of our existence. It is this that we fear to merge into the Greater Self. "Keep me small and unique and a universe unto myself" unconsciously imposes the kinetics of personal self-consciousness. The new potential is inconceivable to the ordinary consciousness. It can only be perceived as threatening, as death, as an awesome loss of control. We are terrified of that enormity in which we are all so insignificant.

With the repression of death comes also the repression of God. Even our God becomes an idea, an idol. We have an idea of something so far beyond ourselves, so far beyond this world in which we already exist, that we cannot begin to see that it is here with us all the time in all that we perceive and do. To begin to know God we must begin consciously to die to ourselves.

The shift in consciousness that can reveal this to us is not so great as we think but it does take an enormous amount of energy to move into it. Thus our challenge is to heighten the energy of our consciousness. To do so we must appreciate how the psyche ordinarily utilizes or dissipates energy (how we live our lives). But we also will have to appreciate the mechanisms by which we are constantly gathering and heightening energy through various functions and dimensions of consciousness.

The image of a dissipative structure may be helpful as a partial model of the transformational process, specifically the awakening experience where we jump to a new level. For example, there are certain fluids that when heated form a geometric pattern similar to a tic-tac-toe board ### . This particular fluid will demonstrate this pattern across a range of energies. Lower the heat and the crosshatch pattern grows faint; increase the heat and it becomes more pronounced. The system can be said to be dissipating a range of energy through this pattern. However if too much energy is added (the heat is too high), the system breaks down. In the case of this particular fluid an interesting thing then occurs. When it reaches the maximum level of energy it can dissipate through its crosshatch pattern, all of a sudden a new pattern emerges, a system of continuous swirls /☺/☺/. This new pattern can handle far more energy than the former pattern. Whereas the crosshatch pattern is rectangular and deals with separate and discrete intersecting lines, the new pattern is infinite. Interestingly, in metaphysics the square is often likened to the personal self-consciousness, while the circle (or in this case the curves, which resemble patterns common to Druidic and Egyptian designs) symbolizes a more eternal consciousness.

Looking at this model, we see that turning up the heat (adding energy) is the essential first phase. In the experience of human transformation the increasing of energy can occur by many routes. There is *solitude*, or any mode of behavior awarely undertaken to diminish energies normally frittered away in lazy socializing. There is *fasting*, which makes energy normally utilized in the physical transmutation of food available for other psychic processes. There is *meditation*, which is the conscious internalizing of the psychic energies. There is the *direct induction* that occurs by proximity to a highly energized individual. There is *spontaneous grace* and, most common of all, *crisis*.

At first this increased energy input results in intensifying the old pattern and it grows more and more extreme. Even latent patterns now come forward as all the ego forces inherent in the old pattern are mustered to maintain the definition of self. While this is happening there is no certain way to know what the new potential will be, despite what we hear from those who have already made the transition. The old psyche inherently filters what it is receiving and translates it into something compatible with its basic state which includes its conception of the next step. This is why so many people back away repeatedly as they approach the gate, the moment of hiatus where the old psychic structure is no longer in control.

The ability to witness this process is essential, because otherwise we do not recognize the augmentation and stress of the basic pattern or appreciate the deeper consciousness in which it is manifesting. Without awareness there is the tendency to remain defined within this process and turn back from the potential to awaken to a new level of consciousness, instead of gradually learning to turn up the heat even more and go deeper. But finally, for reasons that no one really knows but that are somehow related to the love and strength with which one is inwardly motivated, some individuals succeed in letting go into the hiatus and into a wholly new dimension.

When the new level is entered, the process of awakening is far from finished. Now the challenge of basic re-stabilization becomes even greater, for the human system is not a simple fluid. The new awareness must be integrated into a balanced living situation, and this can be as difficult as the initial process of profound letting go. The new consciousness must be mastered moment by moment, for it is so large relative to the old state, and we are creatures of incomprehensively complex relationships that are the summation of our experience. While before the conscious was rectangular, a discrete self, now the moment-by-moment sense of being is a living collective comprised of a vastly interweaving display in which a far greater fragment of the psychosphere contributes to the experience called *me*.

It is at this stage that the tremendous latent personal power, which is so frightening to most of us and therefore must remain repressed, now must come forward to help empower this mastery. The mechanisms of the old self are too feeble to undertake this new statement of Self. Truly the love must be great to invite these forces forward in its service—forces that, without the new expanded awareness and love, would be violent and potentially very destructive. I am regularly approached by people who have followed a transformative path and, having opened, become overwhelmed by the forces they encounter and by their profoundly heightened sensitivity. So many people begin with a romantic dream of a new world and a new self. But inherent in this is a denial of their own personal power in the most primal sense, not to mention the outright rejection of the hidden monsters of the collective psyche which epitomize this repressed power. They dream of being pursued by monsters, dragons, criminals and other symbols of primal (formally uncontrolled) power. Instead of seeing this as the necessary integrating force trying to reach them they become even more frightened of the transformation. Yet after awakening it is this very force that must be wisely and respectfully harnessed to compliment the tremendous expansion, and to act as a precipitating counter-force for manifesting a life in this new awareness.

❖

As an individual begins to gather a higher energy, a recurrent pattern emerges, and we see this same pattern when collective humanity starts to heighten its energy. As we gather the energy that leads to the threshold where a new energy system may emerge (which is a higher harmonic of Beingness that can handle this increased energy in a balanced manner), we repeatedly empower the old energy-dissipating mechanism. The energy turns back and becomes a self-defining stance. We see increased affirmation of the fundamentals of life such as security, sexuality, family orientations or particular personal patterns. The energy tends toward these because they are the states within our ordinary consciousness in which we are familiar with handling the greatest amounts of energy. Or the energy expresses itself as a re-empowering of and acquiescence to the very things one is attempting to stand free of. In the very action of deciding to stand free we begin to gather an energy for transformation. But we cannot keep re-empowering the old energy-dissipating behaviors. At a certain point we must rest into a new mode which is essentially unknown. Otherwise, over and over again the augmented energy becomes expressed though the usual channels but at tremendously increased intensity. As much energy as it appears to take to stand up in our anger, rage, frustration and fear, it always takes less than to move into a harmonic of higher order. Unconditional love is such a state of higher energy. And in my experience it is clear that it takes less energy to become afraid, to hate, to reject—even perhaps to make a cancer—than it does to enter and realize unconditional love. Without a deep commitment to an unconditional state of being, the levels of energy as we approach that which is necessary to empower an awakening of consciousness frequently get expressed as man's greatest potential for selfishness and violence.

With the repression of death and the loss of God or the idolization of God, humankind has created a prison in which our confined consciousness ping-pongs around in ever-growing complexity and intensity. This can seem like a meaningless abstraction, but it comes to the heart of the matter. We have nothing to rest into, no genuine perception of melting and melding, nothing in which to conceive of the new integrating repository of our own or a collective transformation. How can we go forward if we cannot let go enough to intuit a relationship with a greater reality that is intrinsically loving and harmonious. Instead we have so many conditions to negotiate, to argue, to barter; so many ideas and philosophies and cosmologies to legitimize and prove.

There is filter after filter between us and any direct experience of being. I see this all the time in my work. Physicians, for example, have the filter that whatever they are learning should have direct practical application for their work: When they cannot see the immedate practical utility many shut off and thus limit themselves. It is the same with so-called seekers. Over and over again comes the request or plea or challenge "Tell me how to do this." But if one heeds this request, up comes another one. This time it is the authority-that-has-just-told-them-something filter and out comes the rebellion response—all the stored away authorities that can now be called upon to argue or debate the validity of what they have heard. But the one place where all conditions converge, where we are all humbled and united is beyond any distinctions or philosophical and theological conditions. True transformation will turn you inside out before you arrive at a new wholeness. The direct realization of this state of unity is very rare. We are terrified to abandon ourselves to it, to discover and begin to carry the energy of it.

We are still fighting "holy" wars in which the real God is a state of consciousness we swim in and are oblivious to. And, primitively, we evoke our abstract God for *our* cause versus someone else's. This is ever and will always be the mark of the ordinary mind of man, of idol worship, of lack of realization.

The love born of this consciousness is conditional and frequently murderous. It bends back upon itself and competes for its own energy, which leads to terrible crisis, war or disease. Yet it is at these very times that humans individually and collectively reach a potential for the use of our energy that far transcends our ordinary minimal use. And this is what redeems our apparent insanity. I believe it is through this very process that higher and higher energies are coming to animate form. Deplorable as it may seem from one pespective, it may be this very process by which mankind will leap to a new potential.

Where else but in crisis have vast numbers of people participated in augmented collective energy? Where else but in the army did ordinary people in huge numbers experience the power of group ritual and the energy of setting aside self in obedience to higher authority? Where else but in the throes of disease have so many learned the incredible intensities of energy that surround the life/death process, the breakdown of habituated patterns of living, and the incredibly subtle relationship of body and mind?

Of course, there is another place besides crisis and fear of death where we have learned to expand our potential and to experience a heightened state of consciousness. This is in the area of personal love. In the moment of our love affairs we taste slightly of that greater benediction. Here, when we find the appropriate partner, we discover the higher energy—the love—in which we are transcended every time we join with something more than just ourselves. It is a small taste, but enough to be the calling song of all humanity.

All of these ways are the natural, instinctive, physical, sensate and emotional channels by which the psyche of unawakened humankind amplifies and at times tremendously intensifies the energy of its being. They can be examined through two dynamics that I call the *fusion state* and the *fission state*. The fusion process is exemplified by the energy heightening that occurs when two people fall in love. The fission process at the same level can be typified by separation or divorce and the powerful forces this unleashes. Fusion and fission are the dynamics by which we heighten energy through the positive or negative vectors of crisis. At another level we can see this process in any form of self-directed, intentional activity of mastering, winning and achievement (fusion with a goal, image or idea) which automatically evokes an energy flow. Similarly, the frustration or failure or collapse of this effort again releases tremendous crisis energy (fission process). The vast majority of human beings define themselves and mobilize themselves through some form of crisis. It is how most of us gather energy and thereby tap our deeper resources.

These same dynamics can be amplified, intensified or refined through the process of ritual. Ritual activity (although we usually don't recognize it as such) such as sitting with one's doctor, or working with a surgical team, or marching, demonstrating, dancing, playing football games, or leading the military life can be employed to intensify energy toward any end. Whether we call such end good or bad is determined by two fundamental things: the quality of the motivating principle and the state of consciousness that the energy is ultimately consecrated to. The energy itself is neutral. It is how we gather it or receive it, how we hold it or let it pass through us, where we let it flow or how we give it out that determines what it evokes. This understanding and the subtlety with which we can function as multidimensional energy transducers will always be a consequence of our level of consciousness. Individuals of awakened consciousness also use crisis, but they do so consciously and, in addition, they can access energy directly through other dimensions without empowering the crisis mode.

The crisis mode of intensification of energy is unconscious in the majority of people. It is entirely natural, and I suspect it will continue to be impressed on us until through it we gather sufficient energy to rise to another level. And we may be getting close. At our present level of technological sophistication, to continue unconsciously to employ the crisis mode, even though it is a natural path by which the psyche becomes amplified and intensified, may lead us to self-annihilation. Thus we are challenged to find a new way to express energy through our Beingness or use the old ways and accept the consequences. The fact that other ways do exist is clear through the long tradition of transformative spiritual practices and the fact of awakening.

I don't believe that the inspiration of the great spiritual teachers was ever intended to limit us except in such a way as to help us gather energy to heighten into our highest potential. But it is certainly understandable that humanity in its ignorance would take these guidelines as Commandments and Laws instead of signposts of how one would want to interact with life after having touched a higher dimension. In the meantime the truth of the awakenings exist everywhere and reflect in everything, once we learn how to look.

To break free of our narrow unconsciousness is not easy. Yet we can be led gently, and in my work one of the key experiences that allows this door to begin to open is when individuals can directly experience the flow of energies through their bodies and the patterning of energies around their bodies, and around the bodies of others. To sense directly the magnificence of the interpenetrating force field that unites us all, to be swept up in currents of feeling and sensation never before experienced, and to feel a kind of love unlike any that one has ever known before, leads a person to gradually want to relax the obsession with the low-energy self. Then if we so choose, we can prepare our lives for the wondrous opening of the heart. It is the totality of this very process that is transformation.

# 13 ❖ THE I THAT IS WE

*There is danger here of formation of a separate faction on the basis of personal and egotistic interests. Such factions, which are exclusive and, instead of welcoming all men, must condemn one group in order to unite the others, originate from low motives and therefore lead in the course of time to humiliation.*

HEXAGRAM 13: TU'UNG JEN/FELLOWSHIP
THE I CHING OR BOOK OF CHANGES
WILHELM/BAYNES EDITION

WE HAVE AN EPIDEMIC of high-energy diseases in our world and we also have a tremendous upsurgence of spirituality and human-potential psychologies attempting to heighten our awareness. Are these phenomena related? I am certain they are. As we have seen, the high-energy diseases may be the consequence of a field of energy conceived in our own arrogance of self-awareness. They come back at us seemingly from beyond, but they are nonetheless a reflection of the integrity of the whole of life, an integrity that we unconsciously and consciously violate merely because we are afraid to experience more of it. I believe that the spiritual thrust is another wing of the impulse to recognize a dimension of Self beyond the personal areas in which we are obsessed. The diseases and the spiritual awakening ask for the same thing—the bridging of individual and collective consciousness, the awakening to *the I that is We.*

214

We have thought that to allow the breakdown of a structure results in chaos. We have thought that to allow our spiritual and intuitive dimensions to be admixed with our science or our politics would result in scientific, rational entropy or chaos. We have thought that we must fight to maintain "our" perspective, "our" reality, "our" territory. Recent physical evidence concerning the phenomena of dissipative structures suggests that, as a structure or energy-utilizing system breaks down because it can no longer contain the energies moving through it, it may be replaced by a more subtle structure.

My personal experience, and the observation of transformation in hundreds of people, confirms that the human psyche transforms in a process for which the image of dissipative structures is a valid, though limited, analogy. There *is* another finer pattern that emerges when we take the leap. If sufficient energy can be brought forward, and if this energy has an intrinsic integrity that can honor and embrace the full spectrum of humanness, it is possible for the low-energy reality to let go and permit an experience of a new option for Beingness. It is possible for our grosser level of awareness to break down safely and be replaced by a more subtle level of awareness that can handle and radiate a greater energy. There will still be crisis and great stress, but it will be that of an awakening consciousness. This is the most wondrous, difficult, gracious and creative potential possible for humanity.

In every setting and at every level of human unfolding, the energetic dynamics of consciousness need to be discovered and examined. In one sense all human activity is ritual, if we define ritual as a process of evoking or raising up and thus dispersing a particular quality of energy and being from out of the greater pool of Beingness. Most of the time we don't consider our own activities as ritual, and regard ritual as that activity which consciously evokes a particular quality of sacred energy to give contrast to our regular secular lives. But to the awakened awareness all activity is ritual and, in a sense, sacred, for it evokes and qualifies the deeper energetic process. Our activities and the spirit in which they are undertaken contracts or expands, refines or coarsens this deeper sense of aliveness. There is always an overview that exists energetically and against which the energetics governing our ordinary level of experience or ritual can be elucidated and radiated.

In the body we do not really know why one cellular potential ultimately manifests as a liver cell while another manifests as a muscle or a nerve cell. Yet it is through this process of an essential differentiation within an equally essential unifying overview that we as human beings come to be. It is only when the larger integrity is violated, when one group of cells decides somehow that they want more of the resources or would rather take a different role, that we recognize the result in the form of a cancer. Neither do we really understand the analogous phenomena of human differentiation and individuation. We give different labels to the people oriented to a similar mode of utilizing and expressing the greater energy that is humanity, who unconsciously join in a similar form of ritual. Some drive our trucks, repair our ships, raise our food, heal our bodies, defend our territory. For some reason people of certain intrinsic qualities are brought together to serve life in a way unique to them. But who is to explain the myriad impulses that lead one soul to carry one quality, to perform one role within a certain sphere of reality, rather than another role in another sphere? And wherever and however we gather, there is an inherent freedom to fulfill our unique Beingness in relative isolation, in relative self-definition of role or religious sect or nation, or with a conscious recognition of the essential energy binding us all. Without this deeper recognition, those segments with the greatest fear and the greatest power can define a part at the expense of the whole. This results in unbalanced flows of resources and in patterns of intensity and disease and war.

Without deeper awareness, perhaps this is the best way. Perhaps in this way we gather a vast collective energy charge for the potential of universal change. However, there is no assurance that a system that increases its energy flow to the point of maximum dissipation will in fact reconfigure into a higher expression that we can recognize. If we are, as I believe, gathering the energy for a major collective shift in consciousness, there is some basic wisdom that cannot be overlooked. In my experience of moving into a deeper dimension of consciousness, I have come to recognize that it is the honesty and purity of the motivating force, combined with the deepest embrace of the highest potential of which we can conceive, that somehow influences where we ultimately arrive—or at least the quality of how we respond and begin to integrate our new consciousness. If a deep intuition of the highest unifying context, of the finest kind of love, is not somehow held up as the backdrop in which to express the energy of our being as it moves through the hiatus of transformation, the outcome may be a system of lower energy—a body ravaged and amputated, a mind psychotic or merely animating the safest, most conditioned and instinctive human components, or a culture dispersed or even extinct.

In A.D. 900 the Mayan culture, believed to involve nearly two million people, which had plotted the orbits of Venus and Mars, created a 365-day calendar based on the Earth's circumnavigation of the sun (while Europe was still in the Dark Ages), and built an exquisite display of magnificent pyramids, disappeared in less than one generation. What remained were dispersed village units living at a simpler more basic agricultural level of collective formulation. No one knows why or how this occurred. Perhaps it was a creative evolution. Perhaps the dispersal of the more coherent society into apparently more primitive units was not a regression. Perhaps the outer development of culture with all its sophistication and technical development is not the deeper measure of a growing process. Perhaps those who survived emanate a finer quality of energy and are capable of a more refined ability to transmute reality. Perhaps hidden in their simple culture is a greater love. When love of the whole planet as a single life form is sensed into, we often find ourselves turning to the so-called primitives to study their folklore. And in the end, if truth be allowed, we really don't know where humankind is going and what ultimately is best for it.

Under any circumstances, we continuously gather the potential to tap a greater reservoir of human, or perhaps trans-human energies. The question becomes, can we make this more directly conscious? Must the process continue to be expressed unconsciously, habitually, through repetitive addictions to particular levels of intensity, through powerful epidemics of disease, social unrest, and conflict?

Everywhere love is not allowed in the most genuine and open sense that honors the whole spectrum of the great diversity of humanness, we create conquest and repression. We do this intra-psychically with our own fears and impulses (of which the greatest and most destructive at our present developmental stage is the repression of death and God), and then we do the same collectively in awesome exaggerations of our unconscious individual tendencies. Later the fruit of this action is a force that must re-emerge to create balance. This is not a case of good or bad or of right or wrong. I am not commenting about man's social and political issues. Such issues are always and shall ever remain relative to the level of consciousness that examines them. I am commenting on energy, how it is transmuted through our awareness, and most of all on finding a central space (an unconditional love) in which to begin safely breaking down the compelling identity with the narrow range of Beingness.

Without unconditional love there may be nothing original. No amount of hope or caring or righteousness will suffice if it is not referent to or emanating from a commitment to an unconditional state that transcends the conditional awareness. If we cannot take the leap, we may just replay our lives through every addiction pattern, through our own repressed components, and through the enormous reservoir of deeper patterns hidden within the collective unconscious. The funny part is that in our arrogance we may think that we are choosing to love, but I suspect it is evolution itself that is choosing it for us.

As we begin to allow a sense of unconditional love we are swept into dimensions of ambiguity and uncertainty, of having to learn areas of subtle discernment, of over and over again releasing the relative contraction of the personal, narcissistic perspective and thus learning honesty, humility and compassion. It is an inner path. The first taste can be bequeathed by a teacher, a catalyzing-integrating presence that can also offer certain practical reflections and techniques. Most frequently the first taste comes through some crisis such as an illness. But eventually it is clear that this is a process of communion.

We are all in it together and the most powerful method for deepening the process within oneself is to join together in experiments of collective unification and heightening. This more than anything else empowers the greatest energies and sows the seeds of destruction and growth out of which a new consciousness is born. Meaning and purpose, goal and achievement, rightness and pride, no matter what wonders they appear to be moving us toward, also operate as obvious or subtle mechanisms for self-definition, of self-defense to bulwark against a fuller state of Beingness.

To tap this deeper Beingness means the radical re-evaluation of all psychodirective forces. Now things become less clear. There is a place called the heart, and here we discover a new relationship to life. It is not just a new concept of goodness, some right way for the "evolving" human being to be. It is a space of tremendous enhancement of energy implying greatly increased sensitivity and necessitating great strength and maturity to master even in a limited, miniscule sense. We have to relearn how to use the energy of our Beingness. It is like learning to walk again. Even a brief experience of this dimension can and does radically transform the awareness. Beginning to tap into these areas of consciousness regularly can so transform the body that human medicine is naive if it continues to merely observe biologic processes without appreciating the powerful energies of consciousness in which they operate.

The discoveries that come forth to ultimately cure or master the health challenges of our time may appear to emerge from our science. But, just as Newton reached up out of the collective pool of knowledge of his time and Einstein out of his, so too the great discoveries of any time emerge from and are defined and checked like a gravitational pull by the collective energetic from which they attempt to lift free. The significance of more and more individuals tapping unconditional levels of consciousness, beginning to directly perceive and consciously interact with the field of energy that is the more subtle milieu of their being, is leading us toward potentials we are unable to conceive.

We must be willing to live this potential. It is discovery. What is it like to be a physician and to feel vulnerable to the pain and passion of human suffering and to transmute this to a radiance instead of hiding in technique? What is it like to be both technically proficient and energetically and consciously present in any work we undertake? What is it like to know that all of one's training in whatever field may be nothing more than the preparation or scaffolding necessary to act as a more refined conduit for the demands of an entity or energy which we will never comprehend totally and for which we ourselves are but transient servants? What is it like to stand like a door between life and death, form and formlessness, and thereby consciously transfer an energy into this plane of reality from another dimension—even as one recognizes the arbitrariness of one's activities? And to know that the forms employed for this transfer, though inseparable from the whole experience, of themselves carry little or no inherent value. But also, what is it like to realize that the energetic shift demanded by the challenges we have created (such as our diseases) may be more difficult to undertake for many than to allow the disease itself to take its course? It may be easier, or perhaps one should say more natural, at this point in our development for humankind as a whole to enter into mass extermination rather than to find a way to live together.

Since, either way, we have to give our lives to find out, it might as well be though deep opening and a conscious embrace of a higher energy in whatever walk of life we are involved.

I believe we are at the threshold of what I have referred to as the collectivization of mind. The united personal consciousness is being transcended and a consciousness is being prepared that is capable of handling much higher energies, and directly experiencing its intrinsic connectedness with all humanity, so that it can function as a unit amidst a much greater wholeness. As a physician I saw perhaps 10,000 patients individually. When I left that work and experienced the awakening of higher energies, I found myself in the exploration of group consciousness. Over the past five years I have done hundreds of group sessions that demonstrated the capacity to bring people temporarily into levels of telepathic and energetic rapport. Very few people can stand for long the energy of even twenty or thirty people brought into a unified focus; they must then enter a deep process of rebalancing and integrating that involves the whole of their lives. But already the experiment is entering into work with much larger groups. The energies are astronomical in comparison to the energies of any individual or family cluster. The challenge to find balance and a safe integration of such energies requires one basic realization—unconditional love.

Fellowship with Men → The Creative

*True fellowship among men must be based upon a concern that is universal.*

I CHING
WILHELM/BAYNES EDITION

# Epilogue

SEVERAL YEARS AGO I WAS INVITED to meet a medium who was described as an extremely gifted channel whose vehicle for expression was automatic writing. Her telepathic abilities were impressive and I also witnessed her directing people to specific sentences in books in a home she was visiting for the first time. The sentences gave appropriate answers to their questions. I found the experience intriguing but discomforting. She spoke of earthquakes, floods, economic failure, predictions that are rampant in these times. She urged individuals to migrate, to sell their homes. She pointed out (I would even say played upon) their fears and inadequacies. Throughout this there was a deep pulsing uncomfortable pressure in my solar plexus. I looked for my own fear or judgment and finally accepted that the energy being channeled emanated from the solar plexus and there was nothing to do but be with it.

Finally I requested to ask a question. She asked me to place the question telepathically which was the first time this option had been offered. I inwardly asked what the nature of our communication would be if the solar plexus energy I perceived shifted to heart level? Her pencil danced and the answer was read "It would be telepathic." I asked if a second question was alright and when she assented I inwardly asked what would be the relevance of what she had been channeling if we were to shift collectively to heart level? Again her hand wrote and the man who read the answers replied "It would not ensue." I was impressed.

At this point I began to describe to the other guests the questions for which the answers had been given. As I spoke I could sense the energy shifting in the room. As I reached the description of the second question and its answer, the whole room lifted to heart level. At that precise instant the woman jumped from her chair and shrieked that it had turned into a commode. For the rest of the evening she was clearly disturbed, sometimes irrational, and embarrassed us all by repeatedly insisting that answers existed in books which didn't have the required number of pages.

There are several reasons that I tell this story. I am concerned with how easy it is for people to relinquish their own center and take on another's reality in the face of impressive psi talents, especially when there is manipulation of personal and collective fears. We can enter a spiral of fear and reaction that clouds the larger perspective and creates a dynamic that may eventually fulfill what was only a transient potential. As I've suggested, this may be what we do unwittingly through our problem-oriented political, economic, and medical forecasting and dialectic.

The potential for being manipulated by power and fear usually results from having not looked deeply into oneself. It is not simply a question of valid information—there may be some truth in the medium's information. The telling issue is whether one has perceived the level of consciousness in which such sharing is done. The level of the information may be a problem level that unconsciously presumes an absolute reality (or a more comfortable reality) instead of a changing and unfolding process. To remain centered in a larger appreciation of life can naturally transmute the problem.

This experience showed me something else of great importance. The shift to heart level may appear as a dark and destructive force relative to the psychic integrity of another level of consciousness. I was troubled at the discomfort the energy shift created for the medium. The force she was working with, which moments before had such compelling power, could not function after the shift to heart. A state natural to one person may be destructive to another. This experience also shows how easy it is for what may actually be a transformative shift in consciousness to be intuited and then displayed as outer upheaval and disaster prior to the actual internalization of this shift within one's own being. For the medium, the very upheaval she was predicting occurred as a psychic process when the energy shifted. As we explore more and more at the edge of formlessness and information is brought forward from many dimensions we will need to learn to discriminate that which is wisdom. To do this we must begin by knowing ourselves.

When touching upon higher states of consciousness, I repeatedly see the tendency to add *therefore*: "Therefore I should do this, or be this way . . ." I am coming to experience a world without a therefore, without a rationalization for being. It feels like a process of dissolving. Yet it simultaneously reveals something else—a presence, an aliveness. At times I feel like a living experiment, an alchemist's vessel in which a marvelous, although sometimes painful, mystery is unfolding. On the one hand it is effortless and on the other hand certain patterns of *me* must be relinquished over and over again. One of these patterns—and it is one that we can all pay attention to—is the tendency to seek early or simplistic resolution to states of unknowing or paradox. It is uncomfortable to live at the edge of formlessness, but the longer we can remain in a consciousness that sustains uncertainty the deeper the resolution seems to be when it comes. Practically speaking, this is one of the greatest challenges in any exploration of the transformational process: to let go into the process but not relax the energy and rest into resolution prematurely. To sustain this dynamic of being poised at the edge requires setting aside so much of what we like to think and who we want to be. I had never wanted to be ordinary, but now with each new day a growing simplicity of being is my refuge and joy, for it is here that the presence is most gracious.

I could not understand my own awakening during the immediacy and intensity of the early phases. Over time, as the process continues and as I observe it kindled in others, I have come to see it as a wonderous natural development. We stand, I believe, at the edge of a profound potential to view life anew. I believe there will emerge a medicine and a psychology that recognizes and seeks to serve a great intertwining and evolving wholeness. Less and less do I see disease and despair; what I see is love evolving.

I went to the *I Ching* at the conclusion of the manuscript to see what it would mirror of the endeavor of writing. The result was the hexagrams shown at the end of this book. As I reflect upon the wisdom of the *I Ching*, I am struck by the observation that of the sixty-four possible hexagrams only two represent images of man made origin. All the others derive from nature (i.e., mountains, lakes, wind, thunder, etc.). These two man made images are the well and cauldron.

The well is symbolic of the basic inheritance of all humanity. All of us must receive water and nourishment and this universal requirement reflects in all human activity. It unites us but it crystalizes us in limitations too. The cauldron recognizes something that goes beyond our basic physical and cultural inheritance. It is the symbol of the endeavor that leads to a higher humanness. To this end much that we are granted of security and nurturance must be placed within the transformative cauldron. It is a conscious action and there are no guarantees, no insurance policies.

To me the earth itself is a cauldron. I sense the inflow of wavefront after wavefront of energy that is transforming us all, and I anticipate that this may now be intensifying or at least so it feels. Where there is limited wisdom of the kind born of the cauldron these wavefronts result in polarization and confrontation. The journey of the heart is an inward reconciliation of these forces.

I am not so naive to feel that we are even close to being able to bring the wisdom of inner transformation to a sufficiently universal level that we can be done with power struggles and outer crisis. Crisis is itself intrinsic to the cauldron. Neither am I motivated when I am in my more balanced awareness by a sense of urgency. The sense of immediacy that accompanies the opening into more universal levels of awareness tends to make one feel that the new awareness is birthing everywhere and it tends to make us rush and push for more. It also makes some of the areas of danger stand forward as more imminent. But the urgency this produces is, I believe, a stage of opening itself. In one sense the awakening and the dangers are imminant in life itself. I caution against confusing the motivation for the deeper exploration with a sense of urgency. To do so may render that awakening as always forthcoming, never here and now—and it may stimulate the problems as well.

The impetus for me is the unfolding process itself and a basic sense of inspiration. All I have to do is sense into my own transformation to be filled with wonderment at the incredible potential that resides within us all. How far can we go given the gifts and limits of our natures to cultivate a new aliveness? To live with each other day by day with direct experience of higher awareness—this excites me. I invite you to venture into the challenge and joy of your own awakening.

# RELATED MATERIALS

## THREE MOUNTAIN FOUNDATION

Three Mountain Foundation is a nonprofit organization which invites people into greater aliveness, health and wholeness. The foundation sponsors conferences and workshops for individuals, organizations, and hospitals, including the transformational conferences led by Richard Moss referred to in this book. Its books, tapes and magazine address all aspects of transformation. Based on the work of Richard Moss, the foundation is continuously unfolding in new directions. Its work is timeless and is the basis of a cultural and social evolution revealing new possibilities for life.

## HOW SHALL I LIVE
### Transforming Surgery or Any Health Crisis into Greater Aliveness

A book published by Celestial Arts, 1985 and a cassette tape program.

This book and cassette tape program can be used alone or to augment each other. Their unique approach extends the effectiveness of modern medicine through specific exercises and meditations that invite the healing process and turn health crisis into a time of positive change and growth. Patients, relatives, friends, clergy and health care professionals—all can help and all can benefit. Using health crisis as a metaphor for growth, this book and tape program provide an excellent, practical introduction to the transformational process.

Book $7.95; Tape Program $24.95. Book and Tape Program together $28.00; plus $1.00 postage and handling. California residents add 6% sales tax. Overseas add $5.00. U.S. Funds only.

## THE BLACK BUTTERFLY:
### Invitation to Radical Aliveness

This book expands the theories presented in *HOW SHALL I LIVE*. Dr. Moss asks incisive questions about our personal approach to life and its relationship to our own health and society as a whole. He links our personal aliveness and willingness to embrace the fullness of life to the transformation of society. (Celestial Arts, 1986)


## AUDIO TAPES BY RICHARD MOSS

Talks covering all aspects of the transformational process are available on cassette tapes. These tapes have been heard throughout the world by those who are engaged in the exploration of consciousness. They are recommended by doctors, therapists, and ministers to assist individuals who are in crisis or transition. Each tape can bring the listener into heightened awareness.

$7.50 per single tape. Please contact Three Mountain Foundation for an updated list.

*THE THIRD MOUNTAIN* is a quarterly tape and magazine published by Three Mountain Foundation. The immediacy of the tape and magazine format is an ongoing forum on transformation, aliveness, and consciousness exploration.

Yearly subscription: $40 for tape and magazine. $15 for magazine alone. Canada and Mexico add $7. Overseas add $12. U.S. funds only.

*HOW SHALL I LIVE—Transforming Surgery or Any Health Crisis into Greater Aliveness*
A book published by Celestial Arts, 1985 and a cassette tape program.

This book and cassette tape program can be used alone or to augment each other. Their unique approach extends the effectiveness of modern medicine through specific exercises and meditations that invite the healing process and turn health crisis into a time of positive change and growth. Patients, relatives, friends, clergy and health care professionals—all can help and all can benefit. Using health crisis as a metaphor for growth, this book and tape program provide an excellent, practical introduction to the transformational process.

Book $7.95; Tape Program $24.95. Book and Tape Program together $28.00; plus $1.00 postage and handling. California residents add 6% sales tax. Overseas add $5.00. U.S. Funds only.

For information about the work of Three Mountain Foundation contact the address below.

For books, tapes, and magazine, if not available in your local book store, send check or money order in U.S. funds to:

**THREE MOUNTAIN FOUNDATION**
**P.O. BOX 1180**
**LONE PINE, CA 93545**
**(619) 876-4702**

---

Richard Moss, M.D., released the practice of medicine in 1976 and has since led workshops throughout the world. He is widely regarded as an inspirational teacher and master of awakening individuals into new dimensions of consciousness. His work bridges traditional medical, psychological and spiritual thinking and moves into the direct experience of higher consciousness.

He enjoys rock climbing, sculpting, writing poetry, and tending the orchards of his home at the base of the eastern Sierras. He founded and directed the transformational community at Sky Hi Ranch for three years before moving to Lone Pine, California in 1984. Three Mountain Foundation, a tax-exempt organization, provides workshops, lecturers, tapes and other writings based on Dr. Moss's work.

---